Addicted?

Addicted?

RECOGNIZING DESTRUCTIVE BEHAVIOR BEFORE IT'S TOO LATE

Marilyn Freimuth, Ph.D.

ROWMAN & LITTLEFIELD PUBLISHERS, INC.
Lanham • Boulder • New York • Toronto • Plymouth, UK

ROWMAN & LITTLEFIELD PUBLISHERS, INC.

Published in the United States of America
by Rowman & Littlefield Publishers, Inc.
A wholly owned subsidiary of The Rowman & Littlefield Publishing Group, Inc.
4501 Forbes Boulevard, Suite 200, Lanham, Maryland 20706
www.rowmanlittlefield.com

Estover Road
Plymouth PL6 7PY
United Kingdom

Distributed by National Book Network

British Library Cataloguing in Publication Information Available

Library of Congress Cataloging-in-Publication Data
Freimuth, Marilyn, 1951–
    Addicted? : recognizing destructive behavior before it's too late /
    Marilyn Freimuth.
        p. cm.
    Includes bibliographical references and index.
    ISBN-13: 978-0-7425-6025-3 (pbk. : alk. paper)
    ISBN-10: 0-7425-6025-2 (pbk. : alk. paper)
    1. Compulsive behavior—Popular works. 2. Substance abuse—Popular works.
    I. Title.
    RC533.F744 2008
    616.85'84—dc22   2008006816

Printed in the United States of America

∞™The paper used in this publication meets the minimum requirements of American
National Standard for Information Sciences—Permanence of Paper for Printed
Library Materials, ANSI/NISO Z39.48-1992.

Contents

PART I: GETTING TO KNOW ADDICTION   1

1 The Problem: Recognizing Addiction When It's Too Late   7
2 The New Look of Addiction   18
3 The Making of an Addiction   34
4 The Continuum: Early to Late Stage Addiction   47
5 Addiction's Many Masks   58
6 Addiction's Self-Disguises   70
7 Subtle Signs of Addiction   78

PART II: UNMASKING ADDICTION   87

8   Unmasking Substance Addictions   93
9   Adolescent Substance Use: Experimentation or Addiction? 113
10 The Unseen Faces of Addiction: Older Adults and Women   130
11 Gambling Addiction   141
12 Computer Addiction   156
13 Sex and Cybersex Addictions   169
14 Buying Addiction   183
15 Exercise Addiction   194

PART III: GETTING HELP FOR AN ADDICTION   207

16 Unmasking Addiction and Preparing for Change   211
17 Impediments to Effective Helping   240

Appendix I: An Overview of Addiction-Induced Psychological   255
and Physical Changes
Appendix II: Common Addictive Substances   261
References   265
Index   279

PART I

Getting to Know Addiction

Every day you meet someone who has addiction. In fact, you most likely meet several people, each having a different kind of addiction. These are not strangers you have passed on the street. They are not the stereotypical junkies passed out in doorways. These are people you know, perhaps even well: friends, clients, coworkers, maybe even someone you love. And just as you do not recognize them as being addicted, it is likely that they, too, do not know they have a problem. I know this because it happened to me. I'm a psychologist and trained psychotherapist, a Ph.D., with a thriving private practice. Despite being in practice for twelve years, I had never treated an addict among my many patients. Or so I thought. I was to find out that I was very wrong. It is my hope that the reader will make the same lifesaving discoveries that I have made. This is knowledge you need to have because the people charged by society to identify addictions—health care providers such as physicians, psychiatrists, nurses, social workers, and clinical psychologists—continue to do an inadequate job of diagnosing addictions.

Addiction Is the Number-One Public Health Problem

Most people believe that cancer, heart disease, and obesity are the major health concerns in this country. Yet in terms of direct and indirect costs, addictions are the number-one public health problem (To, 2006). People with addictions make more medical visits than those without addictions. Substance-related disorders are the most frequently occurring mental health problem (Brems and Johnson, 1997). Problematic substance use is implicated in close to one quarter of the annual deaths in the United States. Estimates suggest that one dollar of every twelve spent for health care is related to an addiction (Institute of Medicine, 1997).

Clearly, the impact of addictions spreads far beyond costs to the health care system. Addiction is often referred to as a family disease. Like a virus, the subtle and not-so-subtle effects of living with an addicted family member spread to every member of the family. The emotional toll that addiction-instigated arguments, abuse, and neglect take on families cannot be measured. It is equally reasonable to call addiction a disease of friendship and of the workplace. Addiction's toll at work is measured in terms of billions of dollars in lost productivity. Wherever an addicted person lives, works, or plays, the quality of life narrows.

Here are a few figures for substance addiction:

- On any given day, 8 percent of the population drinks in a manner warranting treatment, and at least 4 percent are addicted to other substances.
- Close to three million women over age sixty are addicted to prescription medications (National Center on Addiction and Substance Abuse at Columbia University, 2000).
- At least once a month, thirty-three million adults drink sufficient amounts of alcohol to impair judgment, leading to accidents, fights, and other harm.
- Seventy-four percent of the general population says their lives have been negatively impacted by alcoholism (To, 2006).
- Today, one quarter of all children live with a parent who is dependent on or abuses alcohol.

Addictions Are Not Confined to Substance Use and Abuse

The number of addicted people keeps getting higher. Virtually any behavior can become a full-fledged addiction, and the list of familiar addictive behaviors is growing. Gambling is the best known of the behavioral addictions. Consider computer games or Internet porn as just a couple of the more recent examples of recreational behaviors that can evolve into destructive addictions. These behavior-based addictions only add to the substantial emotional and financial costs tabulated for substance addictions. These numbers, while enormous, significantly underrepresent the overall problem because they are based on addictions that have been diagnosed. Unrecognized addictions far exceed those that are identified.

Most Addictions Are Disguised

For each person in your life who you know has a substance addiction, you have relationships with nine others whose addiction is not recognized (National Center on Addiction and Substance Abuse at Columbia University, 2000).

Here is a real life example of the damaging effects of alcohol that went unrecognized.

For years Marla had a serious problem with anger. Despite recognizing its destructive effects on her spouse and young children, she struggled to control her behavior. Sometimes she was successful; most often she was not. Her own mother had been prone to unpredictable fits of rage and this only added to Marla's worry. She knew that her mother's angry outbursts had damaged her self-esteem. The last person she wanted to act like was her mother.

I am a psychotherapist who believes the past influences the present, and so it seemed reasonable to me that talk therapy would be just what was needed. While therapy was helpful, anger control wasn't the main issue. It turned out that alcohol had more to do with Marla's outbursts than her history with her mother.

Together we discovered that Marla did not always fly into a rage. Finding herself in a frustrating situation after a few drinks is when Marla's anger came spilling out. Marla didn't have a problem with anger; she had a problem with alcohol. Once Marla agreed to stop drinking, her angry outbursts declined dramatically. We then began to look more carefully into her family history. Her mother had passed away, but there were many clues to suggest that she, too, had a drinking problem. This possibility was amazingly liberating for my patient—perhaps her mother did not really hate her. Rather, like Marla, the disinhibiting effect of alcohol was the reason her mother always seemed to be angry.

Detecting Addiction Early Is Critical

Addictions often masquerade as mental health problems or medical conditions. Addictions also hide behind the stereotypic images of what an addict looks like. When addiction-created problems, such as Marla's angry outbursts, are not correctly tied to their true cause, neither the problems being created nor the addiction itself can be effectively addressed. Today, relatively few people get the benefits of early recognition. On average, more than ten years pass before people seek help for an addiction, and most people never get help (Randall et al., 2002). When an addiction goes untreated, it becomes a more entrenched and detrimental part of the addicted person's life.

How to Use This Book

Part I examines the hidden nature of substance and behavioral addictions, how they develop, and the masks that keep addictions hidden from self, others, and even the professionals that are consulted for help. The more you know about addictions and their signs, from early stages through full-blown addiction, the easier they are to identify.

In part II, you will find descriptions of a range of common addictions— from substance abuse to exercise addiction—and the screening tools for determining if you or someone you know has an addiction. While it's impossible to include every kind of addiction in this book, the general attributes of addiction discussed in chapter 4 are applicable for almost every type of addiction. Each chapter ends with a list of resources that can help you or your loved ones learn about the addiction in greater depth, find support groups, and begin to assess where and how help might be found.

Now that addiction has been identified, part III helps you take the steps necessary to address and treat the addiction. Whether you yourself are suffering from addiction or whether it impacts someone you love, this section is designed to help you identify what might be stopping you from seeking help and how to support yourself and others to begin and stay in treatment.

Undetected addiction is a problem that comes at a great cost to each of us. Unmasking the hidden nature of addictions has the potential to save lives and families and alleviate years of unnecessary heartache. However, unlike receiving a diagnosis like heart disease or cancer, where we are likely to seek treatment immediately, doing nothing is often the initial response to finding out the problem is an addiction. If it appears that you or someone you know is struggling with an addiction, I hope you will find this book a valuable resource in learning more about how to recognize the problem and get help before it's too late.

CHAPTER 1

The Problem
Recognizing Addiction
When It's Too Late

- I would know if a loved one, friend, or coworker had an addiction.
- If I suspect that someone close to me is addicted, there's no use mentioning it. The person will just get angry or deny it.
- I would know if I had an addiction. The only reason I would not know is because I was in denial.
- Addictions entail consuming illegal substance and too much alcohol.
- You either have an addiction or you don't.

The Addiction Stereotype

Early in my career as a psychologist and psychotherapist, I would have readily agreed with each of these well-worn beliefs. Nothing I had learned during my professional education suggested they were not true. What I observed after achieving my Ph.D. and starting a psychotherapy practice only reinforced these beliefs.

How could I *not* know when a person was suffering from an addiction? I would notice the changes in a loved one, a coworker, and most certainly my patients. The signs of addiction are obvious. My graduate training in how to diagnose addictions only confirmed it. Work suffers. Responsibilities are neglected. There are hangovers, bloodshot eyes, and a worn-out, disheveled appearance. I was to learn that when it comes to recognizing addictions, not only had I been misled, but so have you, and many medical and health care professionals.

My initial experiences learning about addiction are typical. I learned from watching a family member. In my case, it was Uncle Ross. Growing up, I didn't have any immediate family members with addictions. Sure, my parents drank socially. They had fun going to Las Vegas every few years. They weren't the type to use illegal drugs. The story was different with my father's older brother, Uncle Ross, who visited once a year, arriving with his favorite Scotch in his suitcase. He began drinking the moment it turned 5:00 p.m. and did not stop until bedtime, despite my mother's obviously disparaging sighs in response to his increasingly slurred speech and sloppy movements.

My experience is not unique. Addiction touches most every family. Seventy-four percent of the general public reports that alcoholism affects their daily life. Forty-one percent have encouraged a parent, child, or close friend to seek help for problematic drinking (To, 2006). These figures, while large, increase 10 to 20 percent by taking drug addiction into account.

Our views on addictions are also shaped by television and movies. Across the decades, different types have been cast in the role of "model" addict. These models—like Uncle Ross—share one thing in common: addiction is obvious for all to see. Alcoholism looks like Jerry Lewis or Dean Martin: eyes half-closed, shuffling, and stumbling across the stage. Drug abuse looks like Jimmy Hendrix and Janice Joplin, whose substance use ultimately led to overdose and death. More recently addiction is represented by Britney Spears's erratic behavior from public ranting to rehab and back. There is Dave Chappel's portrayal of Rick James, the so-called king of funk whose death in 2004, according to the coroner's report, was not necessarily connected to the nine drugs identified in his bloodstream. Chappel portrays James high on cocaine as prone to constant verbal rambling and violence. Interspersed is the real Rick James exclaiming, "Cocaine's a hell of a drug."

At the start of his supposed addiction memoir, *A Million Little Pieces* (2003), James Frey portrays himself as broken, literally and figuratively. Frey comes out of a drug-induced stupor to discover that he is missing teeth, bleeding, smelly, and in ripped clothes but has no idea how he arrived on an airplane or where it is taking him. Our assumption that addictions are easily identifiable can help explain why so many readers found this memoir believable, when in fact it is mostly fiction.

While media portrayals of addiction are often exaggerations, their main lesson—addiction is apparent and easy to identify—influences what we expect to see if someone is addicted. These images shaped what I was looking for when assessing whether a patient I was treating was addicted or not. I had no reason to think otherwise. My graduate school training in addiction assessment supported these impressions. Addictions are medically identified based on signs and symptoms listed in the "bible" of diagnostics: the

Diagnostic and Statistical Manual (DSM) now in its fourth edition (DSM-IV). According to the DSM-IV (American Psychiatric Association, 2000), addiction to a substance creates negative consequences that profoundly affect a person's functioning. From reading the DSM, I expected to see an addicted person with DUIs (drinking under the influence) or arrests. Addicted people would have out-of-control arguments that progressed to physical fights. There would be problems with job performance or even job loss. Physical consequences like hangovers or stomach problems would be apparent.

With these criteria in mind, I would have been confident to say that in my early years of practicing psychotherapy I never treated an addicted person. However, as a professional, I knew I could not rely on impressions and that it was good practice to ask about alcohol use. Then, much like today, one was expected to assess for alcoholism by asking the four questions on the CAGE, a standard assessment for alcoholism. The name refers to the first letter of key words in each question.

1. Have you ever felt you should *cut down* on your drinking?
2. Have people *annoyed* you by criticizing you about your drinking?
3. Have you ever felt *guilty* about your drinking?
4. Have you ever had a drink first thing in the morning to steady your nerves or to get rid of a hangover (i.e., an *eye opener*)?

A point is scored for each affirmative reply; a score of 2 or 3 is indicative of problematic alcohol use (Mayfield, MacLeod, and Hall, 1974).

I would sprinkle these questions among the many questions I asked during an intake and in early treatment. A few patients reported having felt guilty or thought about cutting down on drinking at one time or another. No one's drinking seemed to be excessive. No one demonstrated the pervasive impairments in daily functioning described in the DSM-IV. The people I saw all held jobs. They desired to have relationships or had relationships and sought therapy in order to improve those relationships. Many were depressed. Others were anxiety ridden. No one entered psychotherapy asking for help with an addiction. And then a series of events occurred to transform my thinking and practices.

Developing a Realistic Picture of Addiction

I got to know an alcoholism counselor who had remarkable success in helping people, even those with long histories of addiction. He referred some of his patients to me for psychotherapy when persistent emotional problems surfaced that threatened the success of their addiction treatment. As these new patients related their histories of interpersonal conflicts, low self-esteem, unmet dreams, and emotional ups and downs, I found myself thinking that they were not so very different from my other patients. This thought glimmered on the periphery of my awareness. It took a series of encounters over several months before its full meaning emerged.

The Case of Nancy: Addiction Is Not Obvious

The first encounter occurred when a patient revealed, out of the blue, that she believed she had a drinking problem. Nancy was a thirty-seven-year-old divorced woman, mother of two teenagers, and CEO of a computer company. She had begun therapy eight months before for increasing feelings of loneliness, concerns about how divorce affected the children, and uncertainty about whether she had acted too hastily when she initiated divorce proceedings with her now ex-husband. I asked her to tell me more about this "drinking problem" revelation. Nancy explained that, as best she could recall, two to three months before calling me for an appointment, she had begun a new routine of pouring herself a glass of wine while making supper. When she started therapy, she was having one or maybe two glasses of wine while preparing dinner and another when she ate. She thought nothing of her drinking. Some time after therapy began, she started having one or two more glasses of wine when her children went to their rooms to do homework. She wasn't sure when she began to exceed this amount. Still it didn't occur to her there was a problem. Then came the wake-up call—literally—a few weeks earlier. Her thirteen-year-old son awoke in the night with stomach pain and nausea. He called out to her for ten minutes before she first heard him, and even then, it took her several more minutes to get oriented and go to his assistance. The next morning, while thinking about the previous night, she realized that she had been finishing more than a bottle of wine almost every night. She was frightened. What if something more dangerous had occurred and she could not be aroused? Nancy immediately decided to cut back and limit herself to no more than two glasses of wine an evening. After two weeks of consistently exceeding her self-defined limit, she decided it was time to bring her drinking problem to psychotherapy.

I never expected this funny, articulate, and successful woman to have a drinking problem. There were simply no signs. But should I have been surprised? In school I had learned that close to one third of psychotherapy patients can have a substance use disorder (Kessler et al., 1997). I never took the figure seriously given that my patients did not have the severely limited functioning that I associated with addiction. But what about the patients who recently had been referred to me who had a history of being addicted? They had described being quite functional even during the most active phase of their addiction. Only in this moment did I realize how much Nancy was like so many of them—successful and engaging even while in the midst of addiction. They did not fit the media image of an alcoholic and neither did Nancy.

I was beginning to think that my belief that addictions are readily apparent might be wrong. Furthermore, I wondered if it was possible to not recognize one's own growing addiction. Nancy had been drinking excessively for at least five or six months and only discovered, by accident, that her drinking had reached a problematic level. If this were true for Nancy, then how many other patients might have an unidentified addiction?

The Case of Carl: Even One's Own Addiction Is Not Obvious

Carl, a twenty-two-year-old recent college graduate, already had two job promotions under his belt and was looking ahead to a bright professional career. He came to me to talk about his discomfort in social situations. In one of our early sessions, he mentioned in passing that smoking marijuana had helped get him out of his apartment one weekend. Now, with my emerging sensitivity to the possibility that addictions may be hidden, I returned to the topic and inquired about his recent substance intake. I found out that he socialized primarily at bars and would drink until quite drunk. Sometimes during an evening out he supplemented his drinking with a Valium. I could clearly see a potential danger; not only was he drinking heavily, he was using two sedating substances (alcohol and Valium) that, when taken together, are the most common cause of accidental overdoses. And yet Carl assured me that he had no problems with substance use.

How readily can one self-identify an addiction? A bit of research in the professional literature confirmed what I was beginning to suspect. A recent government survey known as the National Household Survey (NHS) had focused on alcohol use in local communities. Going door to door, people were asked about how much they drank, how often they drank, and if there were any resulting negative consequences. This study revealed that the vast majority of people experiencing the kinds of negative consequences consistent with an alcohol use problem did not consider their drinking problematic (Substance Abuse and Mental Health Services Administration, 2002).

The answer to why they did not recognize their own addiction seemed obvious. They were in denial. Addiction is even referred to as the "disease of denial." But Nancy had not denied her problem once she recognized it. Nor did Carl once I outlined some of the potential negative consequences of his substance use, such as being less attractive to women as a sloppy drunk.

> An addiction that does not fit the stereotype often goes unrecognized, be it one's own or another's addiction.

He simply stated that he had not thought much about this behavior. In fact, he was quite curious to explore why he needed marijuana, alcohol, and Valium to feel comfortable in social situations. While denial is an issue for some people, I realized that failure to recognize one's own addiction was more complicated.

In the case of Carl and Nancy, I had a potential explanation. Like me (and most people), they held a stereotypical view of addiction: for an addiction to exist, it must be creating pervasive and apparent negative effects. Until I outlined some potential harmful effects, Carl had not identified any downsides to his substance use, while Nancy became aware of her problem once drinking created an obvious negative consequence (i.e., she was not readily available for her son when he needed her). Other potential problems of her alcohol use such as disrupted sleep, stomachaches, and feeling more irritable had not captured her attention.

First Nancy. Now Carl. I continued listening in a new way to all my patients. I also actively asked questions any time substance use was mentioned. To my surprise I discovered a number of other patients who were using substances in a potentially harmful manner. What I had suspected was indeed turning out to be true. Not all people with substance abuse problems are obviously alcoholics like Uncle Ross, whose behavior fit the media portrayal of the sloppy drunk.

Addiction: A Matter of Degree

I needed to revamp my thinking about addictions. I recognized that Hollywood images represent addiction in its more advanced stages. But addiction is not an all-or-none kind of problem. It is not as if one day you are addiction free and the next day you are addicted. I realized that an addiction occurs in varying degrees. Addiction can be thought of as occurring along a continuum where one end represents normal behavior and the other a full-fledged addiction. In between are intermediate degrees of addictive behaviors with signs and symptoms that are less dramatic than those portrayed in the media. New questions arose. Are signs and symptoms of earlier stage addictions visible? If so, what do they look like?

One of the more dramatic stories of failure to recognize another's addiction is told by a mother and son team, Chris and Toren Volkmann (Volkmann and Volkmann, 2006). What makes the story dramatic is that this mother was intent on making sure her three sons were well aware of the dangers of drugs and alcohol. Hindsight suggests there were many warning signs that Toren, her youngest, was using drugs in a more-than-experimental manner. However, his ability to keep good grades through it all blinded Chris and her husband to his growing addiction.

Addiction: More Than Substances

Having identified substance-based addictions in a number of my patients, we began working together on these problems. I quickly found that many of these patients reported problems with what they referred to as "overdoing it." For some patients, a frequently occurring behavior had been creating problems before or during their days of active substance addiction. Other times, excessive behaviors emerged during psychotherapy as substance use declined or ceased. As Carl cut back on smoking marijuana, he dramatically increased the distance of his daily runs. The way he ran created the same kinds of difficulties as his substance abuse: running interfered with meeting his responsibilities; he would choose to run rather than socialize. On a few occasions he was so exhausted from running that he was late for work the following morning.

Often these forms of overdoing represented another kind of addiction known as behavioral addictions. Gambling is the most familiar of the behavioral addictions. Other common behavioral addictions include shopping, work, or sex. Newer forms of behavioral addictions involve Internet use and cybersex, one of the fastest growing addictions. While the range of substances to which one can become addicted is large, there is virtually no limit to the behavioral addictions. One can become addicted to most any behavior or experience.

Recognizing behavioral addictions in oneself or others is equally if not more challenging than identifying substance-based addictions. Few people know what to look for in order to decide whether his or her own or another's behavior is occurring in an addictive manner. Is any behavior done frequently and intensely an addiction? Would we say Tiger Woods is addicted to golfing? Do the hours spent instant messaging represent an adolescent's social activity or an addiction? In order to recognize an addiction, we need to know how to distinguish an addictive behavior from a habit or an activity we love to do. Chapter 3 clarifies these distinctions.

Unrecognized Addictions in Health Care Settings

Given that addictions are rarely self-identified, what sort of safety net do medical and health care professionals provide? Herein lies the most disturbing finding of all. As I demonstrated in a previous book designed for professionals (Freimuth, 2005), health care providers—including nurses, physicians, counselors, psychotherapists—routinely fail to identify addictions in their patients. It gets worse: those who fail to identify addictions are the professionals who have the most contact. Physicians and psychotherapists see more patients with addictions than professionals who specialize in addictions. This may seem strange but it actually makes sense. When a person fails to self-identify an addiction, the addiction's adverse physical and emotional consequences are believed to be the problem. Thus, a person seeks help from a physician for stomach ailments or sleep problems, or a mental health provider for help with anxiety or relationship problems (Weisner and Matzger, 2003).

The frequency with which addictions fail to be identified in health care and mental health care settings is startling. Take college counselors who certainly are expected to be attuned to substance use problems. In one study, half of the intake reports did not mention concerns about alcohol use even when a student's self-reported use was worthy of concern (Matthews, Schmid, Conclaves, and Bursley, 1998).

The gatekeepers of health care—primary care physicians—routinely fail to recognize alcohol problems. One study found that alcoholism is missed in 90 percent of patients (J. Johnson et al., 1995). In another report, physicians were given a case study where the patient reported experiencing a number of physical and psychological signs of alcohol abuse (e.g., recurrent abdominal pain, intermittent elevated blood pressure, trouble sleeping, irritability). Ninety-five percent of these physicians failed to even suspect the problem.

Koren Zailckas, in her autobiography *Smashed: A Story of a Drunken Girlhood* (2005), presents the typical story of a missed addiction. Her drinking begins in high school and intensifies dramatically in college. During her sophomore year, she experiences crying spells when drunk and sober. A visit to her pediatrician just before starting her junior year of college yields the following "diagnosis":

> I burst into tears during the depression-screening bit of my yearly physical, when she asked me if I felt "hopeless about the future." She'd wheeled her stool up close, and said, "That's your menstrual cycle talk-

ing." She wrote a prescription for the oral contraceptives meant to harness my hormones and give my black moods the dependability of modern medicine. . . . She didn't ask me how often I booze. (Zailckas, 2005, p. 248)

It is certainly a disquieting notion that most health care providers are as poorly equipped to identify addictions as are people in general. Keep in mind that the previous research only addresses health care providers' skills (actually lack of skills) in recognizing alcohol use problems. The studies omit the myriad of other substances and behaviors that one can become addicted to. Behavioral and drug addictions that are even less familiar than alcoholism are being missed in far greater numbers.

How I Came to Write a Book

I took stock of what I was learning. Professionals, like myself, and people in general expect addictions to look like long-held stereotypes shaped by media "models" of addiction. No wonder addictions so often go undetected.

A Note of Optimism?

In a creative study by Weisner and Matzger in 2003, sixteen hundred people, about two thirds of whom had been treated for alcoholism, were asked if they had made a medical or mental health visit in the past year. If they said "yes," they were asked if their health care provider had asked about drinking. Relative to other studies, these physicians were more likely to ask patients about their drinking although the figure is still low—24 percent. The results for mental health providers appeared quite promising. Sixty-five percent of people making a mental health visit had been asked about their drinking. But these percentages are misleading. The people who were asked most often about their drinking were those with a known history of addiction treatment. Physicians and mental health professionals would look in a patient's chart, see an addiction history noted, and then ask about a patient's drinking. Those without a preexisting addiction history cannot rely on health care providers to recognize a problem. In general, it is believed that only one in ten alcoholics are correctly diagnosed in any health care setting (National Center on Addiction and Substance Abuse at Columbia University, 2000).

Stereotypes are based on a grain of truth that becomes distorted or exaggerated. They serve as a lens that shapes what we expect an addiction to look like. It was this lens that blinded me to recognizing Nancy and Carl's addictions sooner.

Stereotypic images of addiction portray a person, usually male, whose salient symptoms are more representative of the later phases of the addictive process. Neither Nancy nor Carl had a long history of substance use. Nancy had been drinking for less than a year while Carl had been mixing substances for eighteen months. While Carl's gender and behavior when under the influence was somewhat consistent with the media's image, his addiction did not fit the rest of the stereotype. He was successful, functioning well, and the negative consequences of addiction had a limited impact on his life.

Professional training and the media's representation of addiction provide an extremely narrow way of defining addiction. They completely fail to address most behavioral addictions, provide no clues to the appearance of early stage addiction, and in many cases, do not even apply to later stage addiction.

Continuing my quest to become more adept at recognizing addictions, I began reading extensively on addiction treatment and assessment. Most books began with the assumption that addiction was self-identified—that a person came to treatment asking for help with an addiction or a significant other had identified addiction as the problem. The goal of assessment was simply to confirm that the person was indeed addicted. I already knew that identification of addiction by self or other was the exception rather than the rule. None of this literature captured what I was looking for: What are the clues to revealing an addiction in its earlier stages of development?

When I could not find the answers in the existing literature, I decided to discover them for myself. I started with my patients with a known addiction history. In the early stages, their lives sounded very much like Carl's and Nancy's. It was when the addiction progressed that the pervasive functional impairments reported in diagnostic manuals appeared for some—though not all. Many described having successful and productive work lives, marriages, and children along with active participation in their communities while all the time drinking in the evenings until passing out or doing heroin on the weekends or snorting cocaine daily.

I began taking copious notes on patients whose substance use turned out to be problematic. At the same time, I began a research project with my students who were working on their doctorate at the Fielding Graduate University. We interviewed health care providers who were experts in the addiction field. We asked them about the full range of signs and symptoms they used to identify addictions. From these interviews, we distilled a list of what came to be called "subtle signs of addiction." To further understand addictions, I began reading autobiographical accounts of how people develop and recover from addiction. I focused on whether their experiences of living with addiction provided clues that could facilitate earlier identification.

I learned that stereotypes are but one of a number of factors that hinder recognition of addictions. The addictive process has the unique capacity to disguise itself. One of the most typical disguises takes the form of emotional problems. Depression and anxiety are a common outcome of addictive behaviors. This emotional distress, created by an addiction, leads a person to seek help from a general practitioner or mental health provider. Too often, the provider accepts the patient's definition of the problem as anxiety or depression, and the underlying addiction remains hidden.

Looking back, I wondered if the concerns Nancy expressed at the start of psychotherapy were influenced by her growing alcoholism. Alcoholism is known to have a sedating effect that enhances feelings of depression, especially for a person already feeling depressed. Enhanced sadness and loneliness were two reasons Nancy came to therapy.

Recognizing addiction is further hindered because it manifests itself differently depending on gender, age, and race. A woman's addiction looks different from a man's. Addiction during adolescence greatly differs from addiction in an older person.

A limited view of what qualifies as an addiction is extremely costly because it hinders the recognition of addiction in less extreme forms. As with most health care problems, early recognition is critical. The sooner an addiction is recognized, the less likely it is to become severe and treatment will be more effective. Early identification can save lives that would otherwise be lost due to drunk driving, HIV contracted due to unclean needles, unprotected sex while under the influence, and accidental overdose or suicide. Early recognition also lowers the extensive financial and emotional costs of addiction that arise from decreased work performance, lost jobs, physical and verbal abuse in the home, and divorce.

It is time we see addiction not unlike the way we see diseases such as cancer where millions of dollars are invested in early detection. If we can learn to see the early signs of addiction, then there is hope that the problem will not become so severe. William Cope Moyers, in his autobiography of addiction, wonders how his life course would have differed if those around him had recognized his problematic substance use when he was arrested for breaking and entering during his college years—an incident that would not have happened if his judgment was not impaired by alcohol. "To this day I wonder how much agony might have been spared if, after I got busted, the judge, the prosecutor, the probation officer, or my own attorney had insisted on an assessment to determine if my temporary drug problem was actually a progressive drug addiction" (2006, p. 73).

CHAPTER 2

The New Look
of Addiction

It wouldn't be the weekend if Eric weren't drinking. He easily consumes six or seven beers on a Saturday afternoon. During the workweek, he has one or two beers a day.

Tanya is always talking about how stressed she feels juggling the demands of her work and family life. She thinks a lot about taking one of the pain relievers (left over from a back injury last year) in her medicine cabinet. But she usually doesn't take any except for once or twice a month.

Molly has always had a tendency to be a little overweight. She drinks at least four cans of soda and chews four to five packs of gum daily. When it comes to soda she likes the diet kind, but she prefers gum with real sugar because it has more flavor. She has put on six pounds over the past nine months, and her dentist has expressed concern that her teeth are being adversely affected by all the sugar. Molly shares his concern but hasn't reduced her sugar intake.

Cara has always shared one computer with her parents and younger brother. She just bought her own computer. Every night she is up until 1 a.m. instant messaging friends and exploring the latest "in" websites. She forgot to study for a test, and because of oversleeping, she missed the school bus three times.

Matt snorts heroin on the weekends. He doesn't do this every weekend, and he never uses heroin during the week.

Craig loves to gamble. Poker is his favorite game. He is a pretty good player. His winnings usually exceed his losses. He is on a losing streak right now and will miss making this month's mortgage payment.

Jean has a healthy glow all year round. She is proud of her tanned appearance. No matter what else comes up during the week, she makes sure to make her weekly Wednesday tanning sessions. On the rare occasion that she misses a week, she doesn't feel quite right and senses something is missing. She doesn't feel normal again until after her next visit to the tanning salon.

People become overly involved with many different kinds of substances, behaviors, and experiences. Which of the above people are addicted? Is excess what distinguishes a behavior as addictive? Are addictions more than bad habits? Is there a difference between a compulsive behavior and an addictive behavior? Keep these cases in mind as you learn more about addiction. At the end of chapter 4 we will revisit these cases to look more closely at which people are addicted.

Diagnostic Manuals Shun the "A" Word

Under the letter "a" in the index of the major diagnostic manuals, such as the DSM-IV and ICD-10, you will not find a section on addiction. Addiction is a term that has been dropped completely from current editions of these professional texts. This omission came about, in part, as a way to avoid the stigma that is attached to the term "addict." The change was also motivated by the fact that the term has lost its medical connotation. Addiction has entered our everyday vocabulary where it is equated with any behavior done in a repetitive, excessive, or overzealous manner. There is no question that alcohol and other drugs are something people can become involved with in an addictive manner. In the DSM-IV these addictions are renamed "substance-related disorders." But addictions are not just confined to substances. In women's magazines, in self-help books, and on reality TV shows, addictions come in many varieties. There is gambling addiction, buying addiction, love addiction, sexual addiction, eating addiction, and football addiction. The book *Beauty Junkies* (Kuczynski, 2006) suggests that even plastic surgery is addictive.

Where common parlance draws these behaviors together under the umbrella of addiction, only a small number of these behaviors are included in professional diagnostic manuals. The few that are included are placed in distinct diagnostic categories so that their differences, not similarities, are emphasized.

Diagnostic Categories and Addictive Behaviors

Diagnostic category	Diagnosis
Substance-related disorder	Substance abuse
	Substance dependence
Impulse control disorder	Pathological gambling
	Common parlance
Anxiety disorder: compulsion	Computer addiction
	Exercise addiction
	Sexual addiction
	Buying addiction

Gambling, the best known of the behavioral addictions, is named pathological gambling. Pathological gambling has no connection to substance-related disorders in the DSM-IV. Pathological gambling belongs to a totally separate diagnostic category called "impulse control disorder" and is classified with kleptomania (stealing), pyromania (starting fires), and other behaviors that have no obvious connection to addiction.

The proliferation of computers has brought a new form of behavioral addiction involving high levels of interaction with this technology. There is nothing close to a computer addiction in current professional diagnostic manuals. Computer use, along with most any other kind of behavior that occurs in an excessive, repetitive, and uncontrollable manner, is usu-

---

Excessive food intake is often referred to as an addiction. In the DSM-IV, eating disorders have their own category, with the two major subtypes being anorexia (food avoidance) and bulimia (eating with purging). Bulimia, along with binge eating, involve excessive food intake and, of all the forms of disordered eating, are the most like addiction.

Eating disorders, along with smoking, are not covered in this book for two reasons. First, the emphasis here is on facilitating recognition of addictions that are easily hidden from self and others. For most people, smoking is an obvious behavior; likewise, the negative consequences of over- or undereating are apparent over time. Second, questions have been raised about whether eating disorders are best understood as addictions (von Ranson, McGue, and Iacono, 2003).

ally referred to as a compulsion. Compulsions are part of an obsessive-compulsive disorder, one type of anxiety disorder.

With easy and anonymous access to pornography through the Internet, sexual addictions are receiving increased attention. Under the DSM-IV general heading "sexual and gender identity disorders," there is no diagnosis that captures the notion of a sexual addiction. There is a diagnosis for a lack of sexual desire, but none for the other side of sexual desire and behavior captured by the lay terms "nymphomania" for women and "satyriasis" for men. These problems are usually considered to be a compulsion or a symptom of manic-depressive illness.

The variety of behaviors that popular vernacular labels as addictive, professional practice places in distinct diagnostic categories or simply ignores. This gives the impression there is no such thing as addiction—a conclusion I heartily disagree with. The challenge is to identify the attributes shared by all forms of addictive behavior.

Addiction: Nothing More Than Excess?

A behavior that routinely occurs too frequently, too intensely, or in larger amounts than expected is usually the first sign to elicit concern that an addiction is developing. A commonsense understanding of addiction is a behavior done to excess—too much alcohol, too much gambling, too much shopping. But what qualifies as "too much"? In the case of alcohol consumption, the government provides standards that should not be exceeded.

Moderate or Non-Hazardous Drinking Limits

Men under sixty-five:
  Two standard drinks* per day
  No more than fourteen drinks per week
  No more than five drinks on one occasion
Women (all ages) and men over sixty-five:
  One standard drink* per day
  No more than seven drinks per week
  No more than three drinks on one occasion

*Standard drink: 12 ounces of 4.5 percent beer; 5 ounces of 12.9 percent wine; 1.5 ounces of 80-proof liquor. (U.S. Department of Health and Human Services, 2000).

Exceeding these amounts puts you at risk of experiencing the adverse effects that result from alcohol-induced changes in judgment, reaction time, and motor control.

So is a person who drinks a six-pack every day an alcoholic? This level of consumption, which greatly exceeds safe limits, does not necessarily make a person an alcoholic. Whether a set amount of alcohol is hazardous depends on many factors, one of which is body size. This point is portrayed in a story told by Jim Ramstad, a Minnesota congressman in recovery from alcoholism. The day he decided to get sober, he was flying home with the friends he had been partying with the night before. He was surprised to discover that even though they had consumed as much as he did, they were able to recall the details of the evening while he could not. His friends were Minnesota Viking players (Stromberg and Merrill, 2005).

The point of this example is not to challenge government standards on safe alcohol consumption but to emphasize that what qualifies as "in excess" varies from one person to the next. "In excess" is even less useful in defining addiction for substances other than alcohol. There are no government standards for unsafe use of illegal substances or the variety of legal substances that are used addictively (e.g., cough medicines, airplane glue). Deciding if a certain behavior is excessive is equally challenging. Is six hours a day on the Internet excessive but four hours is not? Is routinely losing $4,000 at gambling excessive but $100 is not worthy of concern?

If this is your first day with a computer, then six hours is not necessarily too much. After a year, this kind of daily time spent on the computer could be considered excessive unless you are doing it for work. Losing $4,000 on a regular basis may seem excessive, and yet, for a multimillionaire, this amount of money is insignificant.

Whether referring to substance use or a behavior, routinely doing something "too much" or "in excess" is not a reliable way to identify an addiction. While "safe" drinking limits have been defined, and it may be possible to create "safe" limits for other behaviors, lower levels can be "too much" for some people but not unsafe for others. As a result, "in excess" is not a good measure of what makes a behavior addictive.

Addiction as Physical Dependence

At one time, only certain substances were believed to have the capacity to engage a person in an addictive manner. Addiction arose when ongoing substance use altered physiological functioning so that a person came to be physically dependent on the drug. Alcohol and heroin are two such substances.

The two observable correlates of physical dependence—tolerance and withdrawal—came to be the hallmark signs of addiction. Tolerance is demonstrated when (a) the usual level of a substance leads to diminished effects or (b) a person needs more of the substance in order to achieve the desired effects. The heroin user shows signs of tolerance when the dime bag of heroin no longer provides a satisfying high. Alcoholics demonstrate tolerance when they need to drink greater quantities in order to achieve the same good feeling.

Withdrawal appears when substance use is reduced or stopped. An alcoholic who abruptly stops drinking can experience life-threatening withdrawal symptoms that include delirium tremens (DTs). A person with DTs shakes uncontrollably and may hallucinate. People who are dependent on alcohol only have these dramatic withdrawal symptoms when alcohol is stopped totally, and there is no medical intervention to manage the resulting effects. However, less dramatic symptoms of withdrawal often occur but are not recognized as such. A headache after a night of drinking is one kind of minor withdrawal symptom. A feeling of discomfort or sense that one is not "quite right" in the substance's absence is another form of withdrawal.

Confining addiction to substances that create physiological dependence became a problem in the 1960s when the range of drugs that people used was expanding to include marijuana, hallucinogens such as LSD, and inhalants such as airplane glue. None created the biological changes associated with the two classic signs of physical dependence, and yet, people came to depend on these substances in much the same way as heroin or alcohol. In response, professionals expanded the notion of dependence to include psychological dependence. Withdrawal and tolerance could be psychological or physiological in nature. This new line of thinking not only expanded the range of potentially addictive substances but also opened the door for addictions that were not substance based.

As it turned out, behaviors that are done intensely and for long periods of time can, like substances, create tolerance and withdrawal. Runners are known to go for longer and longer distances before feeling that the workout is complete—a sign of tolerance. Buying addicts begin spending more and more money before their binge comes to an end. Withdrawal symptoms, similar to those for alcohol, have been described by long-distance runners who are prevented from running due to injury (Chan and Grossman, 1988). Likewise, addicted gamblers experience agitation and anxiety if going too long without placing a bet.

The centrality of dependence, whether physical or psychological, in defining an addiction no doubt influenced the choice of "dependence" as the term to replace "addiction" in diagnostic manuals. And yet just around the time of this name change in the mid-1960s, the idea that tolerance and withdrawal were fundamental to addiction was called into question. Addiction specialists observed that frequent and intense use of sedating substances that were believed to inevitably create dependence sometimes failed to do so. Researchers were surprised when Vietnam veterans who used heroin or opium daily while overseas could stop cold turkey without major adverse consequences once they returned home (Robins, Davis, and Goodwin, 1974). These observations were enough to raise questions about whether physiological and psychological dependence were necessary signs of addiction. The search for the defining criteria began again.

Addiction as Behavior Gone Wild

Returning to a commonsense understanding of addiction, it seems that being "out of control" of a behavior could be the common core of this problem. People who have lived with an addiction frequently link recognition of a problem to the fact that their behavior has gotten out of control. Nancy, from chapter 1, first mentioned her drinking in therapy because she felt it had gotten "out of control." For her, "out of control" meant that despite her wish to cut back from a bottle of wine a day to two glasses, she had been unable to achieve this goal. For others the realization that a behavior is out of control arises after a near-fatal accident or extensive financial losses followed by failed promises to reform and start a new life. The "out of control" aspect of an addiction is acutely felt by loved ones. They support and encourage change only to have their hopes dashed as the self-destructive behavior returns.

For John Moriarty, in his memoir, *Liquid Lover* (2001), "out of control" meant more than being unable to reduce or stop a behavior: "I try to remember when drinking became the focus of my life. When it evolved from a social activity to an act that defined every day of every month" (p. 45). Others, like Caroline Knapp (1996), describe the out-of-control nature of her alcoholism in terms of its overwhelming allure: "It's about passion, sensual pleasure, deep pulls, lust, fears, yearning hungers. It's about needs so strong they're crippling" (p. 7). Life centers around the addictive object: it defines the purpose of each day. This subjective component of the addictive experience often becomes a person's first acknowledgment that there is a problem.

George Vaillant's (1995) classic research into the natural history of alcoholism found that much like "excessive," "out of control" is not conducive to reliable measurement. Who defines whether a behavior is "out of control"? A loved one's evidence often differs from that of the addicted person.

Alison had been trying for years to get her husband Jim to stop drinking. She hoped that maybe a third party could help so she asked him to come with her to therapy. Very carefully, Alison explained how Jim would retire to the living room after she and the children went to sleep and drink until he stumbled to bed. When he came to bed drunk, he would burp and toss and turn until she had to leave for the spare bedroom. Of greater concern to Alison was that on several occasions he had left the house late at night to buy more alcohol and failed to close the front door. He had no recall of leaving the door open. Alison feared for the safety of the children and herself. Jim was not impressed by these facts and considered himself to be totally in control of his drinking. He explained that Alison was a light sleeper and leaving the door open was simply a mistake. He had closed the door but not tightly enough and the wind must have blown it open. He assured Alison that there was really nothing to fear. It was not until he fell down the back stairs when drunk and badly sprained his arm that he was willing to consider that his drinking might be problematic.

Alison concluded that Jim's drinking was out of control because he endangered his family and continued drinking despite the conflicts it created in their marriage. For Jim, the wake-up call came after spraining his arm. Because each person's experience of being out of control has a different meaning, Vaillant argued against defining addictions as out-of-control behavior. Instead, he suggested that a better approach would be to look at the adverse events people use to conclude that a behavior is out of control.

Addiction: A Behavior That Creates Negative Consequences

Despite the wide array of behaviors and substances that can be addictive, the negative consequences are surprisingly similar. Negative consequences common to many addictions include emotional distress, legal and financial problems, health problems, interpersonal conflicts, and failure to meet life's obligations.

Like the other attributes of addiction that I have presented, defining addiction solely in terms of negative consequences has its limitations. Lifestyle and personality variables can serve to prevent negative consequences, make them slow to develop, or make them difficult to recognize. A wealthy individual can easily avoid the financial strain that a person with fewer means would experience after intensive gambling or shopping. Many of addiction's negative consequences emerge in the interpersonal realm. As

Addiction literature refers to good or positive addictions. The most common example is exercise addiction. Apparently, what is meant by a positive addiction is a repetitive or habitual pattern of behavior that is done with intensity or passion. A good addiction is beneficial, or at least without negative consequences, and may be associated with a feeling of craving, need, or strong desire to do the behavior. Because addictions are partly defined by their negative consequences, I prefer to avoid the term "positive addictions" and instead consider these positive habits.

a result, an older retired person who lives alone can drink every night until he passes out with little or no negative reverberations. There is another reason that defining addictions solely on the basis of negative consequences is problematic. Many people continue to repeat behaviors that have adverse effects (e.g, polluting the environment, fighting with a spouse, eating trans-fatty acids), but we don't consider these behaviors an addiction.

Recognizing an Addiction When You See One

No one quality defines a behavior as an addiction. An addictive behavior cannot be defined solely in terms of its frequency, capacity to create dependence, our ability to control it, or its creation of adverse effects. Rather, an addiction is defined best based on meeting a number of criteria.

The two approaches I present allow for any substance or behavior to be addictive as long as it meets the specified criteria. This means it is possible to become addicted to orange juice, although addiction to alcohol is more likely. Similarly, addictions are not confined to certain behaviors such as sex, exercise, or work. Any behavior, even raking a lawn, has the potential to develop into an addiction. However, an addiction to orange juice or lawn raking is unlikely. This is because substances and behaviors need to create certain kinds of effects if they are to become addictive; the nature of these effects and how an addiction develops are addressed in chapter 3.

The Three C's That Identify Addiction

Howard Shaffer of Harvard Medical School (1999) outlines the three C's of addiction: "(1) some element of craving or compulsion; (2) loss of control;

and (3) continuing the behavior in question in spite of associated adverse consequences" (p. 1445).

The three C's provide a simple heuristic to remember the central attributes of addiction. These are most readily identifiable by the person who has an addiction. I have discussed all but the first—cravings.

It is difficult to know whether another person is experiencing cravings unless they are overtly acknowledged. Cravings are a critical clue to self-identifying addiction. Cravings make it difficult to concentrate on anything else. Cravings leave one with the feeling that the only purpose in life is the addiction. One professional describes the subjective tug of cravings: "There is an unnamable quality that an addiction has, a quality of urgency, a no-delay-tolerating quality, wiping out all differentiations. For example, for an alcoholic, alcohol is the important thing. It does not matter whether it is good or bad bourbon, good or bad wine" (Kohut, 1987, p. 118). It is the cravings that often make an addictive behavior so difficult to control. Cravings can be the most personally bothersome and, hence, most salient clue that a behavior has become problematic.

The Addictive Disorder Approach to Identifying Addiction

Physicians discover an underlying disease process by looking for observable signs and symptoms. Professional diagnostic practices take the same approach to addictions. What can be observed in a person's behavior to suggest that an addiction is present?

Addictive Disorder

Addictive disorder is a maladaptive pattern of behavior, leading to clinically significant impairment or distress, as manifested by three (or more) of the following, occurring at any time in the same twelve-month period:

(1) Tolerance, as defined by either of the following:
(a) need for markedly increased amount or intensity of the behavior in order to achieve the desired effect
(b) markedly diminished effect with continued behavior at the same level of intensity
(2) Withdrawal, as manifested by either of the following:
(a) characteristic psychophysiological withdrawal syndrome . . . and/or psychologically described changes upon discontinuation of the behavior

(b) the same (or a closely related) behavior is engaged in to relieve or avoid withdrawal symptoms

(3) The behavior is engaged in over a longer period, in greater quantity, or at a higher level of intensity than intended

(4) A persistent desire or unsuccessful efforts to cut down or control the behavior

(5) A great deal of time is spent in activities necessary to prepare for the behavior, to engage in the behavior, or to recover from its effects

(6) Important social, occupational, or recreational activities are given up or reduced because of the behavior

(7) The behavior continues despite knowledge of having a persistent or recurrent physical or psychological problem that is likely to have been caused or exacerbated by the behavior (Goodman, 1998, pp.15–16)

An addictive disorder is in evidence when three of the seven criteria are met. However, once introduced to the continuum of addiction in chapter 4, you will also see that meeting fewer than three does not rule out a problem.

One of the greatest challenges to identifying an addiction is that each person's presentation is a unique mix of idiosyncratic characteristics alongside some characteristics common to addiction. This menu-like approach allows for people's addictions to differ. For some, addiction is possible even if the behavior is under control. For others, addiction is present despite the absence of negative consequences. The earlier one is in the addictive process, the more individualized are the signs and symptoms. The longer an addiction goes on, the more commonalities appear.

Am I a Shopaholic? A Shopping Compulsive? Hopefully, It's Just a Bad Habit!

Repetitive behaviors that generate negative outcomes are as likely to be labeled as an addiction as a habit or a compulsion (Dodes, 1996). Being able to distinguish the three makes recognizing an addiction easier.

Habits and Addictions Habits, like addictions, involve repetitive behaviors. Good habits like brushing your teeth and regular exercise have desired outcomes. Most habits are probably neutral and involve routine behaviors such as weekly golf outings, picking up groceries each night on the way home from work, or a healthy person having one drink before dinner. Bad habits, like addictions, create negative consequence.

To distinguish bad habits from addictions, begin by imagining a typical bad habit: chewing with your mouth open or forgetting to put down the toilet seat. It doesn't make sense to refer to these habits as addictions, even though both involve repetitive behaviors and result in similar negative consequences—others responding with anger, being asked repeatedly to stop, and perhaps, feeling badly. Another similarity between bad habits and an addiction is difficulty controlling the behavior. However, "difficult to control" is not the same as an addictive behavior being "out of control." Herein lies the difference between addictions and run-of-the-mill bad habits.

The person who has a bad habit does not feel out of control. When asked why he leaves the toilet seat up, he is likely to apologize and say, "I forgot." A habit is an automatic behavior that occurs with little or no awareness. In contrast, once a behavior becomes addictive, it rarely occurs automatically. The alcoholic is aware of urges to drink (cravings) and struggles (usually unsuccessfully) against them. Despite promises made to her husband not to spend more money, a wife is overcome by a need to go out shopping. With an addiction, there is a conscious struggle to control the behavior. Habits lack this kind of internal struggle; the behavior just happens.

Nail biting, which usually is referred to as a bad habit, may in fact meet the criteria for an addiction. There are negative consequences: increased risk of illness due to putting hands in the mouth, unattractive appearance of one's fingers, and social disapproval from others. The nail biter, when caught with hands in his mouth, might say, "Oops, I forgot again!" But the real test comes when you try to prevent the behavior (e.g., cover the nails with bandages or using foul-tasting polish). A felt need to continue nail biting (craving) and awareness of difficulty controlling this behavior, despite the mechanisms intended to stop it, are evidence of addiction.

Sometimes what appears to be an addiction will turn out to be a habit. Having a drink every night with dinner or daily exercise is usually just a habit that creates no harm. But once a habit is not always a habit. A behavior can gradually increase in frequency until adverse effects occur, or a person may undergo changes due to age or declining health where a once routine behavior becomes a source of harm.

During our first meeting, a woman I was treating in her late seventies for moderate depression told me how much she enjoyed her two nightly glasses of wine, which were the equivalent of two standard drinks. Knowing that this amount exceeded the government recommended safe maximum

---

Distinguishing Bad Habits from Addictions

Shared Attributes of Bad Habits and Addictions
Repetitive behaviors
Negative consequences
Others are critical of the behavior

Distinctive Attributes of Bad Habits
Bad habits are automatic and occur without awareness
With awareness comes the possibility of control
Cravings are absent

---

of one standard drink a day for someone her age, I wondered if drinking had any harmful effects such as contributing to her depressed feelings. I asked if she recognized any of the other common consequences experienced by older adults with drinking problems: falls, stomach problems, falling asleep before bedtime. This list jarred her. In fact, she had been feeling less steady on her feet and falling asleep earlier than planned.

Ultimately, I decided that her drinking, while unsafe, was simply a bad habit. Signs of craving, dependence, or being out of control were absent. During the summer months, she preferred lemonade to wine and had no trouble making the switch. Her ability to stop drinking for long periods of time indicated the absence of physical or psychological dependence.

Her response to our discussion of negative consequences further supported my decision that her drinking was a bad habit. She promptly cut back. Awareness that her behavior was creating problems was sufficient to make a change. The change was not without a few "slips" when she forgot to stick to her limit of one glass, but overall she achieved her goal. I would have concluded differently if she had insisted on minimizing the problems created by drinking two glasses of wine nightly. I would have wondered if this attitude masked a fear that she would be unable to cut down on drinking.

Compulsions and Addictions One of the best-known compulsions is portrayed in Shakespeare's *Macbeth*. Lady Macbeth repeatedly washes her hands raw after complicit involvement in her husband's murder. A compulsion is usually one half of an obsessive-compulsive disorder, a type of anxiety disorder.

On the surface, her compulsive behavior seems quite distinct from the shopping addict who feels compelled to visit clothing stores every night on the way home from work, leaving her children hungry at home. Yet addictions and compulsions have a great deal in common (Dodes, 1996).

Both create negative consequences. Lady Macbeth, who never felt her hands were clean, continued washing even after they were raw. The inner experience of a compulsion has the same driven, out-of-control quality that characterizes an addiction. The pull to do a compulsive behavior, often described as an "urge," is really no different than a craving. In fact, cravings are often defined as a compulsive need to do a behavior.

Compulsions often are accompanied by obsessive thoughts and worry. Obsessive-like thinking occurs with addictions as well. A person with a checking compulsion ruminates about whether he locked the doors and worries about the dramatic (and often unrealistic) consequences that will ensue. An alcoholic is preoccupied with thoughts about drinking and worried about the realistic consequences (e.g., a spouse's anger). Given these overlaps, it is not surprising to find that urge-driven repetitive behavior is as likely to labeled an addiction as a compulsion. One author's sexual addiction is another's sexual compulsion. "Compulsive Internet use" in one article is described as "Internet addiction" in another. Shopping that creates negative consequences is as likely to be named a shopping addiction as a shopping compulsion.

Despite the frequency with which the terms "addiction" and "compulsion" are used interchangeably, some contend that distinguishing the two simply requires knowing a behavior's motivation. Compulsions "are repetitive behaviors . . . the goal of which is so to prevent or reduce anxiety or distress, not to provide pleasure or gratification" that comes with an addictive behavior (American Psychiatric Association, 2000, p. 457).

By this definition, Lady MacBeth's hand washing is without doubt a compulsion. There was no enjoyment in trying to rid her hands of the imagined blood of her murdered husband. Likewise, a compulsive need to check if the doors are locked or if the gas is turned off is not intrinsically pleasurable. On the other hand, drinking makes a person feel good, at least for a while. The gambler enjoys the rush of placing a bet.

Addictions are pleasure driven while compulsions are stress reducing seems like a reasonable distinction. However, as will become apparent in subsequent chapters, addictive behaviors can also serve to reduce stress and anxiety. Who isn't familiar with the idea of having a drink after work in order to relax? Behaviors that have the potential to become addictions have a unique quality; they "can function both to produce pleasure and to provide escape from internal discomfort" (Goodman, 1993, p. 226). This dual motivation

Distinguishing Compulsive and Addictive Attributes of Behavior

Compulsive behavior: (1) is driven to reduce distress and/or avoid imagined harm; (2) sometimes experienced as unwanted, odd, or crazy (e.g., hand-washing, neatly aligning objects); and (3) in combination with obsessive thoughts, is directed at imagined or unrealistic negative consequences that could arise if the compulsive behavior does *not* occur (e.g., the house will burn down if any lights are left on).

Addictive behavior: (1) occurs for pleasure, for its distress-reducing effects, or for both; (2) in the beginning, is not considered problematic; (3) in combination with obsessive thoughts, takes the form of realistic worries about the negative consequences that are likely to arise if the behavior continues (e.g., "I really want a drink but I really shouldn't. What if my wife gets angry again? Will she take the kids and leave? I can't stop thinking about having a drink.").

Another characteristic that distinguishes addictions from compulsions can only be applied after successful resolution. As one psychotherapist I interviewed reported, "One rarely hears of a person lamenting the absence of a compulsion, but often those with history of addiction mourn its loss" (Freimuth, in press).

appears in the addictive behaviors of Nancy and Carl from chapter 1. Nancy drank as a way to deal with the stress and loneliness she experienced as a single mother. Carl drank in order to alleviate social anxiety. However, there is a unique aspect to the discomfort-alleviating function of addictive behaviors and substances. Relief from a negative mood state rarely occurs in isolation. At almost the same moment that a behavior or substance alleviates distress, it is also creating a good feeling. Carl's drug consumption served to remove his social anxiety as well as to make him feel more relaxed and confident. In contrast, the stress-relieving function of compulsive behavior removes unpleasant feelings but without providing good feelings.

Repetitive Shopping: Habit, Compulsion, or Addiction?

Is it more fitting to say a person who continues shopping despite negative consequences is a shopaholic, a shopping compulsive, or simply a person with a bad habit? Several studies that have looked at women repetitive shoppers and buyers concluded that shopping was not simply a habit (Christenson et al., 1994; LeJoyeux, Ades, Tassain, and Solomon, 1996; Mitchell et al., 2002). These women reported experiencing an urge to shop: some even referred to this urge as a craving. Despite trying to resist, they were unable to control their behavior.

The researchers then looked into the reasons for shopping. Shopping was initially done for pleasure, although over time, some women felt that shopping became a way to alleviate unpleasant emotions, the most common being sadness, low self-esteem, loneliness, anger, and hurt. As a source of stress relief, shopping is consistent with either an addiction or compulsion.

But there were other feelings associated with shopping. Many women reported a sense of high or rush after making a purchase. This dual function of a behavior—generating pleasure and alleviating stress—fits with an addiction. Obsessive thinking, when present, also was more fitting of addictions. Women who obsessed about their shopping focused on its realistic negative consequences (e.g., debt). Obsessive thinking that accompanies a compulsion revolves around imagined consequences that will arise if the behavior does *not* happen (e.g., "If I don't own this bracelet, my friends will reject me"). Another interesting characteristic of this group of shoppers and buyers was the higher-than-average lifetime history of other additive behaviors, especially substance dependence and abuse.

The more you understand addictions, the easier they are to identify. To better understand addictions, the next chapter reveals how a routine, repetitive behavior can evolve into an addiction. This discussion illuminates why certain people are more prone to developing addictions and explains why some behaviors are more apt to develop into addictions than others. Understanding the origins of addiction makes them easier to recognize.

While this book's focus is on improving the recognition of addictions, ultimately any person whose repetitive behavior is creating negative consequences deserves to get help for the problem. In other words, if you or someone you know continues to repeat a behavior that is creating adverse effects, it matters less that it is a habit, a compulsion, or an addiction. What is important is that you identify the existence of a problem and consider getting help—the sooner the better.

CHAPTER 3

The Making of an Addiction

Any behavior has the potential to become an addiction and yet certain substances and activities are more apt to be addictive. An addiction to alcohol seems more likely than to lemonade. An addiction to exercise or sex seems more probable than an addiction to doing laundry. The behaviors and substances most likely to become addictive share a common effect: an ability to induce desired psychological changes in consciousness, mood, and behavior. Hence, the typical substances of abuse are known as psychoactive substances. Addictive behaviors also have this psychoactive property. However, not all people who use psychoactive substances or do psychoactive behaviors develop an addiction. The evolution of a nonproblematic behavior into an addiction shows how the risk of becoming addicted involves a mix of biology, psychology, and our social world.

A Few Parts Biology: Neuroadaptation and Genetics

Initial explanations of addictive substances focused on something inherent in the substance itself that would necessarily create psychoactive effects. This inherent something seemed to reside in a substance's ability to alter brain functioning. The area most affected by substance use is the reward/pleasure center.

What makes heroin more addictive than milk? Surfing the Internet more addictive than window washing? Addictive substances and behaviors have psychoactive effects; these are appealing or desired temporary changes in feelings, perception, and consciousness.

In the absence of psychoactive substances, the reward center responds to experience by producing chemicals—neurotransmitters—that are the basis for gratification, satisfaction, enjoyment, and reduction of discomfort. Routinely ingesting psychoactive substances alters the brain's reward system. It begins to produce less of its specialized neurotransmitters, and over time, the brain comes to rely upon external sources for these chemicals. This substance-induced change in brain functioning is known as neuroadaptation.

Neuroadaptation explains how an initial interest in a drug develops, with repeated exposure, into a dependence on the drug. Neuroadaptation makes stopping or reducing substance use more difficult; just as it took a long time for the nervous system to adapt to its ingestion, it can take weeks and even months for the nervous system to return to its previous way of functioning. This is yet another reason why early detection is so important—to catch the addiction before neuroadaptation sets in. The strongly addictive nature of heroin and morphine resides in their ability to quickly bring about neuroadaptation.

Despite heroin's high addictive potential, repeated use does not necessarily end in addiction. As mentioned previously, soldiers returning home from the Vietnam War were able to stop using heroin without displaying evidence of dependence. Even today, some people are able to use heroin on a fairly regular basis (known as weekend warriors or controlled users) and not become addicted (Shewan, Dalgarno, Marshall, and Lowe, 1998).

A behavior that is repeated frequently over a period of time or a substance that is routinely taken into the body has the capacity to alter how the nervous system functions even when the substance is absent. This is known as neuroadaptation. Once neuroadaptation sets in, going without the behavior or substance for a period of time can lead to withdrawal symptoms.

These examples do not rule out the fact that substance dependence involves substance-induced changes in the brain's pleasure/reward system. Nor do these examples negate the fact that for many—if not most people— heroin, oxycodone, and other opiate derivatives are highly addictive. However, the fact that repeated use of opiates does not necessarily create addiction means that a fuller understanding of addiction requires looking beyond biological changes created by psychoactive behaviors and substances.

The next place to look is genetics. There is no doubt that coming from a family in which there is addiction increases the likelihood of becoming addicted. Having an alcoholic parent does not ensure you become an alcoholic but it does make you more vulnerable. The effect of genetics is stronger for boys than girls, especially when their father is alcoholic. Sons of alcoholics develop alcoholism 25 percent of the time while daughters become alcoholics 5 percent of the time (Schuckit, 1998).

Genetic makeup does not cause an addiction; rather, it makes one vulnerable to developing an addiction by altering biological processes that, in turn, influence how a person responds to and experiences the world. For example, genetics can alter how the body metabolizes alcohol. Right from the start, a person with this genetic makeup consumes more alcohol. Here is a typical story.

> I discovered drinking as a teenager. . . . I was happy for the first time in my life. I loved it. . . . I never even drank socially. Right from the start, I used it as a drug . . . and people . . . would look at me and say, "You know, Franz, you're going to get drunk," and I'd say, "No shit. Like, why do you drink?" It never occurred to me you would drink for any other reason." (Stromberg and Merrill, 2005, p. 262)

Genetics have little to do with the tendency to experiment with addictive behaviors or substances. Rather, they influence whether, once initiated, the behavior evolves into a full-fledged addiction. The relative contribution of genetics and environment varies depending on the substance. When averaged across the more common addictive substances, genetics contribute one third and family contributes another third. The remaining third involves one's environment including neighborhood, economic conditions, and peers. (Goldman and Bergen, 1998; Rhee et al., 2003).

Some genetic vulnerabilities are addiction-specific, like the previous example. Other pathways are nonspecific; they increase one's proclivity to develop any kind of addiction. One proposal is that a person inherits the tendency to be a sensation seeker (Grucza, et al., 2006; Zuckerman and Kuhlman, 2000). Sensation seekers get bored easily, like variety, and are attracted to highly intense experiences like bungee jumping, skydiving, and traveling to unusual places. Sensation seekers may be more prone to addiction because many psychoactive substances and behaviors (e.g., gambling, sex, exercise) are stimulating, alleviate boredom, and provide high levels of input and novelty.

Many Parts Psychology: Reinforcing and Robust Experiences

Substances with the greatest addictive potential generate a sense of pleasure or escape from distress. An adolescent's first can of beer is associated with various good feelings—there is the buzz from the alcohol, the sense of camaraderie with peers, and the pleasure of declaring independence from one's parents' rules. This is how Anne Lamott describes her early experiences with hard liquor: "I loved it. It sort of gave me a chance at a real life. . . . Those first few sips felt like the oxygen tube had been untangled, and I could breathe again" (Stromberg and Merrill, 2005, p. 65). The emotional appeal of addictive substances is aptly captured in the titles of autobiographies about addiction such as *Liquid Lover* (Moriarty, 2001) or *Drinking: A Love Story* (Knapp, 1996).

Behaviors with the greatest addictive potential are likewise associated with pleasant experiences or stress reduction. There is the runner's high or the shopper's pleasure of finding a sought-after piece of clothing that not only fits but is on sale. There is a sense of mastery that comes from achieving the next level of a computer game or the pleasures of sex. All of these behaviors also can be a source of distraction and means of escape.

The Role of Reinforcement

Behaviors that are reinforced are more likely to be repeated.

Reinforcement comes in two forms: positive and negative. Positive reinforcement or reward involves receiving something that is desired or pleasurable. Money, food, praise, and sex are a few examples of positive reinforcement. Negative reinforcement involves taking away something undesired or unpleasant. Shopping or having a drink after work, as a way to

> ## Positive and Negative Reinforcement
>
> Behavior A followed by **Reinforcement** → Behavior A is *more likely* in the future
>
> **Positive Reinforcement:** desired/pleasant stimuli
> **Negative reinforcement:** removal of unpleasant stimuli
>
> Behavior B followed by **Punishment** → Behavior B is *less likely* in the future
>
> **Punishment:** removal of desired/pleasant stimuli or presentation of unpleasant stimuli

alleviate stress, is an example of negative reinforcement. The addictive potential of pain relievers rests in their ability to negatively reinforce usage by doing what they are supposed to do: eliminate pain.

Negative reinforcement often is confused with punishment. The difference rests with the effect the two have on behavior. Whereas negative reinforcement supports a behavior's reoccurrence, punishment decreases its occurrence in the future.

The Unique Role of Intrinsic Reinforcement

When learning a new behavior, reinforcement usually comes from outside the self; another person provides the reinforcement. Most adolescents experiment with drugs because they want to fit in. The praise and camaraderie of peers serves as a positive reinforcement that makes drug use more likely in the future. Adolescents who initially resist peer pressure may relent and do drugs to stop being harassed by drug-using peers. Drug use, in this case, is rewarded by negative reinforcement through the cessation of bullying.

External reinforcement rarely results in a behavior becoming addictive. Behaviors and substances with the greatest addictive potential have a unique property—they generate their own positive or negative reinforcement. These behaviors are said to be intrinsically reinforcing. Alcohol has this self-reinforcing quality. Drinking alcohol is positively reinforced by the pleasant buzz alcohol creates or negatively reinforced by reducing stress. Heroin users speak longingly of the intense pleasure of the original high. Intrinsic

Psychoactive substances and behaviors create a variety of effects: a buzz, a high, excitement, escape, mastery, relaxation. You cannot always predict in advance which of these experiences will be reinforcing. One person's reinforcement is another's punishment. Snorting cocaine increases arousal and alertness. For one person, this feeling is associated with a sense of being fully alive and powerful (positive reinforcement). For someone else, this aroused feeling is simply experienced as jitteriness and worry (punishment) and cocaine will be avoided.

reinforcement is involved in behavioral addictions, as well. Prolonged exercise sets the endorphin system into action, which in turn creates a pleasant, high feeling. The act of gambling is intrinsically rewarded by the exciting feelings it creates or its ability to help one forget problems (negative reinforcement). Any behavior that is associated with feelings of power, alertness, aliveness, excitement, mastery, or relaxation has the potential to become an addiction.

The power of intrinsic reinforcement is aptly illustrated in a discussion of what distinguishes the addicted exerciser from the committed athlete (Terry, Szabo, and Griffiths, 2004). When asked why they exercise, committed athletes say they strive for health benefits, status, prestige, money, and the social companionship of fellow athletes—primarily external rewards. Those addicted to exercise provide a very different rationale. The appeal of exercise rests with its ability to create internal changes in their mood, improve self-esteem, or to create a "buzz."

Paradox of Addiction

In the absence of social sanctions that counteract behavior's intrinsically reinforcing effects (see below), a behavior becomes more and more frequent until, at some point, adverse consequences arise.

One of the sinister things about an addiction is that it actually enables you to function for a while. If it made you horribly sick from the start, who would do it? The reason you do it is it literally improves your life for a number of years, and then you reach a point where it slowly dawns on you that you cannot function without it. (Stromberg and Merrill, 2005, p. 262)

And the quality of life declines. This is known as the paradox of addiction—a behavior that initially is experienced as improving life ultimately becomes a source of pain, hurt, and distress.

Now here is the odd thing about addiction. You would expect that once adverse effects set in, they would serve to punish the addictive behavior and it would stop or decrease. The relatively low rate of alcoholism among certain Asian populations is attributed to a genetically based flushing of the face that occurs with alcohol consumption. This very visible physiological reaction, which can be quite embarrassing, acts as a punishment and yet some individuals continue to consume large amounts of alcohol, despite reddened faces. An even more extreme example of punishment failing to control an addiction is drug overdose. Despite the punishing effects of multiple overdoses (e.g., facing possible death, having your stomach pumped, the cost of being hospitalized), the addiction continues.

Regretfully, punishment rarely is effective in curbing an addiction. There are several reasons for this failure. Whatever immediately follows a behavior, be it reinforcement or punishment, has the greatest effect. With addiction, reinforcement wins this race. A person drinks and within a relatively short time feels more relaxed and confident. The punishing negative consequences, in the form of a spouse's anger, threat of job loss, inability to pay the bills, come much later. Not only does punishment come later in time, but it also is less reliable than the intrinsic reinforcement arising from the substance or behavior. Sometimes you drink and have a hangover and other times you do not. One's partner does not get angry after every shopping spree. The overall result is that reinforcement is far more effective than pun-

How Reinforcement and Punishment of Drinking Should Affect Drinking Behaviors

Drinking that is routinely, positively reinforced by pleasant feelings created by alcohol and/or is negatively reinforced by alcohol-induced stress reduction → more likely to drink again

Drinking that is routinely punished by getting sick or caught by the police → less likely drink again.

In reality, the effects of reinforcement more strongly influence drinking than punishment.

ishment when it comes to controlling behavior. This is a familiar tenet of child rearing.

It is true that like punishment, the reinforcing effects of an addictive behavior are not always reliable. The gambler only wins sometimes. But when it comes to reinforcement, inconsistency enhances its power. Reinforcement that occurs intermittently—even if interspersed with punishment—creates a behavior that is more resilient and harder to stop than a behavior that is always followed by reinforcement.

The fact that reinforcement influences a behavior more than punishment explains the paradox of addiction: an addictive behavior continues despite adverse effects. But ultimately this principle does *not* explain why an addiction develops. Everyone who gambles experiences the intermittent reinforcement of winning but only a very few become pathological gamblers. Imagine if every person who was exposed to the intrinsically reinforcing effects of alcohol became an alcoholic! Addictive potential does not reside in a behavior or substance but in the person. Two aspects of a person that make addiction more likely are (1) limited coping mechanisms and (2) the need to escape or alter oneself.

So Few Ways to Feel Good: Addiction as a Coping Mechanism

Addiction can be one's primary way of coping with life's challenges. The idea that an addiction is a coping mechanism seems ironic when faced with its self-destructive effects. And yet, a person who has no alternative means to relax other than to drink will turn to alcohol whenever stressed. Should this person's life be filled with daily stress and strain, alcoholism is a strong possibility. Imagine a woman who feels chronically bored and detached from life. She has tried working, sports, and going out with friends, but nothing has really engaged her. Then one day she discovers that shopping for bargains provides what has been missing. Shopping is at risk of become addictive because it helps her cope with feeling lifeless.

Christopher Kennedy Lawford (2005) recalls how addiction helped him cope with the demands of being a part of the Kennedy clan and the son of the famous actor, Peter Lawford. With one exception, nothing he did removed his sense of failing to live up to the expectations bestowed by his heritage. The one exception was using multiple substances: "The best thing was this sense of being apart from reality coupled with a sense of well-being" (p. 112). Despite the punishing effects of his substance use (overdosing, lying, lack of money), his addiction was maintained by its ability to help him escape the unbearable feelings of inadequacy he would experience in moments of sobriety.

Neither hangovers, nosebleeds from cocaine, bedwetting when knocked out on Valium, nor the risks to his professional life when driving drunk or carrying illegal substances to work stopped William Cope Moyers (2006). "Whether I was using them to highlight the pleasure or blot out pain, alcohol and other drugs automatically did for me what I could not do for myself: They gave me confidence, boosted my self-esteem, erased my shame, eased my despair" (p. 80). Addiction was Moyers's way to cope.

Addiction is less likely if you have an array of alternatives for coping with life's difficulties (e.g., support of friends, ways to relax). Coping capacities distinguish regular heroin users who became addicted from those who do not. For controlled users, heroin is not their primary means of coping; drug use is secondary to their larger values, personal relationships, and activities (Zinberg, 1994).

Genetics can contribute to whether alcohol becomes a primary means of coping (Dai, Thavundayil, and Gianoulakis, 2005). When stressed, the body produces a special type of endorphin that dampens unpleasant feelings. Those with a family history of alcoholism inherit a lessened ability to produce this endorphin. As a result, day-to-day hassles, which are easily tolerated by those with normal endorphin production, are experienced as unpleasant and possibly intolerable. Not able to rely on the body's internal mechanism for managing stress, other means of coping are sought. Drinking or consuming sedating substances becomes one means to feel "normal" in response to daily hassles.

Independent of genetics, simply growing up in a family with an addicted parent can limit one's coping skills. Children first learn how to cope with unpleasant events in the family. Growing up with alcoholic family members means fewer effective coping mechanisms will be observed. The coping mechanism most likely to be learned is the one observed most often—substance use. Combine limited coping skills with a genetic proclivity to feel more stressed and the result is a greatly increased risk of developing an addiction.

So Few Ways to Feel Good: Addiction and the New You

There is more to an addiction than a behavior that creates its own reinforcement. For some people, an addictive behavior has the capacity to create highly desirable experiences. One addiction specialist has described these experiences as "potent" (Peele, 1985). And what makes an experience potent? Potent experiences create "desired or sought after shifts in subjective experience that are reliable and robust" (Shaffer et al., 2004, p. 368).

It is not simple to capture in words the difference between a substance or behavior's capacity to create reinforcing effects and "potent" experiences that reliably shift subjective experience. A person who gambles for the pleasure of winning is less likely to become addicted than a person who feels chronically empty except while gambling, when he feels emotionally deep and fully alive. A behavior is most likely to be addictive when it primarily serves as a means to regulate the emotional well-being of a person who has few or no other ways of managing well-being.

Addictive substances are psychoactive; they create significant and powerful alterations in subjective experience. Heroin's strongly addictive capacity is said to reside in its ability to alter the brain's reward system, which brings a sense of bliss and calmness that is otherwise difficult to self-generate. Certainly sex has the capacity to create "potent" and "robust" experiences. So why do only some people become addicted?

The difference is that for the sex addict, sex provides a robust and reliable shift in experience that alters his or her sense of self. A woman who experiences herself as invisible, vulnerable, and powerless is a budding sex addict if these feelings vanish and she becomes a diva whenever men find her desirable.

An addiction emerges out of the interaction between a given individual's psychological needs, lifestyle, and the particular behavior or substance. This point is aptly illustrated by the frequency with which successful people become addicted. Why do people who have wealth, power, fame, or talent become dependent on one source of reinforcement? Firsthand accounts of addiction (Wholey, 1984; Stromberg and Merrill, 2005) reveal that the external trappings of success do not alleviate feelings of being incomplete, empty, or convinced that something is missing from life. A behavior, or more often a drug, becomes a way of regulating a sense of well-being that neither wealth nor power nor success supplies.

A Few Parts of the World We Live In

Vulnerability to addiction—whether genetic or psychological in nature—does not necessarily mean an addiction will develop. Here is where sociocultural and environmental factors play a role. Some of these situational variables are "in the air" so to speak; these are the salient cultural values at this time in history. Other situational factors that influence addition's

How Vulnerable Are You to Addiction?

If you have ever wondered if you are likely to become addicted or are addicted to a substance or behavior, first ask yourself: What does this do for me? Good feelings fall across a wide range. At the normal end of the spectrum, there is a sense of pleasure or gratification. This is not the kind of "robust" experience that supports development of an addiction. Robustness refers to a behavior's ability to create intense excitement, a "rush," or an altered and preferred sense of self.

Robust feelings also arise from the alleviation of negative experiences. These, too, fall along a range. It is one thing to take a drink to relax after a stressful day; it is another if drinking transforms the painfully shy introvert into an extrovert. The woman who feels meek and worthless snorts cocaine and feels talented, competent, and on top of the world. An awkward adolescent who avoids social activities at school finds himself outgoing and funny in the chat rooms he visits online. Anne Lamott, who has written a number of books about her life before and after addiction, describes her transformation after drinking beer as an adolescent: "I felt like I had been given a new lease on life. I felt like I could breath. I felt like I was prettier, and I just felt that the real me had finally arrived" (Stromberg and Merrill, 2005, p. 64). Behaviors that create these kinds of transformations are at risk of becoming addictive.

development—accessibility and economic/living conditions—are more tangible.

Access to a substance or behavior contributes to addiction by providing the opportunity to experiment and be exposed to its reinforcing effects. Not surprisingly, there is more alcoholism in areas with more liquor stores. Rates of pathological gambling increase in closer proximity to casinos. The significance of accessibility is reflected in the dramatic increase in sexual addictions because of easy access to pornography on the Internet. The role of accessibility is discussed further in relation to adolescent addiction in chapter 9.

Consuming psychoactive substances is not new to human life. From the start of recorded history, mood and mind-altering substances have been a significant component of ceremonies and rituals. We still toast to newlyweds and the New Year. Rituals and ceremonies have the potential to serve an important purpose: they provide social mechanisms for controlling substance use. When the tribal structure was strong in American Indian life, alcohol use was confined to ceremonial events. As traditional tribal leaders lost their authority, alcohol began to be used outside these socially sanctioned situations and alcoholism rates soared.

Similar changes have occurred in Western society as a whole. Having an alcoholic drink is normative, a socially appropriate way to behave. Not drinking is considered outside the norm. As a result, most people will take the opportunity to try alcohol when it is available. Alcohol is consumed in most any place and at any time, given the relatively few legal or social sanctions that confine consumption.

Without social sanctions or government edicts (e.g., prohibition), the individual is responsible for deciding how much is enough or too much. How is this learned? Schools, family, and church are a few of the social institutions that help the individual develop such control. For example, when parents convey that drug use is unacceptable, children are less likely to get into trouble from substance use. If a parent or social institution is to have an influence, a child must feel some sense of bond or attachment. A child who feels connected to family or church is more amenable to incorporating the values it represents. Those with poorer attachment are more prone to addiction in part because they are less likely to incorporate the messages of school and family (Flores, 2004).

Self-regulation or behavioral control also is learned by internalizing the values reflected in our culture's worldview. Control is *not* a salient message. The modern Western world has been referred to as the culture of consumption (Starace, 2002). While Americans initially lived by an economic principle involving unchecked consumption of goods, we have turned to consuming the environment, food, psychoactive substances, and behaviors. Materialistic values, so often portrayed in the media, prize immediate gratification and consumption over control and delayed gratification. Television ads portray credit card debt as the route to a better marriage and happier children. In the presence of such cultural norms, unregulated consumption, typical of addictive behaviors, becomes acceptable.

In the culture of consumption, only the affluent are believed to have enough, although research shows that they do not feel this way (Csikszentmihalyi, 1999). Everyone else is left to feel that their economic and living conditions and they, themselves, are "less than." These cultural forces have given rise to the age of narcissism, the empty self-living in a society without a moral or spiritual anchor (e.g., Lasch, 1978; Kohut, 1987). This lost and empty self tries to escape its discomfort either through repetitive, numbing activities or filling itself up with overconsumption.

Add to these emotional tensions the stress of actually living in poverty, struggling to make ends meet, and constant exposure to threats of violence.

This kind of environment takes its toll even on those who have effective ways to manage stress. For the many who are without such coping skills, chances are high that substance use will be discovered as one of the few effective means to escape from an otherwise inescapable situation.

So What Causes Addiction?

This chapter has focused an answering two questions: why some behaviors are more likely to develop into addictions, and why certain people are more prone to becoming addicted. There is no single answer to either question. What forms the basis for an addiction and whether a person develops an addiction involves the complex interaction among biological, psychological, and sociocultural factors, where the nature of each and their relative importance vary from individual to individual.

CHAPTER 4

The Continuum
Early to Late Stage Addiction

Recreational Level . . . At-Risk Level . . . Problem Level . . . Dependence

Taylor is an alcoholic. Bonnie is addicted to cocaine. Kim is an exercise addict. Typically we think about addictions in a dichotomous manner: yes, you are addicted, or no, you are not addicted. This approach fails to capture the full range of addictions. An addiction does not emerge fully formed. It begins small just as an infection begins in one part of the body. A doctor does not wait until the infection has permeated all bodily systems before addressing the problem. And yet, this is effectively what happens with addictions. Before the problem is recognized, the harmful effects of addictive behavior have permeated the person's life. Addictions can and should be recognized long before this happens.

The future alcoholic rarely begins the path to alcoholism by drinking until blacking out. Initially, he drinks to be social and on an intermittent basis. If alcohol proves to be an effective coping mechanism or provides desirable potent experiences, the frequency of drinking can increase rapidly. The first adverse effects to emerge are relatively minor, intermittent, and easy to overlook: a hangover, waking up in the morning having fallen asleep on the couch, a coworker's annoyance at not being fully prepared for a joint presentation. For some, the problems get no worse or go away. For others, the added stressors created by these minor problems become more reason to drink. Negative consequences multiply. It is at this point that some hear a wake-up call and recognize the need to change. For others, alcohol's ability to make life more manageable—at least temporarily—takes precedence over the negative effects drinking creates. After prolonged periods of consuming large amounts of alcohol, tolerance develops and more alcohol is needed to achieve the same good feelings. Life is becoming less manageable and more time and energy go into feeding the addiction. Despite recognizing that drinking has gotten out of hand, verbal resolutions to stop rarely are implemented; cutting back even a little results in severely uncomfortable withdrawal symptoms. This is a fully developed addiction.

As another example of a developing addiction, consider a woman who decides to lose weight and get in shape through exercise. She does not begin exercising for the rush that comes after a sixty-minute aerobics class. She begins to exercise in order to be healthier and more attractive, but soon discovers that aerobics not only burns the most calories but creates a delicious high that provides relief from the low mood that permeates her day. She has tried medication, but only exercise is able to eradicate her sad, low energy moods. An injury to her knee does not deter the time she commits to exercise. In fact, she spends more time at it each day and shrugs aside her boyfriend's complaint that she seems more interested in exercise than him. This is an exercise addiction in the making.

Steps along the Addiction Continuum

One end of the addiction continuum is marked by nonuse or nonoccurrence of a behavior and the other end represents a fully developed addiction. This section describes the general characteristics of behavior at each addiction level. Part II illustrates these levels with reference to specific addictions: substance use, gambling, computing, sexual behavior, shopping, and exercise.

Recreational Level

Repetitive behaviors that occur fairly regularly and in "moderation" are described as recreational, social, or experimental. This is the person who snorts cocaine to see what it is like or the woman who goes shopping because she enjoys it as a pasttime. The term "social" is a very apt descriptor because such behaviors primarily occur within a social context. Adolescents join with peers to experiment with drinking alcohol. A person only smokes marijuana on weekends when out with a group who smokes. The recreational gambler enjoys a monthly trip with his wife to Atlantic City.

At the recreational level, the behavior is shaped primarily by the situation and the reinforcement it provides. Reinforcement comes from being part of a group, fitting in, or enjoying a change of pace from daily routine. The social drinker enjoys alcohol because it is a way to fit in and share an activity that enhances the social nature of the event. This motivation for drinking is distinguished from drinking with the goal of getting drunk. Likewise, an adolescent's first experimentation with an illegal substance is often more about fitting in or being cool than getting high.

The recreational level is not without danger; it provides an opportunity to discover whether a behavior or substance has intrinsically rewarding effects. Drinking or smoking marijuana with friends exposes you to the relaxation such substances can provide. You search the Internet to accomplish a task but in the process discover you have forgotten your financial worries. Reinforced behaviors are likely to continue. At the recreational level the frequency and quantity of a behavior is constant and not on the increase. Whether a behavior becomes at risk for addiction depends a great deal on who you are and what a behavior's intrinsically reinforcing effects do for you.

At-Risk Level

Feeling more relaxed after a drink or two is not necessarily a problem. However, the story is different if, after a few drinks, you realize, "Finally, I have found a way to chill out." This kind of "robust" feeling, if difficult to create without alcohol, can represent the start of an addiction. Take viewing online pornography as another example. Pornographic materials can be used in a recreational manner. However, if the ensuing sexual fantasies and arousal provide a means of escape or the pleasure far exceeds what is experienced in face-to-face interactions, then there is risk of a sexual addiction. When the rewarding effects of the behavior serve a larger purpose—as a means of coping that is otherwise unavailable or to alter one's sense of self—the behavior is at risk of becoming more than recreational.

Problematic Level

At the mid-range of the addiction continuum, a behavior becomes increasingly repetitive and problematic, but is distinguished from full addiction because the negative effects are relatively specific and have yet to impede quality of life (see types of negative consequences, p. 51). Problematic behaviors are driven by their intrinsically reinforcing effects. For the problematic drinker, relaxation is the primary motivation, and people, if they are even around, are simply a good excuse to drink. In contrast, the social drinker finds the company kept while drinking is as or more important than alcohol's stress-reducing properties. For the recreational computer user, this

Factors Associated with Increased Risk of Full Addiction

Looking at addictions as occurring along a continuum does not mean that everyone will inevitably progress from one end of the continuum to the other. Being a recreational gambler is not necessarily the first step to becoming a pathological gambler. Social drinkers do not inevitably evolve into problem drinkers and then alcoholics.

Behaviors most at risk for becoming addictive
(1) have intrinsically rewarding effects;
(2) provide reinforcement not available elsewhere;
(3) have the potential to reliably and robustly shift subjective experience;
(4) serve as a primary means of coping.

The person who is most likely to respond to these experiences by becoming addicted
(1) has a genetic predisposition to addiction;
(2) has an addicted family member;
(3) lives in highly stressful, dangerous, unpredictable conditions;
(4) has limited coping skills other than addictive behaviors;
(5) is seeking to repair a sense of sense of self that is damaged, empty, worthless, or powerless.

machine provides a pleasant way to pass the time by searching for information, accessing friends, or playing games. The computer becomes problematic when used as a way to escape a difficult family situation or to find pleasure activities that are otherwise unavailable.

Dependence/Fully Addicted Level

For the person who has limited alternatives for reinforcement, a strong genetic proclivity for addiction, or whose sense of well-being depends on a substance or behavior, the frequency of a behavior will continue to increase. Gradually, addiction is becoming life's central organizing principle. Even after achieving the desired effects from the substance or behavior, it continues. This is the alcoholic who, although quite drunk, continues to consume more alcohol. Other people and activities are a distant second to thinking about, preparing for, doing, and recovering from the addictive behavior.

Addiction at this level is the addiction we are most likely to recognize. However, at this point, our expressions of concern are likely to be dismissed.

How Close to Full Addiction Is a Behavior?
Degrees of Negative Consequences

The nature, frequency, and severity of negative consequences (NC) are another way to assess how far along the continuum of addiction a behavior has traveled. It is important to remember that the mere occurrence of negative outcomes is not the same as an addiction. Behaviors that are social or recreational can have negative consequence. A social drinker wakes up with a hangover or a recreational gambler loses more money than planned, but these are intermittent and minor in nature.

NC 1: Negative consequences arise directly from the addictive behavior itself. There is impaired motor control and poor judgment while drunk or a hangover the next morning. There is an ankle sprain from too much exercising. Sexual gratification in response to viewing pornography impedes sexual performance with a partner. To determine if an adverse event represents a direct negative consequence, remember that these kinds of effects will cease when the behavior stops or within a short time thereafter. There is no hangover without alcohol. Ankle sprains heal by taking a rest from exercise. Money is not lost if gambling ceases.

NC 2: Secondary negative consequences represent the physical, personal, or interpersonal reactions to NC 1. These reactions may be private. A woman feels guilty for things she said and did while intoxicated. A computer user worries about the work that is left incomplete after hours online. Often NC 2 involves others' reactions to NC 1. Alcohol-induced impairments in judgment and control (NC 1) lead to a DUI (driving under the influence). A wife becomes upset due to the money her husband loses playing poker (NC 1). A boss notices a decline in work performance that the employee knows is due to lack of sleep (NC 1) after many late nights on the computer.

Other people's reactions to NC 1 give the person an opportunity to learn from his or her "mistakes." However, if NC 2 continue to accrue and occur more regularly, the stage is set for next type of negative consequence to emerge.

NC 3: Functional consequences occur when the capacity to fulfill life's roles and to meet responsibilities is compromised. A marriage is threatened due to continuous fights about drinking. There is a complete loss of sexual intimacy in a marriage due to pursuit of prostitutes. The effects of substances compromise a parent's responsibility to his or her children. Gambling-related credit card debt is not just a source of family distress (NC 2), but threatens a family's financial well-being.

	Drinking	**Computer Use**
NC 1	Hangover Poor night's sleep	Miss a child's sporting event Sore neck

As NC 1 increase in frequency, NC 2 emerge.

	Drinking	**Computer Use**
NC 2	Guilt about actions taken when drunk Less effective at work	Family becomes distressed Chronic neck and back pain

The regular, ongoing occurrence of one or more NC 2 leads to NC 3.

	Drinking	**Computer Use**
NC 3	Job loss is possible Depressed	Not meeting one's role as parent or spouse
NC 4	Job loss	The addictive behavior becomes the center of daily life

By the time NC 3 appear, the person has begun to wonder, "Am I addicted?" By the time NC 4 appear, the true nature of the problem—addiction—is apparent (but not necessarily admitted).

NC 4: Secondary negative consequences (NC 2) and functional impairments (NC 3) become more persistent, severe, and frequent.

The Continuum of Addiction

Social/Recreational Level
Behavior is social or is contained to leisure time.
The situation is the primary reason for the behavior.
The "amount" of the behavior is normative for the situation.
The behavior's frequency and quantity is fairly constant.
The behavior does not merit worry.
Negative consequences are minor, rare, and unexpected.
If adverse effects occur, they are limited to NC 1.

At-Risk Level

The behavior is done alone sometimes.

Behavior is controlled more by its intrinsic reinforcement than the situation.

Negative consequences are intermittent and often unexpected.

The behavior may create some harm.

Negative consequences are primarily the NC 1 type.

Occasional NC 1 is noticed by others (NC 2).

Open to other people's expressions of concern about the behavior.

Problem Level

The behavior is more important than the people it is done with.

The behavior is increasingly done alone.

The behavior occurs primarily for its effect (i.e., as a way to cope, escape, provide potent experiences, or alter experience of self).

Negative consequences are apparent to others (NC 2) and becoming more frequent.

A problem is recognized but may not be identified as an addiction.

Other people's expressions of concern may be accepted but more often are dismissed.

Fully Addicted Level

The behavior continues even after the desired effect is achieved.

The addiction is life's organizing principle.

Life without the substance or behavior seems unmanageable.

The behavior is "out of control."

There are signs of tolerance and cravings.

Negative consequences (NC 1, NC 2, NC 3) occur frequently and are becoming more severe (NC 4).

A problem is recognized but it is hidden or kept secret.

The harm created by the behavior is minimized or denied.

Three or more of the criteria for an addictive disorder are met.

Is It an Addiction?

Having defined different levels of addiction and discussed how to distinguish an addictive behavior from habits and compulsions, let's return to the examples from chapter 2 to see which represent addiction and where each behavior falls along the continuum of addiction.

It wouldn't be the weekend if Eric weren't drinking. He easily consumes six or seven beers on a Saturday afternoon. During the workweek, he has one or two beers a day.

On the weekends, Eric is exceeding the safe drinking limit of no more than two standard alcoholic drinks per day. To know what this means for his life, we would need to know more about Eric, the nature of his drinking, and how alcohol effects him. How large is Eric? How many hours does it take to consume this much alcohol? Most importantly, are there any negative consequences? Eric does not seem to be "out of control" of his drinking; during the week he easily cuts back to safe drinking levels. In light of the common assumption that people with substance problems stay intoxicated all the time and can rarely control their substance use (addiction myth 3, chapter 5), we might mistakenly conclude that there is no problem. Yet it is possible that Eric's reasonable drinking during the week is a way manage cravings and withdrawal. While the information provided does not allow for the conclusion that Eric is addicted to alcohol, this pattern of drinking qualifies him as a frequent binge drinker. Binge drinking is a form of problematic substance use, which I'll discuss further in chapters 8 and 9.

Tanya is always talking about how stressed she feels juggling the demands of her work and family life. She thinks a lot about taking one of the pain relievers (left over from a back injury last year) in her medicine cabinet. But she usually doesn't take any except for once or twice a month.

Taking one or two pain relievers a month does not seem excessive. However, according to the diagnostic criteria for substance-related disorders, using a prescription medication in a way other than prescribed is substance abuse. It would be important to find out more about what is motivating her use of pain relievers. Does she have limited ways of coping with stress? If so, her use of pain relievers is at risk of increasing. Or perhaps she is already further along the continuum. Despite the absence of apparent negative consequences and infrequent use, she thinks a great deal about taking the medication. These ruminations may be an expression of cravings.

Molly has always had a tendency to be a little overweight. She drinks at least four cans of soda and chews four to five packs of gum daily. When it comes to soda she likes the diet kind, but she prefers gum with real sugar because it has more flavor. She has put on six pounds over the past nine months, and her dentist has expressed concern that her teeth are being adversely affected by all the sugar. Molly shares his concern but hasn't reduced her sugar intake.

Molly is experiencing two negative consequences of her gum chewing—weight increase and tooth decay. She is well aware of the problem; her behavior is not automatic, so it cannot be considered a bad habit. The problems being created are frequent and a direct negative consequence of chewing gum (NC 1). NC 2, defined as reactions to NC 1, are present in her dentist's warnings and her own expression of concern. Despite acknowledging a need to stop or cut back, she is not able to control how much gum she chews. Her gum chewing is at least at a problematic level.

Cara has always shared one computer with her parents and younger brother. She just bought her own computer. Every night she is up until 1 a.m. instant messaging friends and exploring the latest "in" websites. She forgot to study for a test, and because of oversleeping, she missed the school bus three times.

This example of computer use highlights the importance of context in understanding whether a behavior is addictive. Cara's computer use could be described as at risk because it has resulted in a rash of reoccurring direct negative consequences (NC 1): forgetting to study and missing the bus. There is no indication of an NC 2, such as lower grades as a result of not studying or missing school. However, it may be a mistake to conclude that her computer use is at risk. Much like a child with a new toy, adults can become highly engaged with new things and spend a great deal of time interacting with them. To decide if Cara's involvement with the computer represents an addictive behavior will require following her over time. If current negative effects are simply the result of her initial engagement with a "new toy," they will decline over time. Distinguishing a highly engaging behavior from an addictive one is a topic in chapter 11.

Matt snorts heroin on the weekends. He doesn't do this every weekend, and he never uses heroin during the week.

Heroin has the reputation of being one of the most addictive substances. There is no evidence here that Matt is fully addicted, no evidence that he is out of control or having negative consequences. Despite his highly controlled use, we would want to find out if he is experiencing any cravings. One sign of cravings would be that during the week he spends a great deal of time thinking about his upcoming heroin use on the weekend. Also, it would be important to assess what snorting heroin does for Matt. If heroin serves as a means of coping or to create a sense of self he cannot otherwise experience, his heroin use will likely increase and have the potential to become unmanageable, as was the case for Ann Marlowe as shared in her autobiography, *How to Stop Time: Heroin from A to Z* (1999).

Craig loves to gamble. Poker is his favorite game. He is a pretty good player. His winnings usually exceed his losses. He is on a losing streak right now and will miss making this month's mortgage payment.

Craig's gambling would qualify as problematic because of the kind of negative consequences being created. If he were simply losing money (NC 1), his behavior would be described as at risk, but because this loss is affecting a specific area of his life—not being able to pay the mortgage—it qualifies as NC 2. It would be important to know if this is the first time gambling losses led to his inability to pay the mortgage. It would also help to know more about how it came to pass that he is missing this month's mortgage payment. Continuing to gamble while aware that mounting losses will have adverse financial effects would suggest that he is losing control of his gambling.

Jean has a healthy glow all year round. She is proud of her tanned appearance. No matter what else comes up during the week, she makes sure she can make her weekly Wednesday tanning sessions. On the rare occasion that she misses a week, she doesn't feel quite right and senses something is missing. She doesn't feel normal again until after her next visit to the tanning salon.

I have included tanning as a potentially addictive behavior as a way to reemphasize that any behavior has the potential to occur in an addictive manner. Jean's friends laughingly refer to her tanning as a compulsion because Jean never makes plans that conflict with her weekly Wednesday appointment. There could be compulsive aspects to her tanning. We would want to know if Jean has obsessive thoughts that focus on something bad happening if she does *not* go tanning. Maybe she imagines that by missing a tanning session she will be less attractive and lose her boyfriend.

Ultimately, I think Jean's tanning is more prone to be addictive than compulsive. Usually, behaviors that later become addictive initially appear normal and socially acceptable (e.g., social drinking, recreational exercise). This is not true for a compulsion such as hand washing, which, from the start, is unwanted. There are addictive-like qualities to her tanning. The discomfort she experiences when missing a tanning session suggests Jean may be experiencing withdrawal. A return to the tanning salon makes her feel

Research suggests that tanning has the kind of psychoactive effects common to addictive substances and behaviors (Feldman et al., 2004). Over a period of six weeks, a group of regular tanners were exposed to identical tanning booths, but sometimes it was the real thing (emitting UV radiation) and other times it was a fake. Participants reported feeling greater relaxation and less tension whenever they had been in the real tanning booth.

better. It would be important to know why this is. Has she become dependent on tanning as a way to relax? Is tanning a way to make her feel attractive and thus manage low self-esteem? If either question is answered with a "yes," tanning could be creating a fairly strong shift in subjective experience that places Jean's tanning at risk of moving further along the addiction continuum. Also it would be important to assess that her time spent in a tanning booth is not placing her at risk for adverse health consequences.

Right now Jean's tanning seems to be a recreational activity. There is no evidence of tolerance, given that the frequency of her tanning sessions is stable, and she is not tanning more often or for longer periods of time. But there are potential risk factors (e.g., tanning as mood altering). Should Jean's tanning become more frequent, begin to create reliable negative consequences, or become out of control, it matters little whether it is an addiction or compulsion—she will need help.

CHAPTER 5

Addiction's Many Masks

The vast majority of people whose drinking and drug use meets diagnostic criteria are unaware of having a problem (Substance Abuse and Mental Health Services, 2002). Even health care professionals miss addictions more often than they recognize them (Freimuth, 2005). Behavioral addictions, being less well-known, are even more hidden. What makes an addiction so difficult to identify? The first explanation to come to mind places responsibility on the addicted individual. Addicts are said to be deceitful, untrustworthy, and in denial. Denial and addictions are so strongly linked that addiction has been referred to as the "disease of denial."

Denial is one way that a person keeps an addiction hidden from self and significant others. Ultimately, however, I think denial is too simple an explanation for why addictions go unrecognized. Denial plays a role but a small one. I will show that addictions are difficult to recognize—even in oneself—because of our assumptions and expectations about addictions and addiction's disguises.

The Mask of Denial and (More Often) Lying

Denial is a defense mechanism that people use to protect themselves from seeing some part of reality that is too anxiety provoking or unacceptable. Denial is not unique to addictive behaviors. It is a defense familiar to us all. In the shock of suddenly losing a loved one, we can deny that this has happened. Many of us deny the consequences of our less-than-optimal eating habits. Ernst Becker reminds us that we all are adept at using denial in his book *The Denial of Death* (1973).

As a defense mechanism, denial is relatively automatic and occurs with limited or no awareness. A person *really* believes in that moment what he or she is saying. Faced with a terminal illness, a common initial response is to deny that death is near (e.g., "The diagnosis is wrong, I will beat this") as a way to manage the shock and distress of the prognosis. This is not a lie or conscious intent to distort. In that moment, the situation is truly believed to be hopeful.

The distorted reality created by denial of an addiction rarely takes the form of saying the behavior never happens. Confronted with yet another enormous credit card bill, a shopping addict who protests, "The credit card company must be mistaken, I never spent that money," is lying about having run up the bill. This is not denial. What is denied in addiction is the extent to which the behavior occurs or the impact the addictive behavior is having on self and other. "You're right, I went shopping. But there is no need to worry. I'm sure to get a raise at the end of month. By next month, there will be money to spare." Denial is exemplified by this shopping addict's belief that overspending was just a quirk with minimal long-term effects.

This segment from Susan Cheever's memoir illustrates how denial is directed at the consequences of addiction and not the addictive behavior itself.

> I had no idea that the problems I had with men, with marriage, even with my work had anything to do with drinking. I had watched my father think the same thing. . . . Even then, after all the AA meetings I had been to with my father, and after I had betrayed my husband and little girl over and over again, I still didn't see any connection between my drinking and my problems. I thought men were the problem. . . . I thought that drinking was a wonderful way I had of dealing with my problems. (Cheever, 1999, p. 158)

Denial is not restricted to the addicted person. Those who live and work with an addict will deny an addiction if identifying it comes at too high a personal cost. When Rose expressed concern to her husband about the quantity of alcohol she consumed, his response was, "'Aah, you don't drink that much.' Six months later, when she tried to once again convince him, he told her that it was summer, and it made sense that she would drink at least a six-pack of beer each day" (Fletcher, 2001, 46). I wonder what motivated Rose's husband to so baldly dismiss her concerns about drinking. My guess would be that as long as he could convince himself (and Rose) that she drank normally, he did not have to face his own alcohol abuse.

Other times the motivation behind family members' denial is more transparent. An elderly woman is allowed to misuse pain medication or to drink alcohol in amounts dangerous to her health because doing so makes her easier to manage. A wife convinces herself that her husband's drinking alcohol before going to work as a machine operator is not a problem. She accepts his rationalization based in his own denial, "Drink steadies my nerves so my hand is better at the wheel." If she were to stop denying his alcohol abuse and acknowledge that his drinking increases the risk of accidents, she would feel impelled to inform his boss and her husband could lose his job. Work colleagues are known to deny a fellow employee's addiction in order to avoid the guilt that would arise should their acknowledgment of the addiction contribute to a friend's job loss. In chapter 17, I will discuss other ways significant others cooperate in keeping an addiction disguised.

Denial is easily confused with lying; distinguishing the two can be challenging. A lie implies a conscious intent to distort. Confronted with having an affair, a spouse is likely to deny the accusation. In this case, denying is actually lying. A spouse knows full well if he or she is sexually involved with another person. When an adolescent insists that the beer cans found in his room are not his but were left by a friend, this, too, is most likely a lie.

Common practice uses lying and denial interchangeably—even addicts do it. When patients in an addiction treatment facility formed focus groups to discuss what denial meant to them, three different kinds of denial emerged (Howard et al., 2002). Only one fits the defense mechanism described above. Two other forms of "denial" sounded much more like lying because the person was consciously distorting reality in order to manage interpersonal relationships. Denial appears in quotation marks below to distinguish it from the defense mechanism denial.

"Denial" as a Means to Avoid Stigmatization

An addicted person easily feels stigmatized and ashamed of substance use. Shame is shaped in large part by negative societal attitudes toward addictions that an addict has internalized (see "The Many Masks of Misconception" p. 63). When first facing the reality of his alcoholism, Wilbur Mills, a former congressman from Arkansas, expressed his shame in the following manner: "My concept of an alcoholic was such that I felt lowered in my own estimation. I was the lowest thing that God let live. I was lower than a snake that crawled on its belly, because I was an alcoholic" (Wholey, 1984, p. 55). Other times truth is distorted in order to avoid being judged as weak or defective. As one focus group participant reported, "Your denial runs stronger in different circles, too. There might be this family of people that I

Fear of stigmatization is one reason why addictions are underreported. When patients in early recovery were asked why they had not received treatment sooner, 84 percent acknowledged that they had not told physicians about their addiction because they felt too ashamed (National Center on Addiction and Substance Abuse at Columbia University, 2000). Lying in order to save face no doubt explains why family members are not told about an addiction. The addicted person fears that this self-disclosure will be met with anger and criticism.

Stigma and associated shame also contribute to a family member's hesitance to label another's behavior as an addiction. For example, in the competitive atmosphere of some communities where every moment of high school counts as a step closer to being admitted into a good college, having a child with an addiction is an embarrassment. The autobiography, *Smashed: A Story of a Drunken Girlhood* (Zailckas, 2005), reveals how easily parents are willing to believe that an overdose is an accident of first-time use (much like getting pregnant the first time one has sex) and a child's increasingly erratic and volatile behavior is just typical adolescent behavior.

deal with where denial is going to be real strong, whereas for this friend that drank with me [it] is gonna be a lot less" (Howard et al., 2002, p. 375). Although described as denial, this sounds much more like lying.

"Denial" as a Response to Actual Judgments and Accusations Received from Others

Many focus group participants had been aggressively approached by family members or exposed to confrontational forms of addiction treatment. They reported being upset after having been told that they were "in denial." This was experienced as the equivalent of being called a liar and they became defensive. This defensive posture became a self-fulfilling prophecy as the substance user lied about the degree of use and its consequences in order to avoid further accusations.

The Mask of Ignorance

The lying and denial that hide addiction are often confused with another mask that arises from lack of knowledge or misconceptions about addictions. Until made to face the damage created by an addictive behavior, a person may

When a health care provider fails to see an addiction, do we call it denial? No, we call this a mistake, but when the addict does not fess up to an addiction, we accuse him or her of being in denial or lying. In my mind, the professional community places too much significance on denial. It is one way that professionals get themselves off the hook for so often failing to recognize addictions. It's a way to blame the client. Sixty-one percent of physicians say they don't want to waste valuable time during a brief appointment to ask patients about addictive behavior, because if there really is an addiction, patients will deny it (National Center on Addiction and Substance Use at Columbia University, 2000). In fact, I believe that just as professionals make mistakes when it comes to recognizing addictions, failure to recognize an addiction in oneself or another is, similarly, often a mistake. This mistake is the result of a lack of knowledge about the adverse effects, misconceptions, and self-disguises of addiction.

be truly unaware of being addicted. No distortion of reality is involved. Having lived with a behavior for a long time, an addicted person can be ignorant of the behavior having evolved into an addiction. "I try to remember when drinking became the focus of my life. When it evolved from a social activity to an act that defined every day of every month. When it grew into an obsession that influenced my every move" (Moriarty, 2001, p. 45).

No one starts to use drugs, to gamble, or to cruise the Internet with the intent of becoming addicted. Instead, in the beginning, the behavior is associated with positive experiences (e.g., feeling relaxed, more sociable). Only over time do problems emerge—problems sleeping, faulty concentration at work, irritability around the house, difficulties remembering details.

The first few times a behavior has a negative effect, it rarely is taken seriously. Imagine if you did not know that a headache is one sign of a hangover. Upon waking up with a throbbing head, you would not necessarily connect it to your drinking ten hours earlier—it will take a number of hangovers before this happens. It takes time to learn that you are acting in a self-destructive manner. At first, a blackout is attributed to being tired or an unusual mix of wines. A stress fracture from addictive running is explained away as a result of extremely rough road conditions or old shoes. Only after numerous occasions are adverse effects reliably connected to a given behavior pattern.

More subtle and idiosyncratic consequences of addictive behaviors may never be linked to their true cause. Imagine that you are experiencing a growing sense of unhappiness, occasional crying, and hopeless thoughts. You are most likely to conclude that you are depressed even though these experiences can be due to addictive behavior.

Although addiction is referred to as the "disease of denial," ultimately denial has relatively little to do with the frequency with which addictions go unrecognized by self or others. Denial, understood as an unconscious distortion of reality, is strongest for a person with a long addiction history who wishes to avoid recognizing how unmanageable life has become. While the term "denial" is also used to describe why a person hides an addiction earlier in the process, this "denial" is better understood to result from ignorance about addiction's consequences or a conscious attempt to control others' shaming or stigmatizing reactions.

The Many Masks of Misconception

In exploring the meaning of denial, researchers found that a large proportion of participants believed that they were not denying anything; they truly believed that their behavior did not qualify as an addiction because their experiences did not match their expectations. As one woman expressed, "I thought that everybody who drunk [sic] alcohol blacked out. Anybody who drank alcohol would wake up with someone they didn't know and you know I thought that everybody did that, you know wake up on the roadside. . . . I mean it's like raisin' your first child, if you're doing something wrong, do you know it? I wasn't aware of it for a long time and when somebody started puttin' the idea to me you know that you're an alcoholic, well then I thought, well you know, I don't drink now like I did when I was younger" (Howard et al., 2002, p. 376).

Each of us has our own mental image of who is most likely to be addicted, what substances and behaviors are addictive, and how a person who is addicted will behave. To get a better sense of how misconceptions can mask our own and others' addictions, take a moment to identify your "model" addict. Who first comes to mind? What kind of person is this? Man or woman? How old? How does the person behave when under the influence? Our image of a model addict is shaped by stereotypes, culturally based beliefs, and firsthand knowledge of others who we know are addicted. These expectations influence which patterns of behavior we label as addictive. Addictions remain masked when the reality of addiction does not fit our preconceived images.

The Mask of Demographics

Who is more likely to be an alcoholic? A married man in his forties in a three-piece suit carrying a briefcase? A twenty-five-year-old married female homemaker? A Hispanic day laborer with a wife and three children? Or, is it a single man in his thirties who has difficulty holding a job? If you said the single man, then your hunch is supported by demographic data. Statistics on the incidence of alcohol dependence show that this diagnosis is more likely for men than for women, for whites than for nonwhites, and for those who are single rather than married. Addiction is more common among unemployed than employed men (Substance Abuse and Mental Health Services Administration, 1999).

Based on these statistics, you might imagine that the most common type of alcoholic is a white unemployed single man—well, you are wrong. This is because conclusions drawn from demographic comparisons like the above are deceiving. As a group, married men have a lower rate of substance dependence than never married men (10 vs. 24 percent). However, conclusions about the actual number of people cannot be based on percentages. This is because there are more married men in the United States. As a result, the actual number of married men who are addicted to substances exceeds the number of unmarried men. Don't be deceived by demographic information: most people with substance addictions will be employed, married, and living with their children.

The Mask of Stereotypes

Can a physician, lawyer, priest, or psychotherapist be addicted? Whenever I ask this question, I get the same reply, "of course." You just need to think about the number of professional athletes, actors, politicians, musicians, and writers who have acknowledged being addicted to realize that no one is immune (Wholey, 1984; Stromberg and Merrill, 2005). While everyone *knows* this, success, wealth, and being a competent professional interferes with the ability to identify an addiction—even one's own addiction.

Bob Welch never realized he was an alcoholic. "I thought an individual who had a problem with alcohol could not be successful, especially as a major league pitcher who could purchase anything he wanted at a very young age, as I could. I thought an alcoholic had to be lying on a street corner on skid row. That was my definition of an alcoholic" (Wholey, 1984, p. 202).

When I think about my patient Nancy (introduced in chapter 1), what remains salient in my mind is how surprised I was when she first revealed a drinking problem. I have to admit that my first response was skepticism. I thought that this bright, funny, successful businesswoman must be overreacting. Her success in the world, competent functioning, and even her gender was totally inconsistent with my belief about what it meant to have a drinking problem. And yet as she explained her nightly drinking patterns and difficulty cutting back it was clear that she was abusing alcohol. This experience led me to scrutinize my assumptions about who is addicted and what an addict looks and acts like. I discovered that Nancy had four out of the five attributes most commonly associated with a missed addiction: employed, white, insured, and female (Schottenfeld, 1994). The fifth attribute associated with a missed diagnosis is being married; Nancy was divorced.

So what does the typical drug addict or alcoholic look like? Is it Kurt Cobain or other members of a Seattle-based grunge band? Or is it a homeless man sleeping on a grate? The typical drug addict is described as a disoriented, unhealthy, thin, low-class, male "hippie" (Dean and Rud, 1984). The stereotypic alcoholic is described as "uncontrolled, negligent, insensitive, irresponsible, self-centered" (Forchuk, 1984, p. 57).

While these attributes describe some people who are well into the addictive process, they do not describe all. As a patient, a successful stockbroker, once told me, "The best disguise for addiction is a businessman in a suit." This disguise worked against Bill Lee, a severe pathological gambler, when he sought help from a coworker. Being thousands of dollars into debt, "I was desperate, reaching out for some support; what I got in return was denial. He didn't believe me. Jerry saw me as one of the most disciplined people he'd ever met, someone who had everything going for him. Besides, he couldn't see how it was possible based on all the hours we were putting in" at work (Lee, 2005, p. 101). The so-called denial of Lee's coworker has little to do with unconscious or conscious attempts to distort reality. Failure to see an addiction results from an inconsistency between the coworker's beliefs about addiction and Lee's actual behavior.

Stereotypes that mask addiction are derived from cultural images mixed in with one's own personal experiences with addicted people. When an addictive behavior does not match beliefs about what an addiction entails, the problem remains hidden. Jersild, in *Happy Hours*, a book on women's drinking, describes Daphne's experience of her alcoholism:

> When it fleetingly occurred to her that she could have a drinking problem, she let the thought pass without investigation. After all, she never drank before four or five o'clock. . . . She didn't do all those things that alcoholics did, like keeping tiny bottles of liquor in her purse or getting up in the middle of the night to take a swig. She did take a prescribed tranquilizer at three in the morning, however. Occasionally she

stopped drinking for a week—not even a wine at dinner—just to test herself and found that she could do it. She regarded this as another sign that she didn't have a problem. Alcohol was a helpful friend, an ally in her battle against depression. (Jersild, 2002, pp. 54–55)

Susan Cheever (1999) makes a similar point in her autobiography. Even while attending Alcoholics Anonymous meetings with her father, John Cheever, her definition of an alcoholic distinguishes her excessive drinking from others at the meeting.

I loved the stories I heard about hiding bottles, and about the ways people disguised their drinking while leading apparently normal lives as bankers or teachers or housewives. . . . Sometimes the stories sounded like my story, but there was always some detail that was too bizarre to fit into my life. There was always something that allowed me to keep my distance from the idea that I might be an alcoholic. I thought to be an alcoholic, a person had to be in terrible trouble. I was fine, I thought. . . . I thought that alcoholics were told again and again by their friends and doctors that they should stop drinking. No one had ever said much about my drinking. (Cheever, 1999, p. 123)

It is probably true that no one ever suggested to Cheever that she had a drinking problem. Her role as a successful writer disguised her addiction from others.

The Mask of Family Excess

Some families hide addiction by making excess the norm. Quite often my patients refer to their parents' nightly ritual of two or three drinks before dinner and more later. Growing up with parents who routinely exceed recommended drinking levels but are never diagnosed as addicted leaves a person genuinely unaware of the serious risks being created by exceeding safe drinking limits.

Tom, a young man I treated, felt as if life held no pleasure even though good things were happening. In an early session, I asked how much he drank and he said "a few" beers a day. When asked to define "a few," he answered, without a bit of self-consciousness, that it was between five and eight bottles. Tom had no idea that this amount was well above the government limit of two beers a day. As a young boy, it was his job to put a six-pack of beer in the refrigerator each evening before his father arrived home from work. When his father finished the first six-pack, Tom would put another in the refrigerator for later in the evening. Based on how his father drank, for Tom, "a few" beers meant a six-pack.

Family norms also affect recognition of behavioral addictions. Family standards shape attitudes toward what qualifies as reasonable or moderate levels of spending, exercise, gambling, and so on. A woman whose family overspent and then went to the credit union for temporary relief is unlikely to consider her unmanageable credit card debt, a result of constant shopping, to be indicative of a possible addiction. A child who observes a parent routinely absenting him- or herself from family life in order to work on the computer does not learn that one can spend "too much" time with these machines.

The Mask of Addiction Myths

In addition to misrepresentations regarding who is addicted and how they behave, there are several myths about the nature of addiction that further contribute to keeping an addiction hidden (Schuckit, 1998).

MYTH 1: People with substance problems stay intoxicated all the time and can rarely control their substance use.

Even the most ardent alcoholic can have some sober time during the day. A person may only drink in the evenings or on weekends and still be an alcoholic. Others will routinely be abstinent for a designated period of time that they believe demonstrates that they are "in control." Others have rules for when they can use substances or do a certain behavior: not before dinner, only at parties, not on work nights, only on weekends. Jim Ramstad, the Minnesota congressman, carefully monitored his drinking. "Because of political concerns, I would limit my drinking to only in the company of very close friends, or when I am out of town" (Stromberg and Merrill, 2005, p. 40). At these times he drank to the point of blacking out.

Most are able to cease the addictive behavior for some part of a day or even months before a return to drinking. Susan Cheever recalls,

> That summer I stopped drinking again. Sarah's new pediatrician suggested that I stop drinking. I didn't pause to wonder what made him suggest that. It wasn't hard to do. I remember one day [later in the summer] when we were giving a dinner party and I went in the morning to buy wine at the Sakonnet Vineyards. I tasted this and that and then I walked out into the sun, just vibrating with fullness. I had started drinking and I didn't even know it. I thought of it as tasting. (Cheever, 1999, p. 158)

REALITY: One of the hallmark signs of addiction is lack of control. Lack of control is often mistakenly taken to mean that the addictive behavior occurs all the time. However, ceasing substances for a period of time does not rule out an addiction. Rather, "out of control" refers to a person's inability, over an extended period of time, to follow their self-made rules about the quantity and frequency of a behavior.

MYTH 2: Severe drug problems require using drugs intravenously.

The original model of addiction was derived from intravenous heroin use and included signs of physical dependence: tolerance and withdrawal. Since most people do not enjoy being pierced by a needle, even when in a physician's office, the image of routinely injecting oneself with a drug conveys the sense of power that a substance has over a person.

REALITY: Severe drug problems can arise from drinking, smoking, snorting, or injecting. Addiction increases the more effective the route of administration. Injecting a drug is only one means to lose control over substance use quickly. Inhaling into the lungs, like injecting, rapidly brings the chemical to the brain. That is why use of crack (a smoked form of cocaine) is more addictive than powder cocaine, which is taken nasally.

MYTH 3: People with substance abuse problems can't have decent moral standards.

The sociopathic personality is the most common psychiatric diagnosis to accompany addiction (Reiger et al., 1990). A sociopath has low moral standards and will lie, cheat, and take on different personas in order to achieve desired goals. If someone else is hurt while the sociopath is in pursuit of these goals, the sociopath experiences no guilt or remorse. Those living with someone who is addicted are often more aware of the sociopathic behavior than the substance abuse.

REALITY: Having a sociopathic personality is associated with greater risk for addiction but most persons with addiction problems are not sociopathic. Many are productive and ethical members of their communities. One needs only to read the book *The Courage to Change* (Wholey, 1984), which presents personal interviews with many well-known and productive individuals with addiction histories (e.g., Elmore Leonard, Jean Kirkpatrick).

MYTH 4: Addictions are confined to substances.

The word "addict" is more likely to conjure up the image of someone who is drunk, stoned on marijuana, or nodding off from heroin than a person running long distances daily or repetitively shopping or going to a casino. The myth that addictions are only possible with certain substances means that many people fail to recognize that difficult-to-control behaviors that are creating negative consequences in their own or others' lives could be a sign of addiction.

REALITY: Any behavior with psychoactive effects has the potential to become addictive. Those most likely to become addictive are self-reinforcing and serve as coping mechanisms, and/or create desired changes in one's sense of self.

A Tale to Counter Addiction Myths

One of my patients began his path to addiction with a twenty-tablet prescription of oxycodone for recurrent neck pain. When his pain abated in a week, he had six pills left. He was happy to have them in case the pain returned. However, the remaining pills were never used for this purpose. He valued his weekends as a time to rest and relax from the demands of his work. One weekend he found himself ruminating on a meeting he had with his boss regarding needed improvements in his work performance. Worried that he would not get enough rest and be able to work effectively in the coming week, he remembered the oxycodone in his medicine cabinet. He didn't think much when taking one, just this one time, just to relax and get thoughts of work out of his head.

Gradually, over the next four years, he became psychologically and physically dependent on the medication. To maintain his supply, he began seeing different doctors, often in towns he traveled to for business, where he complained of intractable headaches. When out of town, he would tell a doctor that his luggage had been lost. Most physicians were kind enough to provide him enough medication until his return home. Today such scams would be unnecessary. He could just order his medication online.

This man's addiction not only illustrates the development of substance abuse and then dependence through misuse of prescription medication, but it aptly challenges a number of the addiction myths. He did not live on the street. He was a successful businessman living in an upper middle class suburb. He was neither intoxicated all the time nor out of control. In fact, his family did not know about his addiction. Although he experienced cravings after four or five days of nonuse, he was able to manage these by taking oxycodone on weekends, perhaps once during the week, and when traveling out of town.

Is his behavior of scamming doctors consistent with the myth that addicts lack moral standards? For this businessman who lied to physicians to procure oxycodone, it was his addiction that led to his immoral behavior. In other areas of his life he was a model citizen. He was known in his community for his generosity helping out local charities by giving of his time and money.

CHAPTER 6

Addiction's
Self-Disguises

A ddictions create their own disguises! Addictions mimic the symptoms of common psychological and physical problems with the result that addiction is mistakenly identified as some other kind of problem. The other self-disguise takes the form of moderation. No one behavior is problematic, rather, a combination of moderate behaviors creates an addiction.

Addiction Dresses Up as Mental Health and Physical Disorders

How do you feel today? Elated, invulnerable, on top of the world? Depressed, sluggish, disoriented, jittery, anxious, preoccupied, tired? All these experiences can be created by excessive behaviors, active substance use, or withdrawal. When checking in on our emotional lives, positive feelings rarely call for an explanation, but we are prone to asking "why?" when feeling bad for any period of time. Typical explanations include: it's a bad day, a bad week, my boss is giving me a hard time, my girlfriend is nagging me, it's that time of the month. Few would consider that psychological distress is a symptom of addiction—although it can be.

Linking an addictive behavior to its psychological or physical aftereffects is no simple task. Who would imagine that the alcohol used to relax at the end of the day can, over time, create feelings of anxiety and depression? A man who has sworn off gambling would never think that his low mood and difficulty concentrating reflect withdrawal symptoms. Similarly, a person who drinks to get relief from insomnia may never figure out that alcohol exacerbates sleep problems. For an overview of substance-induced physical and psychological effects, see appendix I.

When addiction-induced psychological or physical symptoms persist, some decide that it is a good idea to talk to someone about their problems, usually a medical or mental health professional. As these practitioners listen to their new clients talk about an increasing number of days with low moods, anxiety, difficulty sleeping, digestive problems, or sinus conditions, they diagnose problems consistent with their training. Addiction's disguise is successful when the medical practitioner (mis)diagnoses a physical disorder and a mental health provider sees an emotional or relationship problem.

Misdiagnosis by medical professionals is common. Ninety-five percent of physicians missed a diagnosis of substance abuse in a case vignette containing signs and symptoms of abuse. Instead of alcohol abuse, the most common diagnosis was physical in nature: irritable bowel syndrome and ulcers (National Center on Addiction and Substance Abuse at Columbia University, 2000).

Psychotherapists are equally susceptible to addiction's disguises. In a study I conducted, mental health providers reviewed case summaries in which the client reported feelings (e.g., depression or anxiety), experiences (e.g., isolation, weight loss), and behaviors (e.g., socializing at bars) consistent with substance addiction. When asked for their initial diagnostic

Addiction's disguises might be less effective *if* health care providers routinely assessed for addictions. Despite the fact that health care providers are well aware of the significant role they have to play in prevention and early identification of addiction, assessment of addictions is the exception not the rule. Eighty-two percent of physicians "avoid" or are "hesitant" to raise issues about addictions with their patients (Recovery Institute, 1998). Surprisingly, even when a drinking problem is suspected, more than half of all physicians remain hesitant to ask patients directly about the problem (Thom and Tellez, 1986). Others worry that asking might frighten or anger a patient who would find such questions insulting because of the stigma of addiction (Johansson, Akerlind, and Bendston, 2005).

impressions, few providers suggested a substance use problem. Depression was by far the most common first diagnosis followed by adjustment disorder and anxiety. In fact, distinguishing substance-induced states from psychiatric conditions is said to be one of the greatest diagnostic challenges (Myrick and Brady, 2003).

The Mask of Moderation

"I don't drink much—never more than two glasses of beer, two or maybe three times a week." Is it safe to conclude that Craig does not have an alcohol problem? The answer seems to be "yes" given that further inquiry reveals that Craig drinks beer by the bottle and each bottle is equal to one standard drink. He is in good physical condition with no known medical condition that alcohol consumption could complicate. In terms of standards defining nonhazardous drinking, Craig's overall alcohol consumption sounds reasonable, nothing more than social drinking. But this conclusion could be an error without knowing his involvement with other potentially addictive substances or behaviors. What appears to be moderate substance use or occurrence of a behavior can be part of an addiction's disguise. The mask of moderation takes three forms: (1) polysubstance use, (2) cross-tolerance, and (3) cross-addictions.

Polysubstance Use and Dependence

"Poly" means "many," and most substance abusers are polysubstance users. Availability is a major reason for using an assortment of substances. Despite preference for one substance, which one is used ultimately depends more on access than preference.

Polysubstance use greatly increases the chance of an overdose. Carrie Fischer, in *Postcards from the Edge*, a semiautobiographical reflection on her drug dependence, aptly conveys the danger of polysubstance use. Upon admission into a hospital following an accidental overdose, she recalls the following: "One of the therapists came in to admit me and asked how long I'd been a drug addict. I said that I didn't think I was a drug addict because I didn't take any one drug. 'Then you're a *drugs addict*,' she said" (Fischer, 1987, p. 10).

Like Fischer, taking numerous substances can mask an addiction from self and others because each substance is used in moderation. The typical polysubstance user consumes alcohol and a number of illegal drugs. Frequent misuse of prescription medications and over-the-counter medications are mixed in with this combination. Vicodan, oxycodone, and Valium are a few of the more commonly misused prescription drugs, while cough syrups are the most frequently abused over-the-counter medication. Inhaling household products can also play a part in polysubstance dependence. Sources of readily available inhalants include airplane glue, hairspray, paint thinner, and fingernail polish remover. A person using a little of this and that, here and there, may not be addicted to any one substance, yet taken together, the combination of substances interferes with normal functioning and can be lethal.

A formal diagnosis of polysubstance dependence is made when multiple substances (other than nicotine or caffeine) are creating problems consistent with three or more of the criteria for an addictive disorder (see p. 27). Take as an example someone who is mixing alcohol and cocaine. Alcohol is exacerbating preexisting stomach problems (criteria 7); attempts to cut back on alcohol have failed (criteria 4); and cocaine, which is being used to counteract the sedating effects of alcohol, requires a great deal of time to acquire (criteria 5).

Relative to those who are dependent on a single substance, polysubstance dependence is typical among the kind of people for whom an addiction is most likely to be overlooked. This diagnosis is more common among women and, independent of gender, more common among those who have a more stable lifestyle and are married, highly educated, and employed (Schuckit et al., 2001).

Let's return to Craig, mentioned earlier, whose daily alcohol intake seemed reasonable. When asked what other drugs he used regularly, he reported that on most days he was taking at least five milligrams of Valium. When prescribed this medication for a bout of lower back pain, Craig had discovered how nicely Valium mixed with alcohol. Now he buys it from an acquaintance with ready access to the drug. Misuse of prescription drugs combined with alcohol use puts Craig at risk of developing polysubstance dependence. His particular mix of drugs is especially dangerous in light of what is known as cross-tolerance.

Cross-Tolerance

Cross-tolerance is another way in which moderate substance use disguises an addiction. With cross-tolerance, two or more substances from the same class of substances (see appendix II) are taken together. Each is taken at moderate levels, but because they work in a biologically similar manner, the effect is cumulative.

Cross-tolerance is observed most often with substances with sedating or depressant effects. Craig's mix of drugs represents the most typical combination; alcohol is combined with a sedative such as a barbiturate or benzodiazepines (Valium). Each drug alone may not be harmful, but when their separate sedating effects are combined, consciousness, judgment, and reaction times are severely impaired.

Over-the-counter and legally prescribed medications that have sedating effects can create adverse cross-tolerance effects. Among the elderly, such medications—when combined with alcohol—increase the risk of injury and impaired judgment. Substance users who are unaware of cross-tolerance effects are at greater risk for accidents and accidental overdose, evidenced by how often media reports of drug-related deaths involve substances with depressant effects. The reason overdose is so common with sedating substances is because they have a long half-life (the time it takes for the drug to reach half potency). With a long half-life, toxic levels begin to accumulate even if drinks and pills are taken at different times.

Cross-tolerance is a term not usually applied to behavioral addictions. However, something similar occurs when a series of comparable behaviors are combined. A person who spends a reasonable amount of money on scratch cards and who also plays poker and slot machines during the week can end up with an overall negative effect on finances. When wondering whether a behavior is addictive, it is necessary to be attuned to the many forms the behavior can take. If comparable behaviors—each one of which is unremarkable—are working together to create negative consequences, then there may be a behavioral addiction.

Cross-Addictions

Researchers have documented that a person who uses substances addictively is prone to behave excessively in other areas, such as sex, work, gambling, eating, shopping, exercise, and playing video games (Christo et al., 2003; Greenberg, Lewis, and Dodd, 1999). Among one group of sex addicts, 32 percent also had an eating disorder, 13 percent were addicted to shopping, and 5 percent had a problem with gambling (Schneider and Schneider, 2004). Those addicted to shopping have an increased incidence of bulimia (Faber, Christenson, de Zwaan, and Mitchell, 1995) and substance use (Mitchell et al., 2002). The occurrence of multiple addictions is known as cross-addictions. When addictions overlap in this way it is possible for one addiction to be recognized while the others remain hidden.

There are many possible permutations of substance and behavioral addictions. A common pattern is for the substance and behavioral addictions to occur simultaneously. Alcoholism and gambling is a typical example

(Petry, 2002). Other common forms of cross-addictions are drinking and shopping, abuse of steroids and exercise, and cocaine and pornography.

Sometimes cross-addictions develop because one addiction facilitates the occurrence of a behavior that, over time, becomes addictive. Early recognition of this co-occurrence can prevent the second behavior from becoming addictive. This did not happen for Daron, who came to treatment with a drinking problem and an addiction to Internet pornography.

Daron would end his day by drinking beer. By the time he was on his second beer, his wife and kids were usually in bed. He would then get on the computer to check stock quotes and, later in the evening, he would search the Web on a topic of recent interest at work. Sometimes he ended the evening at a pornographic site. For a long time he did this once or twice a month. After one prolonged stressful period at work, he discovered that he was drinking close to a six-pack nightly as he stayed up later and later visiting pornographic sites. The result was that he rarely went to bed with his wife, their sex life declined, and he was often too tired to function effectively at work the next day. Daron attributed his cybersex addiction to the easy access of pornography on the Internet and the lack of inhibition he felt after drinking alcohol.

For Daron, substance use facilitated the development of a behavioral addiction.

Another common form of cross-addiction involves a sequential shift from one addiction to another. Julia had a history of drug addiction. As drugs left her life, she began "overdoing" certain behaviors.

Six months into recovery from drug addiction, Julia started overeating. Within a year, she gained twenty-five pounds. Having always been concerned about her appearance, Julia was appalled at what was happening to her body so she began a rigorous, two-hour-a-day exercise program. She exercised in what commonly would be described as a compulsive manner—never deviating from the schedule, no matter what other demands were made on her time. Once she was satisfied with her appearance, she began buying clothes and expensive make-up until the stress of not keeping up with her credit card payments brought her to psychotherapy.

Julia seemed to recognize this sequential shifting of addictions. When she began therapy she said, "I don't have drugs anymore; there is no food, no exercise, so now I have shopping."

We may all know someone like Julia who never seems to do things in moderation and becomes highly engaged in many different activities. Despite concerted efforts, science has yet to find evidence to support an addictive personality type. The point remains, however, that as one addiction declines, the possibility that another is emerging can't be overlooked.

The Mask of No Physical Markers:
Behavioral Addictions

Compared to substance addictions, behavioral addictions are more easily hidden because we are less sensitive to their signs and symptoms. Further complicating the recognition of behavioral addictions is the absence of apparent physical markers. Substance addictions leave no discernable physical signs. The drunk stumbles and slurs. There is the smell of alcohol. Needle marks and bruises line the arms of the heroin user. Even when these physical signs are absent, substances leave behind physical traces that can be identified by toxicology screenings. There is no equivalent to the breathalyzer or urine screen for behavioral addictions. Because they don't leave any unique physical traces, behavioral addictions, especially in their early forms, go unidentified.

Seeing the Addiction behind
Its Masks and Self-Disguises

Failure to identify an addiction—be it one's own or another's—is complicated by stereotypic misconceptions about who is addicted and how an addicted person behaves. An addiction is present long before the appearance of pervasive functional consequences more typical in later stages of the process. Those whose addictions are most often missed are employed, married, white, insured, and female (Schottenfeld, 1994). Recently, old age has been added to this list (Weisner and Matzger, 2003). Further masking an

Questioning the role denial plays in keeping addictions hidden has significant implications for how to approach a discussion of another's addiction. Traditional forms of addiction treatment believe that denial is at the core of addiction. Denial is a defense that is like a wall; confrontation is the means to breaking it down. Other treatment options become available when we consider the possibility that denial is not the reason why a person disagrees with a loved one or professional assessment that he or she may be addicted. What appears to be denial may in fact be a function of addiction's masks and self-disguises. Unlike the wall of denial, masks can be lifted (see part III: "Getting Help for an Addiction").

addiction are beliefs originating in one's family and culture that do not fit the realities of an addictive behavior.

The addicted person has other reasons for keeping an addiction hidden; there is fear of another's anger and avoidance of shame or the negative consequences that can arise if an addiction is revealed (e.g., job loss, loss of custody of a child). These conscious forms of avoidance need to be distinguished from classic denial, which involves an unconsciously motivated distortion of the scope of an addiction. Once you understand these various masks and disguises, addictions aren't inherently difficult to recognize.

CHAPTER 7

Subtle Signs
of Addiction

As I've already discussed, any repetitive behavior that has the capacity to powerfully modify subjective experience has the potential to become addictive (Shaffer, 1999). Despite the significance of subjective experience in the development of addictions, current diagnostic practices emphasize "objective" and readily observable signs. These signs are consistent with a mature or fully developed addiction.

It seems reasonable to expect that long before the appearance of obvious signs of late-stage addiction, there are more subtle signs indicative of an addiction in its earlier stages. Identifying an addiction early on has the potential to decrease the chances that a more serious problem will emerge.

Imagine a doctor looking at an unevenly colored patch of skin and remarking, "Well, it could be bruise or rash," rather than considering whether this discoloration is an early warning sign of skin cancer. The equivalent of this exchange routinely happens with addictions. Health care providers notice the physical and psychological consequences created by addiction but miss the addiction itself. They listen to reports of stomachaches and look for ulcers rather than alcoholism. Complaints of poor sleep, low moods, and diffuse anxiety point the way to mental health disorders rather than the addiction that creates such symptoms.

I have been guilty of looking past an addiction to see a psychological problem. Psychotherapy patients seek my help because they identify their problem as psychological in nature. If there is an addiction, they are not seeing it as the source of life's complications. At one time, I would follow their

Subtle Signs of Addiction

A behavior that

has unexpected consequences
occurs primarily for its effect
creates a "new me"
routinely exceeds normative levels
shapes my choice of friends
is usually social but is done alone
you seem to be "in love with"
is indiscriminant
continues even though the romance is gone
you would never consider cutting back
you worry is a problem

is an addiction.

lead and only see a mental health problem, but now, based on my own observations and discussions with master clinicians specializing in treating substance abuse, I recognize the following subtle signs. I think of them as subtle signs because they are subjective in nature and not covered in diagnostic manuals. Although the initial studies for these subtle signs focused on addictive substance use, many signs are relevant for identifying any kind of addictive behavior.

Subtle Signs

Unexpected Consequences

Negative consequences created by a behavior are a defining attribute of an addiction. As the person experiencing these consequences, you may not define them as negative. Instead, you will experience it as something unexpected that has happened to you. For this reason, instead of looking for negative consequences, you may want to consider asking yourself or the person you are concerned about, *Has anything happened lately that you would consider as "unexpected"? If so, was the unexpected outcome in any way linked to something you were doing?*

Unexpected consequences may be relatively minor, such as coming home later than intended or telling someone "I love you" when you had not planned to. Other unexpected outcomes have more serious implications, such as having unsafe sex or putting out so much money for gambling, shopping, or Internet pornography that financial security is threatened. At times, unexpected consequences will be less apparent than the feelings they leave behind: regret and remorse. "I wish I hadn't said all those nasty things. I was just trying to be funny." " I can't believe I forgot to come pick you up."

Taking stock of unexpected consequences is important for several reasons. First, this act of reflection can prevent exposing you or a loved one to more serious harm. Second, unexpected consequences often arise when a behavior is not planned. While there is a place for spontaneity in life, doing a behavior that routinely creates unexpected outcomes can be the first sign that you are losing control of a behavior.

One expert in the addiction field that I interviewed described how unintended outcomes often mean that an addiction is growing in severity. "When it comes to abuse [or problematic levels of a behavior], people talk about knowingly 'choosing' to get wasted. The dependent person may say the same, but their [sic] stories indicate that the drinking is much more compulsive; in their stories things just seem to happen, out of control, unpredictable things happen" (Freimuth, in press).

A Behavior Engaged in Primarily for Its Effect

Social drinkers have no other reason to drink than the setting they are in—a dinner party, meeting friends after work, a wedding. A behavior that is primarily social in nature is different from a behavior done for its effect. For some, alcohol is a way to cope. Alcohol dissolves the day's tensions or provides a sense of calm before heading into an anxiety-producing situation. Probably most everyone who drinks will from time to time use alcohol as a coping mechanism. That is different from using alcohol *primarily* as a way to cope. A behavior that occurs primarily because of the effect it creates is at risk of becoming an addiction.

A Behavior or Substance Creates a "New Me"

Listening closely to my patients' descriptions of the experiences following substance use helps me to distinguish normal from potentially addictive patterns. Reflecting what has already been said about how to define an addiction, one addiction specialist I interviewed emphasized, "It is *not* about how much one drinks but how it affects one's life, relationships, work, and relationship with self (drink to avoid being with ones self)" (Freimuth, in press). The

Only you can judge if the psychoactive effects of a substance or behavior provide potent or desirable experiences. Are you a different person with someone you encounter in cyberspace than you are when you are interacting face to face? It is also worth wondering if you are different after several days of foregoing a certain behavior.

Often, significant others are in a better position to recognize the exact nature of the changes. Bill Lee (2005), a gambling addict, senses that gambling transforms him. Whenever he is "comped" by one of his regular casinos (where the casino covers the expense of his food, drinks, and room), he brings a date:

> I wanted to impress them with my status at the casino.
> Instead, they were exposed to the side of me that one would describe as a "monster" and the other as a "sick bastard." ... Victoria Lew was more perceptive. She noted that the minute we entered the casino, my demeanor completely changed. I became distant and mean. As far as Victoria was concerned, I became possessed by the devil. (p. 87)

If you are wondering if a behavior is addictive, ask someone close to you if there are any observable changes when you become involved with that behavior.

latter—relationship to oneself—is overlooked in diagnostic manuals although this change will be most salient to the substance user.

By emphasizing "relationship to self," this clinician is calling attention to the desired subjective changes that keep drawing one back again and again to a behavior. Does the addictive behavior replace a self that is empty with a self that is filled with excitement or completeness? Does a sense of fragility and insignificance disappear behind a newly formed powerful and potent self? Or perhaps the addictive behavior transforms a self that is filled with worry and uncertainty into one that cannot be ruffled.

A number of master clinicians looked at how an addiction creates outward transformations that others are prone to call a "personality change." Substance use or a behavior is potentially addictive or already addictive if the person (it may be you) you know on a day-to-day basis is not the same person who is "under the influence." The most familiar example is the introvert who becomes an extrovert when drinking. Personality changes also occur with addictive behaviors. A woman who is shy and reticent with men becomes emotionally open and vulnerable with a man located somewhere in cyberspace. Several master clinicians speculated that such personality changes occur because addictive behaviors "filled in something that was otherwise missing for a person" (Freimuth, in press).

Routinely Exceeding Normative Behavioral Levels

Drinking is a routine part of many social occasions. Because some lifestyles provide more opportunities to drink than others (e.g., college, business meetings over meals), frequency of drinking by itself is not a reliable indicator of a problem. Instead, pay attention to the amount of alcohol that is consumed. Excessive alcohol can be defined as consuming more than the standards for safe drinking. However, a better measure may be how often you exceed the norms set by your social or peer group.

How often do you or someone you know drink more than the others around you? The businessman who has one martini at lunch with all the other one-martini drinkers is a very different kind of drinker than the businessman who orders two additional martinis. Routinely drinking more than the norm in a given situation is a sign of problem drinking. Alcoholics, once sober, often remark with surprise that they never realized how much more they drank than those around them. Next time you are out drinking, pay attention to how the amount you consume compares to others.

Social groups also define when a behavior is considered excessive. While engaging in a behavior more than one's peers is not necessarily a sign of addiction, it is still worth paying attention to. For example, if you have always followed your friends who limit their gambling losses to $300 and

There is one caveat to the rule that drinking within the limits of one's social group's norm represents normal alcohol use. Binge is normative in college and club settings. Men who have five or more drinks in a row and women who have four or more drinks at least once every two weeks are considered binge drinkers (Wechsler and Nelson, 2001). Master clinicians emphasized that, despite being the norm, this level of alcohol intake must always be considered as risky drinking because of the impaired judgment and loss of control that ensues.

you begin to exceed this norm, it is time to reassess whether your gambling is becoming more than recreational.

My Only Friends Share My Habits, Hobbies, and Addictions

A person whose friendships primarily revolve around people from bars may not be an alcoholic now, but keep an eye on that person's drinking. The memoir *The Tender Bar* (Moehringer, 2006) illustrates how limiting one's social life to bars contributes to becoming an alcoholic. Runners whose social life is confined to other runners are at greater risk of an exercise addiction. The same is true for women with spouses who are prone to gambling or drinking problems. Their risk of addiction is much greater than women married to men without these problems. For men, an addiction is shaped more by their friends than spouses.

A Social Behavior Done Alone

Part of what makes "normative" drinking normative is that it occurs with other people. Drinking or using other psychoactive substances alone on a regular basis is a sign of a potential problem. For adolescents, drinking alone is always a sign of problematic use. While adolescent experimentation is normative— insofar as it occurs with peers—drinking alone is not.

Gambling, shopping, and work are also behaviors that regularly occur within a larger social context. An addiction is more likely when gambling with friends is replaced with gambling alone or when working alone on weekends becomes preferable to being in the office among people during the week. A behavior that originates as part of a social activity but later occurs primarily in isolation is a behavior that is at risk.

"To My Love—Addiction!"

A number of master clinicians distinguished normal from problematic drinking by closely examining the person's relationship to the substance. Substance use is problematic when the attachment to the substance is stronger than one's connection to people. On his way home from work, a man is more excited about having a drink than seeing the family that is waiting for him. A woman chooses to stay home and drink even though it means being the last one to meet up with her group of friends. Another significant sign of problematic use is when a person has difficulty interacting with others when not under the influence.

It is not uncommon for significant others in an addict's life to feel that alcohol or an addictive behavior has become the primary relationship. No doubt it was this realization that shaped Caroline Knapp's decision to title her book *Drinking: A Love Story* (1996).

Lovelike attachments also develop with behaviors. Many people are attracted to the computer for social reasons, as a means for interacting with other people. However, some find greater enjoyment interacting with people through the computer than face-to-face. A woman I treated provides a typical example: she found it difficult to maintain female friendships and rarely if ever went out with a man for more than a few dates. Her anxiety and anger made her difficult to be with. However, when typing on the computer, she displayed more self-control and was quite charming. The result was that many men courted her online. Gradually she cut off all social contacts outside of work so she could go home and to be with her men on the computer. The men of cyberspace became her primary relationships.

Although It's Love, Any Lover Will Do

The psychoanalyst Kohut (1987) has written about addiction's ability to wipe out all differentiation. In the urgency to gratify a craving, any kind of alcohol will do for an alcoholic. As applied to addictive relationships, feeling loved or desired by another person, any person, becomes more important than the quality of the relationship. For the person addicted to buying, there is little enjoyment in searching for the right thing. Rather, there is a driving need to make a purchase, even if it is not needed or really liked. The injured athlete who can no longer run and spends hours doing ungratifying bench presses reveals a similar attitude.

The Behavior Continues, but the Romance Is Gone

Master clinicians said they could distinguish someone who is fully addicted from someone who is an at-risk or problem drinker based on how the person responded to a substance's psychoactive effects. A problem drinker drinks until the stress is relieved and replaced by good feelings. Drinking is a way to cope. In contrast, when the addiction is fully developed, drinking continues even after the desired effect is achieved. Recognizing that a behavior that once facilitated coping continues, despite the absence of any gain in pleasure or relief from distress, is a sign that a behavior is moving toward being fully addictive.

Continuing an activity after achieving the desired effect is a warning sign for behavioral addictions as well. For the social gambler, the excitement of taking a risk is just a part of the pleasure. For problem gamblers, excitement is the primary reason to gamble. This excitement lifts depression or provides an escape from problems; gambling is a way to cope. By the time gambling is fully addictive, there is little pleasure left. The behavior continues long after the excitement is gone. From the addicted person's perspective, the behavior continues with a single-minded intensity in an attempt—ultimately futile—to regain the pleasure that has been lost.

Bill Lee's (2005) evolution into a pathological gambler followed this route from pleasure, to coping, to days and nights of relentless betting devoid of any benefits. Lee finds out early in life that gambling helps him to cope. Through gambling he escapes his profound sense of worthlessness. Winning a bet provides momentary escape from this emotional poverty. When Lee's gambling becomes addictive, it is a behavior that transcends its ability to help him cope. There is nothing exciting or engaging about winning or losing. Gambling becomes simply a means to place the next bet.

I Would Never Consider Stopping or Cutting Back

The simplest way to distinguish a normal behavior from one that is becoming addictive is to consider quitting or cutting back. Is there a sense of panic at the prospect of not having a drink at the end of the day or running daily? Does it seem out of the question to have just one drink rather than three or to forego gambling this weekend? If a request to stop or cut back leads to excuses or explanations about why the behavior is not a problem or there is no need to change, then chances are good that the behavior is already problematic.

Insisting that there can't be a problem because only wine is consumed or the behavior only occurs on an intermittent basis does not eliminate the need to be concerned. Each of these excuses reflects a myth about addictive behaviors discussed in chapter 5; a person who drinks only wine can be an alcoholic just as a person who drinks intermittently can be substance dependent.

Do You Think You Have a Problem?

One clinician I interviewed cuts through the complexities of diagnosis and assessment with the following edict: if you worry about whether you are addicted, then you probably have a problem!

Have you ever thought that you drink too much? That you are an alcoholic? Have you ever worried that you exercise too much? Work too much? Spend too much time thinking about sex? If you answer yes to questions like these, then it is time to make a change.

Unmasking
Addiction

I n part II, you will find a variety of assessment tools to help you decide
if your own or another's behavior is addictive. Given that potentially any
object, experience, or behavior can become addictive makes it impossible to cover all addictions. Instead, I address the most common addictions
and those that are most easily disguised. Substance addictions masquerade as
depression or anxiety. An exercise addiction wears the façade of a "health
nut." A gambling addiction, like substance addictions, may be disguised as
a physical problem, or, like Internet and sex addictions, simply hidden
behind closed doors.

In the case of alcohol and drugs, screening tools have been specially
designed for women, adolescents, and older adults, given that negative consequences of substance use vary based on gender and age. Chapters 9 and

10 provide scales uniquely designed for these groups. Tools that screen for the behavioral addictions do not address specific populations even though age and gender can shape their signs and symptoms. For this reason, I will be describing the ways in which these addictions differ as a function of gender and age. If the behavior that concerns you has no screening tool, you can still see if the behavior has addictive attributes by following the suggestions provided at the end of this introduction.

How Accurate Are Self-Reports?

Most addiction screening tools are blatantly obvious about what is being measured. This means that if people wish to hide the problem, they only need to give false responses. Even when a person is motivated to be absolutely honest, self-reports are not completely accurate. This is just the nature of self-reports. You may have worried about a behavior or wondered if it was "too much," but this is different than "quantifying" it. When asked how much you drink a week or how often you fail to meet an obligation due to exercise, this is likely the first time you are actually being asked to figure out the frequency or amount of a behavior and the nature of its adverse effects. As a result, when asked about the extent of substance use over two or three different occasions, the amount of reported use increases each time (Hodgins and Makarchuck, 2003; Tonigan, Miller, and Brown, 1997). This suggests that the initial questions about an addiction serve as a catalyst to think more about it. As a result, more accurate information is provided when questions are asked again at a later point in time. Improved recall with further questioning can be expected for most anything, assuming the person wants to be honest. Do you know how many light switches are in your bedroom or bottles of mustard in the refrigerator? Once asked, you will begin to pay more attention to these items. How much alcohol do you drink a week? Exactly how much money do you spend on clothes each month? How long do you spend on the computer each night? Once asked, you will pay more attention to your actions and give more realistic answers when later asked, "How much?" "How long?"

Reported negative consequences also change with repeated questioning. As discussed, addictions remain hidden because a person fails to connect their adverse effects (e.g., anxiety, depression, health problems, increased anger) to the true source. Screening tools ask questions inquiring whether a given behavior has had this or that effect. By calling attention to the fact that the behavior can have specific harmful outcomes makes it difficult to ignore those outcomes next time they occur.

My clinical experience supports the research findings: asking the same question at different times leads to a reported increase in quantity and scope of negative consequences.

Upon entering therapy for periodic bouts of depression, a man in his sixties reported drinking five out of seven nights a week with two drinks each night. He was unaware of any adverse effects except falling asleep at his computer. At his age, this level of alcohol consumption was of concern so when he returned two weeks later for a second appointment, I asked again about his drinking. This time he reported daily drinking and the initial report of two drinks a day turned out to be three or four. Likewise, he had begun to connect bouts of indigestion (something I had asked about in the first session) with his drinking. When asked if indigestion was a problem that arose since our first appointment, his response was no, he was just more aware.

The increased accuracy in self-reports with repeated screenings applies to adults but not adolescents. The professionals who work with this age group emphasize that, no matter how often he or she is asked, an adolescent's reported use is underestimated. Adolescents are much less willing to recognize or acknowledge the existence of a problem. The reasons for this are discussed in chapter 9. The full extent of their substance use usually does not emerge until several weeks into intensive treatment. Part of the therapy for adolescents whose drug use is severe enough to require residential treatment involves writing a letter to their parents acknowledging the full scope of substance use. Parents are routinely shocked by the frequency, quantity, and scope of drugs that were being taken (B. Posner, 2005, personal communication; Volkman and Volkman, 2006).

Interpreting a Screening's Outcome

Screening instruments detect the *possibility* of an addiction. I encourage you to use these screening tools in the same way—as a first step in identifying a problem. Approach the score on a screening instrument as an opportunity to learn something more about yourself or the person about whom you are concerned.

If it is your score, look at the specific items that contribute to your total score and consider what they mean for your life. Take time to consider whether the questions that did *not* describe your behavior may in fact have some relevance.

When screening tools are given in health care settings, the only outcome of interest is whether the total score meets or exceeds the cutoff for a fully developed addiction. The continuum view of addiction presented previously provides a different way of thinking about a screening's outcome; meeting or exceeding the cutoff is *not* the only important information. Given the significance of early identification and intervention, any positive response merits consideration. Even if the total score is indicative of addiction, this outcome should not be mistaken for a diagnosis. Even professionals do not use screening tools for this purpose. If the result of a screening is positive, further assessment by an appropriately trained health care professional is strongly recommended. It may turn out that what appears to be an addiction is actually masking another problem. What appears to be alcoholism is a depression or anxiety disorder that is being self-medicated with alcohol. What appears to be a sexual addiction can be the outcome of a brain tumor. An exercise addiction can mask an eating disorder. This point is critical: a positive screening should be followed up with further input from your health care provider.

Addictions without Screening Tools

If this book does not provide a screening tool for the behavior that concerns you, first see if any of the subtle signs of addiction discussed in chapter 7 are in evidence. You can also answer the following questions derived from criteria that compose addictive disorders that were discussed in chapter 2.

> The screening tools in part II have been found to be reliable and valid. Reliability refers to the scale's ability to recognize a problem at different points in time. A scale is not useful if it indicates that you're an alcoholic today, but not when taken next week, even though your drinking habits have not changed. A scale's validity reflects the fact that it measures what it intends to measure. Just as a bathroom scale measures weight, addiction screening tools should be measuring some kind of addiction. A valid measure of work addiction measures an addiction to work, not a habit to work hard or some other kind of addiction or emotional problem.

Addictive Disorder Screen

1. Thinking back to when I first began the behavior,
   (a) I now need an increased amount or intensity of the behavior in order to achieve the same desired effect.
   (b) I am experiencing a diminished effect of the behavior, which has continued at the same level of intensity.
2. Is one or both of the following true for you?
   (a) When I discontinue the behavior, I experience some kind of discomfort (e.g., anxiety, depression, headache, not feeling like myself, flulike symptoms).
   (b) I do the behavior in order to relieve or avoid uncomfortable feelings that would occur if I stopped the behavior.
3. Do you engage in a behavior over a longer period, in greater quantity, or at a higher level of intensity than intended?
4. Have you had a desire or unsuccessful efforts to cut down or control the behavior?
5. Do you spend a great deal of time in activities necessary to prepare for the behavior, to engage in the behavior, or to recover from its effects?
6. Have important social, occupational, or recreational activities been given up or reduced because of this behavior?
7. Do you continue this behavior despite having persistent or recurrent physical and psychological problems that are caused or exacerbated by the behavior?
8. Do you experience some element of craving or compulsion to do the behavior?

SCORING: For questions 1 and 2, score 1 point if either A or B is a yes. For questions 3–8, score 1 point for each yes. A total of 3 or more is indicative of an addictive disorder at the problematic or fully developed level. (Based on Goodman, 1998)

How to Use Part II

Each chapter begins with a general description of the addiction, who is most prone to this addiction, and how age and gender influence what this addiction looks like. A list of common symptoms is provided. This is followed by a description of the addiction's appearance at different points along the continuum from social level to fully addicted. The chapter ends with a screening tool that measures different levels of the addiction. Chapters on behavioral addictions include this information as well as descriptions of the masks and self-disguises that are unique to each addiction.

If you are reading this book because you wonder if someone in your life is addicted, don't be surprised if this person expresses disinterest when asked to complete a screening tool. In this case, turn to part III, where I describe ways to engage a person in becoming curious about his or her addiction. Or, you can consider the person's behavior in light of the questions on the screening tool and what you have learned about addiction's disguises. If an addiction seems likely, part III will help you take the necessary steps to initiate help for the problem.

When using these self-report instruments to assess your own addiction, remember that chances are good that a positive score means there is a problem that is in need of attention. Even low scores have something to tell you. Look closely at the scale items that contributed to your score, whether the ultimate score indicates a problem or not. Carefully consider what problems the behavior is creating. How much danger is this problem creating for you and others? What kind of emotional costs are there to the behavior?

The outcome of these scales is just one piece of the puzzle, not all of it. If you worry about being addicted, then it is time to go for a further assessment.

CHAPTER 8

Unmasking Substance Addictions

In the 1950s, hearing that someone was addicted would conjure up the image of a white middle-aged man who could not control his alcohol intake. Today, you are more likely to wonder which substance it is. Instead of someone middle-aged, a much younger person will come to mind. And while chances are good you will picture a man, in reality women's problematic substance use is quickly approaching the rate for men.

Alcoholism remains the most common substance addiction, although addictions to other readily available products such as airplane glue, cleaning agents, and over-the-counter medications, chiefly cough medicines, are on the rise. Abuse of prescription medications, especially those with stimulating or sedating effects, is approaching epidemic proportions. Despite ready access to these other substances, after alcohol, the two most frequently abused substances are illegal—marijuana and cocaine.

Given the array of substances to which one can become addicted, professional diagnostic manuals strive to create general descriptions that will apply to problematic use of any substance. Thus, in current manuals, there is no diagnosis known as alcoholism. In fact, as mentioned previously, there is not even a reference to addiction. In its place, the DSM-IV, the most commonly used manual in the United States, utilizes the term "substance-related disorders."

Substance-related disorders come in two forms: substance abuse and substance dependence. Substance abuse involves intentional misuse or overuse of a substance that results in negative consequences. Substance dependence carries the connotation of a fully developed addiction. In the DSM-IV, a diagnosis of alcoholism would be "substance dependence: alcohol."

Substance Abuse

Substance abuse is characterized by a pattern of substance use that creates recurrent adverse consequences. These consequences fall into two types: (1) social problems and (2) hazards or harm.

The negative social consequences of substance abuse include (1) legal problems, such as arrests for disorderly conduct or driving under the influence; (2) interpersonal problems, such as frequent arguments with a partner, decline in sexual relations, or loss of friendships; (3) decline in school or work performance; and (4) failure to meet role obligations, such as a parent forgetting to pick up a child after school due to substance use.

The hazards of substance use refer to placing oneself or others in harm's way as a result of substance intake. Hazards include driving or operating machinery while intoxicated, using unclean needles that increase the risk of HIV infection or hepatitis, or unsafe sex when under the influence of a drug.

DSM-IV Criteria for Substance Abuse

A maladaptive pattern of substance use leading to clinically significant impairment or distress as manifested by one (or more) of the following, occurring within a twelve-month period:

1. Recurrent substance use resulting in a failure to fulfill major role obligations at work, school, or home (e.g., repeated absences or poor work performance related to substance use; substance-related absences, suspensions, or expulsions from school; neglect of children or household)
2. Recurrent substance use in situations in which it is physically hazardous (e.g., driving an automobile or operating a machine when impaired by substance use)
3. Recurrent substance-related legal problems (e.g., arrests for substance-related disorderly conduct)
4. Continued substance use despite having persistent or recurrent social or interpersonal problems caused or exacerbated by the effects of the substance (e.g., arguments with spouse about consequences of intoxication, physical fights). (American Psychiatric Association, 2000, p. 199)

A diagnosis of substance abuse requires that adverse effects are "continued" or "recurrent." A one-time alcohol-induced fight with a spouse is not substance abuse. A few Monday mornings of lost work productivity due to a hangover, likewise, does not make you a substance abuser. Using a continuum view of addictions, a few substance-induced detrimental effects places you in the at-risk category.

There is one adverse outcome of substance use that I think should not require repetitive occurrences in order to qualify for a diagnosis: being arrested for DUI (driving under the influence) or DWI (driving while intoxicated). To me, one DUI or DWI qualifies as a recurrent hazardous consequence. Despite protestations that "I am so unlucky; this is the first time I ever drove after drinking!" the lore among addiction professionals is that this person has in fact been lucky—lucky not to get arrested or have had an accident before this time. Given the life-threatening nature of driving while intoxicated, even one such infraction should be considered evidence of substance abuse.

Substance Dependence

The two substance-related disorders are assumed to follow a natural developmental course from substance misuse to substance abuse and ultimately substance dependence. Viewed as a progressive disorder, using substances more than occasionally and/or outside of social situations will gradually result in increasing levels of consumption until the adverse effects associated with substance abuse emerge. Over time, intermittent difficulties in meeting role obligations become functional impairments and potentially hazardous consequences become real outcomes.

This developmental sequence is not supported by research. When it comes to substance-related disorders (and this probably holds true for behavioral addictions), most people do not move from abuse to dependence. Usually, substance abusers remain abusers or overcome their problem by returning to normal drinking or stopping altogether. Those most likely to progress from abuse to dependence have one or more risk factors for addiction: having a family member with an addiction, beginning substance use at an early age (Schukit et al., 2001), using substances as a primary way of coping (M. Cooper, Frone, Russell, and Mudar, 1995), or using substances to create significant shifts in subjective experience.

The distinguishing feature of substance dependence is a cluster of symptoms that conveys the sense that a person has lost control and, hence, is dependent on the substance. Although being "out of control" is central to a diagnosis of substance dependence, this is not one of the seven criteria on which this diagnosis is based. Professional diagnostic practices strive to be objective, and "out of control" ultimately is a subjective judgment. Routinely getting plastered at sporting events may be "having fun" for the drinker, but evidence for the spouse that drinking is "out of control." To avoid such differences of opinion, "out of control" is inferred from actions such as (1) continued use despite negative consequences, (2) the substance takes on a central role in a person's life, (3) attempts to cut back have been unsuccessful, and (4) larger amounts than intended are used. Although the goal is objectivity, these criteria are not devoid of subjectivity. What signifies that substances have taken on a "central role" in a person's life? Who decides if the amount used was larger than intended?

DSM-IV Criteria for Substance Dependence

A maladaptive pattern of substance use leading to clinically significant impairment or distress, as manifested by three (or more) of the following occurring at any time in the same twelve-month period:

1. Tolerance
2. Withdrawal
3. The substance is often taken in larger amounts or over a longer period than was intended
4. There is a persistent desire or unsuccessful efforts to cut down or control substance use
5. A great deal of time is spent on activities necessary to obtain the substance (e.g., visiting multiple doctors or driving long distances), use of the substance (e.g., chain-smoking), or recovery from its effects
6. Important social, occupational, or recreational activities are given up or reduced because of substance use
7. The substance use is continued despite knowledge of having a persistent or recurrent physical or psychological problem that is likely to have been caused or exacerbated by the substance (e.g., current cocaine use

Two of the best-known and most widely used legal, addictive substances are nicotine and caffeine. The only diagnostic option for nicotine is dependence. Most people will be happy to know that although caffeine is considered an addictive substance, there is no diagnostic code for caffeine abuse or dependence.

despite recognition of cocaine-induced depression, or continued drinking despite recognition that an ulcer was made worse by alcohol consumption). (American Psychiatric Association, 2000, p. 197).

Heaps of Substances

The criteria that define substance abuse and substance dependence can be used with any of the multitude of psychoactive (mood- and mind-altering) substances. To create order, this array has been grouped into categories based on a substance's effect. The major categories are alcohol and sedatives, stimulants, cannabis, opioids, and hallucinogens. Appendix II lists common names for substances within each category, typical methods of use, addictive potential, range of effects, and direct negative consequences.

Substances that do not fit into one of these categories are placed in a catchall category known as "other or unknown substance-related disorders." Pharmaceutical companies manufacture many substances in this category. A few common examples are nitrous oxide, anabolic steroids, and over-the-counter cough and cold medicines. The abuse of cough and cold medicines has become common enough to receive its own name: robotripping ("robo" is taken from the name of a popular cough medicine). The active ingredients in these medicines create hallucinations and euphoric feelings. In order to stem the tide of this growing addiction many states now have laws that require drug stores to limit the sale of cough medicine.

Continuum of Substance-Related Addictions

The continuum of addiction is easiest to describe for alcohol because there is accepted terminology and standards for different degrees of use. At one end of the continuum is the abstainer and at the other is the fully developed alcoholic.

The Latest Fad Addiction:
Prescription Medication Misuse

Misusing a prescription drug means taking it on an ongoing basis in any way other than as prescribed. Misuse occurs when a medication is taken in an amount greater than prescribed or used for purposes other than as prescribed (e.g., a muscle relaxant taken to calm anxiety). Medications that are most prone to abuse include opiates prescribed for pain relief, antianxiety drugs prescribed to alleviate stress or sleep disorders, and stimulants given to curtail attention problems. Misuse of prescription medications is considered a form of substance abuse.

Substance abuse through misuse of prescription stimulants is documented in Elizabeth Wurtzel's autobiography, *More, Now, Again* (2002). Wurtzel, a Harvard graduate and best-selling author of *Prozac Nation*, was under the care of a psychiatrist who prescribed Ritalin to alleviate the difficulties she had completing writing assignments. Wurtzel discovered that Ritalin's effects were heightened when snorted. Thus began her odyssey of lying about lost prescriptions to get more of the drug from her psychiatrist while also procuring Ritalin and cocaine through illegal channels. Substance abuse turned into dependence. Snorting turned into intravenous injections, and ultimately ended in an emotional breakdown, hospitalization, and recovery.

Another commonly abused prescription medication is oxycodone, one of the more popular pain relievers from the opioid category. Rush Limbaugh was addicted to this drug. As was the case for Limbaugh, many who become addicted to this medication initially receive it from a physician who prescribed it for relief of acute pain. No doubt the easy access to such substances through Internet pharmacies has contributed to the growth of this kind of addiction.

Social Use

Social drinkers have no other reason for drinking than the setting. They drink with friends before and during dinner or join in on a champagne toast at a fiftieth anniversary party. Substance use is a means to enhance social activity; it is not the primary activity (e.g., getting drunk). Social drinkers do not rely on alcohol as a coping mechanism. Every now and then, alcohol may be used to relax but the primary reasons for drinking remain social in nature.

Social drinking is also distinguished by the absence of repeated adverse effects. This is because the social drinker has control over drinking. This is

Continuum of Substance-Related Addictions

	Social User	*At-Risk User*	*Problem User*	*Full Addiction*
Motivation	situational	situational	coping	avoid withdrawal feel normal
Consequences	none or minor infrequent	mild intermittent	more severe recurring	functional constant
Diagnosis			*Abuse*	*Dependence*

not to say that a social drinker *never* experiences direct negative consequences. There is an occasional hangover or regret for having been less than thoughtful while under the influence. Such negative outcomes are infrequent and more serious effects do not develop.

Social situations have norms for "appropriate drinking." Having one glass of wine at a luncheon business meeting is social drinking; having three vodka martinis is not. Routinely drinking more than is normative for the given social situation is not social use. Be aware when drinking norms exceed what can be considered safe. The best example is binge drinking (consuming large quantities of alcohol in short periods of time), typical on college campuses but certainly not confined to these settings.

Alcohol is unique among the substances of abuse because the government has created standards for defining nonhazardous use.

Moderate or Non-Hazardous Drinking Limits

Men under sixty-five:
Two standard drinks* per day
No more than fourteen drinks per week
No more than five drinks on one occasion
Women (all ages) and men over sixty-five:
One standard drink* per day
No more than seven drinks per week
No more than three drinks on one occasion

*Standard drink: 12 ounces of 4.5 percent beer; 5 ounces of 12.9 percent wine; 1.5 ounces of 80-proof liquor. (U.S. Department of Health and Human Services, 2000).

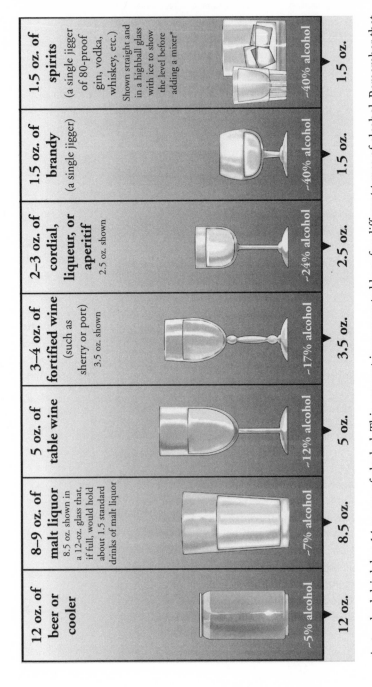

12 oz. of beer or cooler	8–9 oz. of malt liquor 8.5 oz. shown in a 12-oz. glass that, if full, would hold about 1.5 standard drinks of malt liquor	5 oz. of table wine	3–4 oz. of fortified wine (such as sherry or port) 3.5 oz. shown	2–3 oz. of cordial, liqueur, or aperitif 2.5 oz. shown	1.5 oz. of brandy (a single jigger)	1.5 oz. of spirits (a single jigger of 80-proof gin, vodka, whiskey, etc.) Shown straight and in a highball glass with ice to show the level before adding a mixer*
~5% alcohol	~7% alcohol	~12% alcohol	~17% alcohol	~24% alcohol	~40% alcohol	~40% alcohol
12 oz.	8.5 oz.	5 oz.	3.5 oz.	2.5 oz.	1.5 oz.	1.5 oz.

A standard drink has 14 grams of alcohol. This amount is represented here for different types of alcohol. Remember that a "typical drink" can be larger than a "standard drink." A glass of wine is often more than 5 ounces, and many cans of beer are more than 12 ounces.

Courtesy of U.S. Department of Health and Human Services, *Helping Patients Who Drink Too Much: A Clinician's Guide*, 2005.

No other substance has had moderate use quantified in the way alcohol has. It seems odd to refer to someone as a "social user" of marijuana. It sounds even stranger to refer to the "recreational" heroin user. Yet, there are people who use these substances in very circumscribed manners. Often this is accomplished by following "norms" for nonhazardous use set by their substance-using peers. Pot-smoking businesspeople, referred to in *Details* magazine as "white-collar stoners" (Kurutz, 2003), only smoke in the evenings and never during the day when marijuana's effect could impede their acumen. Similar norms of "safe use" have been described for heroin users (Zinberg, 1994).

Drinking within these limits is described as "nonhazardous," "safe," or "moderate" because these amounts are unlikely to create impaired judgment, and there is a low risk of alcohol creating persistent health problems or psychological aftereffects. Social drinkers drink at nonhazardous levels except on rare occasions. Regularly exceeding these levels results in an increased risk of experiencing adverse physical and psychological reactions.

Safe limits are based on the average-sized man and woman. Gender, age, health status, mental illness, and pregnancy are some of the many factors that affect the amount of alcohol that is qualified as safe. Ultimately, whether a given amount of alcohol can be considered safe or not depends on the blood alcohol level (BAL) or blood alcohol content (BAC) it creates.

At-Risk Use to Problem Use

Routinely drinking in a way that exceeds safe levels places you at risk for developing a more serious problem because alcohol impedes judgment and lessens motor control. This means that the at-risk drinker is exposed to alcohol's negative effects but usually these are intermittent and limited in scope. Not so for the problem drinker where negative effects are more routine. At-risk and problem drinkers differ in how they react to the negative effects. An at-risk drinker is truly surprised when substance use creates an unexpected consequence. For the problem drinker, "unexpected" consequences have become sufficiently familiar that they are no longer a surprise.

One's motivation for drinking plays a large role in determining whether intermittent, at-risk drinking becomes problematic. The at-risk drinker, who is like the social drinker and drinks primarily in response to the situation, is not likely to evolve into a problematic drinker. This is the binge drinker who

Blood Alcohol Level

Most of us are familiar with the breathalyzer, a simple and immediate means of measuring blood alcohol level (BAL). To be accurate, a breathalyzer or similar instrument must be used shortly after alcohol consumption because the body rapidly metabolizes alcohol. BAL represents the ratio of alcohol to blood—more specifically, it refers to numbers of milligrams of alcohol per 100 milligrams of blood. A BAL of .1 means that there is 1 milligram of alcohol per 100 milligrams of blood. As BAL increases, so does alcohol's effects.

BAL Level	Alcohol's Effects
.02	Relaxed, decreased inhibitions, good feelings. Anyone in a transportation-related job where safety is an issue would be removed from work. Government standards are based on keeping BAL below this level.
.05	More relaxed, but feeling less alert, less focused.
.08	Coordination is slowed and alertness lessens further. You can be arrested for a BAL of .08 or higher.
.10	Coordination, vision, reasoning, and judgment are impaired.
.15	Reaction time is markedly slowed, behavior is disinhibited; this is a stereotypical sloppy, noisy drunk.
.30	Continued loss of motor control, restlessness, anxiety, confusion, and possible loss of consciousness.
.40	Loss of consciousness.

It is difficult to know in advance just how many drinks will create a given BAL. What qualifies as moderate drinking—a BAL less than .05—depends on numerous variables including age, gender, physical size, health status, medications, and the amount of water and food consumed. Even the type of alcohol can influence how rapidly alcohol accumulates. In other words, before concluding that your drinking or another's is within safe limits, you must consider the larger context in which it occurs. To see if your drinking is within acceptable limits, the following site provides a BAL estimate based on gender, type of alcoholic beverage, and amount of time to consume the drink(s): www.intox.com/wheel/drinkwheel.asp.

consumes alcohol in an unsafe manner but only when accompanied by peers who are binge drinking. In contrast, the at-risk drinker who is on the road to becoming a problem drinker consumes alcohol *primarily* as a way to cope or feel better.

Problem Use to Addicted Use

When alcohol is used to alleviate distress, a person drinks until the stress is replaced by good feelings. The danger in using alcohol to relax is that it takes one or two drinks to begin to relax (.02 BAL), but it takes a BAL of .05 or higher to forget one's worries and feel good. These additional drinks result in drowsiness, fuzzy thinking, and impaired reasoning. These alcohol-induced changes set the stage for more severe and recurring negative consequences.

Problem drinkers are distinguished from those who are fully addicted by the kind of adverse effects created by drinking. The problem drinker experiences the direct negative effects of alcohol on a fairly regular basis (e.g., hangovers, falls). Alcohol-induced impairments in judgment and control create adverse effects that extend beyond the drinker (e.g., fights with a spouse, risky sexual behavior). Problems increase in frequency until they can be considered recurrent. A full addiction is in evidence when substance use results in life-altering changes in functioning described in the criteria for substance dependence (as listed on page 96).

Screening for Alcoholism

CAGE

The most familiar screening tool is the CAGE. Medical providers and psychotherapists, like me, are encouraged by insurance companies to routinely ask the four CAGE questions.

CAGE Alcohol Screen

1. Have you ever felt you should cut down on your drinking?
2. Have people annoyed you by criticizing you about your drinking?
3. Have you ever felt guilty about your drinking?
4. Have you ever had a drink first thing in the morning to steady your nerves or to get rid of a hangover?

A point is scored for each affirmative reply; a score of 2 or 3 is indicative of problematic alcohol use.

Steps along the Continuum of Substance-Related Addictions

Social Substance Use
Motivation: Social use occurs for social reasons, an activity shared with other people.
Consequences: Negative effects are rare and minor.
Frequency/Amount: The amount consumed is appropriate for the setting and within safe limits (i.e., does not impair judgment or motor control).

At-Risk Substance Use
Motivation: At-risk use is primarily a shared social activity but can occur alone occasionally.
Consequences: Intermittent negative consequences are limited in severity. Initially, negative outcomes are unexpected; learning from these "unexpected" experiences means problematic substance use is less likely to develop.
Frequency/Amount: Exceeds safe levels on an intermittent or routine basis.

Problematic Substance Use
See criteria for substance abuse on page 96.
Motivation: Substances are used as a coping mechanism. Substance use stops when the goal of feeling better or coping is achieved.
Consequences: Negative consequences come as no surprise and are apparent to self and others.
Frequency/Amount: Routinely exceeds safe limits; this amount creates impaired control and judgment that sets the stage for more severe consequences to emerge.

Dependent Substance Use
See criteria for substance dependence on page 96.
Motivation: Initially motivated to feel "normal," one's best self. Later motivated to avoid withdrawal.
Consequences: Functional impairments emerge. The user finds it difficult to keep use under control.
Frequency/Amount: Substance use continues even after desired effects are achieved.

Other than the benefit of brevity for the busy physician, I do not find the CAGE a good screening tool. It only identifies later stage alcoholism and does not take degrees of alcohol problems into account.

AUDIT

No screening tool assesses drinking problems along a continuum, but the closest one is the Alcohol Use Disorder Identification Test, better known as AUDIT (Saunders, Aasland, Babor, De La Fuente, and Grant, 1993). The AUDIT identifies whether drinking is problematic, and if not problematic, whether current alcohol consumption can be considered risky or hazardous.

Alcohol Use Disorder Identification Test (AUDIT)

1. How often do you have a drink containing alcohol?
   a. Never b. Monthly c. 2–4 times a month
   d. 2–3 times a week e. 4 or more times a week
2. On a typical day that you drink alcohol, how many drinks do you have?
   a. 1–2 b. 3–4 c. 5–6 d. 7–9 e. 10 or more
3. How often do you have six or more drinks on one occasion?
   a. Never b. Less than monthly c. Monthly
   d. Weekly, daily, or almost daily
4. How often during the past year have you found that you were not able to stop drinking once you started?
   a. Never b. Less than monthly c. Monthly d. Weekly
   e. Daily or almost daily
5. How often during the past year have you failed to do what was normally expected from you because of drinking?
   a. Never b. Less than monthly c. Monthly d. Weekly
   e. Daily or almost daily
6. How often during the past year have you needed a drink in the morning to get yourself going after a heavy drinking session?
   a. Never b. Less than monthly c. Monthly d. Weekly
   e. Daily or almost daily
7. How often during the past year have you had a feeling of guilt or remorse after drinking?
   a. Never b. Less than monthly c. Monthly d. Weekly
   e. Daily or almost daily

8. How often during the past year have you been unable to remember what happened the night before because you had been drinking?
   a. Never b. Less than monthly c. Monthly d. Weekly
   e. Daily or almost daily

9. Have you or someone else been injured as a result of your drinking?
   a. No b. Yes, but not in the past year
   c. Yes, during the past year

10. Has a relative or friend or doctor or other health worker been concerned about your drinking or suggested you cut down?
   a. No b. Yes, but not in the past year c. Yes, during the past year

SCORING: Responses to questions 1–8 are scored 0–4 points (a = 0, b = 1, c = 2, d = 3, e = 4). Questions 9 and 10 are scored a = 0, b = 2, c = 4. For men, a total score of 8 or more is evidence of problematic alcohol use. For women, a cutoff score of 6 indicates problematic alcohol use, although some researchers have argued that for optimal identification, a score of 4 should be used (Bradley, Boyd-Wickizer, Powell, and Burman, 1998). There is one qualification to this scoring system. When scoring question 2, low-risk drinking (the maximum safe amount) is defined as two standard drinks a day for men and one for women and anyone over sixty-five. Remember that even this amount can be harmful (i.e., creating problems) for the elderly, pregnant women, or those with medical conditions.

The first three AUDIT questions measure alcohol consumption to determine whether it qualifies as "safe." The accuracy of the score depends on responses being based on a "standard drink" as stated above. A jelly jar filled with Scotch or a beer stein of vodka is not a standard drink. The AUDIT's other seven questions ask about alcohol-related consequences during the past year. Even if the total score indicates the absence of an alcohol-related problem, answers to these questions provide valuable information about aspects of life negatively affected by drinking.

Quantity/Frequency Questionnaire

Unsafe drinking greatly increases the chance of developing problematic alcohol use. For this reason, the U.S. Department of Health and Human Services

(2000) designed a scale to identify hazardous drinking levels. Appropriately named the Quantity/Frequency Questionnaire, this screen determines if you are drinking within safe limits. While very similar to the AUDIT's initial questions, this scale provides a slightly different set of questions that are more effective in identifying binge drinking. All answers should be based on a "standard drink," as defined on page 100.

Quantity/Frequency Questionnaire

1. On average, how many days per week do you drink alcohol?
2. On a typical day when you drink, how many drinks do you have?
3. What is the maximum number of drinks you have had on a specific occasion during the past month?

SCORING: There is no overall numerical score. Rather, the scale allows you to quantify your drinking to see if it meets the criteria for hazardous drinking.

Question 1: It is recommended that a person abstain from alcohol at least two days per week.

Question 2: Men are not to exceed two standard drinks per day while women and anyone over sixty-five should not have more than one standard drink. Hazardous drinking is in evidence if you exceed these limits on a "typical day" or if you are drinking the recommended amount but also have other risk factors (e.g., mental illness, poor health, pregnant).

Question 3: This question checks for binge drinking. A person who drinks normally and infrequently could still be drinking hazardously by having a large number of drinks on rare occasions. A man who drinks more than five drinks and a woman who has more than four drinks on one occasion is consuming alcohol in a harmful manner.

Another approach to assess unsafe drinking is to calculate how many standard drinks are consumed each week. To do this, multiply the number of days per week that you drink (question 1) by the number of drinks per day (question 2). For men, problem drinking is defined as having fourteen drinks per week. For women the cutoff is seven drinks per week (Substance Abuse and Mental Health Services Administration, 2002). Exceeding these levels is labeled "heavy" alcohol use.

Research on the accuracy of self-reporting indicates that the more often you are asked a question, the more accurate your answer becomes. After taking one of these screening tools for the first time, save your results. Then, after two to four weeks, take it again and see if your answers have changed.

Hazardous Drinking? Alcohol Abuse? Alcohol Dependence?

A forty-eight-year-old mildly obese woman with a history of depression describes herself as a "social drinker." She is married and works as a manager in a department store. She reports drinking "most every evening" with her husband but limits herself to two or three drinks. On weekends, she has been known to drink twice as much. Overall, she reports being happily married, although she and her spouse fight a great deal about money. These fights are more volatile on weekends after she has been drinking. There is no evidence of tolerance or withdrawal; she recently stopped drinking for several days before dental surgery. Is this hazardous drinking? Alcohol abuse? Alcohol dependence?

Despite describing herself as a "social drinker," this woman's weekly consumption (two or three drinks nearly every evening) exceeds safe limits. Her extra body weight might make it possible to drink more with less effect. However, she routinely drinks more than the one drink that is consistent with safe drinking.

There can be little doubt that her drinking is creating problems. The amount of alcohol consumption exacerbates her weight problem, and its sedating effects may be enhancing the depression that preceded her drinking. The intensity of interpersonal conflicts with her husband is increased by alcohol. Based on these observations, her drinking meets at least one criterion necessary to diagnose alcohol abuse: continued use despite recurrent interpersonal problems that are caused or exacerbated by alcohol. A diagnosis of dependence is not warranted because her drinking meets only one of the three criteria needed to make this diagnosis (she continues drinking despite knowledge that alcohol exacerbates psychological and interpersonal problems).

Identifying Other Substance-Related Disorders

The number of substances that can be the basis for an addiction are forever expanding. There are screening tools for some specific substances (e.g., cocaine, marijuana) but given the scope and changing nature of potentially addictive substances, a more useful screen is one that is not substance specific.

The DAST (Drug Abuse Screening Test) is the most widely used general screening instrument for substance use other than alcohol (Gavin, Ross, and Skinner, 1989). Regretfully, its scoring system is binary—either you have a problem or not. However, any answer that contributes to a positive score is worth examining further.

Drug Abuse Screening Test (DAST)

When answering these questions, be sure to remember that reference to "drugs" means all substances other than alcohol, caffeine, and nicotine. For a list of typical substances of abuse, turn to appendix II.

Drug Abuse Screening Test (DAST)

1. Have you used drugs other than those required for medical reasons? Yes No
2. Have you abused prescription drugs? Yes No
3. Do you abuse more than one drug at a time? Yes No
4. Can you get through the week without using drugs (other than those required for medical reasons)? Yes No
5. Are you always able to stop using drugs when you want to? Yes No
6. Do you abuse drugs on a continuous basis? Yes No
7. Do you try to limit your drug use to certain situations? Yes No
8. Have you had "blackouts" or "flashbacks" as a result of drug use? Yes No
9. Do you ever feel bad about your drug abuse? Yes No
10. Does your spouse (or parents) ever complain about your involvement with drugs? Yes No
11. Do your friends or relatives know or suspect you abuse drugs? Yes No
12. Has drug abuse ever created problems between you and your spouse? Yes No
13. Has any family member ever sought help for problems related to your drug use? Yes No
14. Have you ever lost friends because of your use of drugs? Yes No

15. Have you ever neglected your family or missed work because of your use of drugs? Yes No
16. Have you ever been in trouble at work because of drug abuse? Yes No
17. Have you ever lost a job because of drug abuse? Yes No
18. Have you gotten into fights when under the influence of drugs? Yes No
19. Have you ever been arrested because of unusual behavior while under the influence of drugs? Yes No
20. Have you ever been arrested for driving while under the influence of drugs? Yes No
21. Have you engaged in illegal activities to obtain drugs? Yes No
22. Have you ever been arrested for possession of illegal drugs? Yes No
23. Have you ever experienced withdrawal symptoms as a result of heavy drug intake? Yes No
24. Have you had medical problems as a result of your drug use (e.g., memory loss, hepatitis, convulsions, or bleeding)? Yes No
25. Have you ever gone to anyone for help for a drug problem? Yes No
26. Have you ever been in the hospital for medical problems related to your drug use? Yes No
27. Have you ever been involved in a treatment program specifically related to drug use? Yes No
28. Have you been treated as an outpatient for problems related to drug abuse? Yes No

SCORING: "Yes" is scored as 1 point for all questions except 4, 5, and 7. For questions 4, 5, and 7, "no" is scored as 1 point. A total of score of 6 or more indicates a drug problem.

Self-scoring versions of the DAST are available online.

Hazardous Drug Use? Drug Abuse? Drug Dependence?

When an eighteen-year-old high school graduate visited his family physician before leaving for college, he openly responded to his physician's questions about drug and alcohol use. He acknowledged having tried marijuana with friends but had never purchased any himself. He reported drinking with friends most every weekend—usually beer but sometimes tequila. They often drank until drunk (four beers or four shots of tequila) but always made sure to have a designated driver who remained sober.

This physician was well-versed in adolescent drug use and the growing trend to abuse prescription medications. After some probing by his doctor, this young man revealed that he had been stealing Xanex (an antianxiety medication) from his grandmother since his junior year in high school. Since she used the medication intermittently and had some memory problems, she had yet to notice his pilfering. He first started taking the medication "on a lark," but his experimentation on a once-a-month basis had grown to three times a week. Right before high school graduation, he tried to stop the Xanex but was unsuccessful and continues taking one or two on the weekend. Over the summer, he admitted to stockpiling the medication—by buying it from drug-dealing acquaintances—for when he goes to college.

This young man's use of marijuana and underage drinking is illegal, but illegality does not make him a hazardous or abusive substance user. However, this does not mean he is problem free. His level of alcohol consumption on weekends is above safe limits. His misuse of a prescription medication (i.e., using a medication that was not prescribed to him) qualifies him for a diagnosis of substance abuse.

Given his involvement with multiple substances, polysubstance abuse needs to be considered. Polysubstance abuse—where the combined effects of different substances are creating problems—is one way an addiction can disguise itself. Hopefully, his doctor will make him aware of possible cross-tolerance effects that result from taking two sedating substances (alcohol and Xanex). Although this young man does not drive when intoxicated, the combined effects of alcohol and Xanex can impair his judgment, making him prone to poor decisions. One poor decision is stealing from his grandmother. Although both his alcohol consumption and use of sedatives are worthy of concern, in the overall picture, his use of Xanex is the most problematic. Alcohol use with peers is normative for this age group but recreational use of painkillers is not.

Resources

A gateway to an array of twelve-step-based programs:
  www.coping.org/adultlink/step.htm
  www.addict-help.com/
A listing of alcohol- and substance-related twelve-step groups:
  www.addictionrecoveryguide.org/treatment/recovery/12step.html

Rational Recovery offers a treatment approach to change that does not require group participation:

www.rational.org/recovery/

Moderation Management is a change program and national support group network for people who want to reduce drinking. This approach is most effective for at-risk and problematic levels of substance use.

www.moderation.org/

Harm Reduction is a philosophy of treatment designed to reduce the negative consequences of addiction. This may involve cutting back or giving up the addiction. These sites describe the approach that is also discussed in chapter 16.

www.harmreduction.org/

www.habitsmart.com/hrmtitle.html

CHAPTER 9

Adolescent Substance Use
Experimentation or Addiction?

A dolescent experimentation with substances is normal for this life
stage. Experimentation is not the same as addiction, but without
experimentation as its starting point, addiction is not possible. For
some, experimentation starts early and stops; for others it evolves into social
use, while for others, substance use becomes a way of life. Distinguishing
normal experimentation from addiction to drugs or alcohol is a challenge.
To further complicate the picture, there is an alarming increase in addiction
to more dangerous substances (e.g., heroin), and the range of potential
addictions is expanding.

Substance Use Problems
during Adolescence

Fully developed addictions come with extensive physical and emotional
costs. The cost is even higher during the critical growth years of adolescence.
Once an addiction takes hold, healthy emotional and interpersonal development that carries an adolescent from childhood to adulthood begins to
slow. If the addiction goes on long enough, development grinds to a halt.
For this age group, early detection of problematic substance use has the most
far-reaching benefits.

Early detection is critical for another reason. The cycle from experimentation to full addiction is rapid in adolescence. For an adult, the course from

regular use to full dependence takes two to seven years. This time frame is greatly condensed for adolescents. The route to full dependence can occur in as little as twelve to eighteen months.

There is some good news when it comes to identifying adolescent addiction. Relative to adult populations, health care providers are more attuned to adolescent substance abuse. Whereas only 6 percent of physicians recognized alcohol abuse in a vignette describing an adult patient, 59 percent of pediatricians considered a diagnosis of substance abuse after reading a vignette that portrayed a teenager with the following signs of abuse: red eyes, frequent sore throat and runny nose, headaches, fatigue, loss of appetite, loss of interest in school, and worsening relationships with parents (National Center on Addiction and Substance Abuse at Columbia University, 2000). While over half the physicians correctly attributed these signs to alcohol abuse, this still leaves 40 percent who did not.

The Parents' Dilemma

As parents of adolescents know well, identifying whether a child is involved with substances is difficult. Few middle and high school students volunteer information about their drug and alcohol intake. Upon direct questioning or getting caught with a substance, an adolescent is more likely to blame a friend than admit to substance use. "It wasn't me. David left those beer cans here. He didn't know where to get rid of them." Or the adolescent may divulge having experimented with alcohol once or twice or trying a cigarette or even having taken a puff of marijuana. In fact, adolescent experimentation with substances most often involves alcohol, cigarettes, or marijuana.

Having acquired this knowledge, parents feel uncertain about how to best proceed. Many questions arise. Do I get angry? If I do, will I ever hear the truth? Is this just experimentation? For the vast majority of adolescents, experimentation with drugs and alcohol remains experimental. Among twelfth graders, of the 50 percent who use alcohol and the 23 percent who smoke marijuana, 6 to 13 percent go on to develop a substance use disorder (Johnston, O'Malley, and Bachman, 2003). As a parent, any amount of substance use by one's child—no matter how small—can feel like abuse. While chances are good that substance use will not go beyond experimentation, distinguishing normal from problematic use is challenging. The challenge is even greater for parents who have gone through their own adolescent experimentation with drugs and alcohol without any long-term consequences. These parents tend to be more accepting of their children's sub-

"Well, it's *only* marijuana." Parents who have successfully negotiated their own adolescent experimentation without adverse effects underestimate the implications of their child's substance use and are more likely to say nothing. Parents need to realize that the nature of substance use is quite different from when they were growing up. What was age appropriate in the past carries far more dangers with it today due to the kinds of drugs that are available and their devastating consequences.

stance use. However, today's substance use carries with it far greater dangers than when they were young.

The range of drugs has expanded and is available at younger ages. Some of these drugs, such as painkillers and antianxiety medications, are found in the medicine cabinet. As with alcohol, parents have the responsibility to make sure these drugs are not accessible.

Heroin, once thought to be a drug of the urban poor, has become popular in suburban settings among white affluent adolescents who snort rather than inject the drug. Young girls are drawn to heroin as a way to control weight (Rosenker, 2002). Ann Marlowe's engaging memoir, *How to Stop Time: Heroin from A to Z* (1999), explores heroin's allure, its use among the young and affluent, and its ability to rob young lives of their potential.

Today's increased accessibility, especially to "harder" substances, enhances the chance of developing an addiction. Likewise, negative consequences of substance use are expanding and becoming more harmful, even life threatening. The best known is driving while intoxicated. Other severe outcomes arise from unprotected sex while intoxicated and shared needles.

While parents may be uncertain about how best to approach adolescent drug use, an adolescent has no such doubt. From an adolescent's perspective, drug use is normal; it is a way to have fun and be exposed to new experiences. Ultimately they drink and use drugs for social reasons—their friends do it. From the adolescent's perspective, a parent who simply asks about substance use can be chastised as being out of date and prone to moralizing.

Parents have little traction because adolescence is a time of life when adult authority is greatly diminished and replaced by efforts to create one's own identity. Parents, teachers, or health care providers who attempt to teach about the dangers of substances are often ignored or summarily dismissed.

Despite these responses, parents must not underestimate the impact that talking about substance use can have on their child (see the list below).

Wisely, DARE and other prevention programs designed to educate students about drugs begin in elementary school, long before an adolescent experiences the call to independence. These grade school prevention programs teach students about the risks associated with drugs and alcohol. Regretfully, once in middle school and high school, this knowledge is not put to use. Adolescents do not connect the general effects of substance abuse learned in school to their current experiences. In one study, nine out of ten sixteen- to nineteen-year-olds who were classified as hazardous drinkers did not recognize the harmful consequences of their drinking (Miles, Winstock, and Strang, 2001).

An adolescent's failure to connect substance use to its negative consequences may be a result of denial. However, I think a more likely explanation is that they truly do not see the consequences, given the rapid course from experimentation to addiction. The adolescent whose substance use is problematic may have been using drugs for only several months (compared to the adult addict who has been using for years). This relatively brief history—which is occurring amidst the many other changes of adolescence—makes it difficult to reliably link negative effects to substance use.

Signs of Adolescent Addiction

Substance-induced changes to look and listen for include the following.

1. Lower grades or loss of interest in school
2. Decreasing appetite
3. Worsening relationships with parents
4. More frequent illnesses and/or increasing reports of symptoms such as stomachaches, headaches, and runny nose
5. Change in peer group, where friends no longer visit or a new peer group appears to include drug users
6. Large, unaccounted-for periods of time
7. Acting out of character (e.g., secretiveness replacing open conversations or increasing conflicts that include threats or actual violence)

Major changes in the parent-child relationship, when a child no longer seems to be him- or herself, can be a sign that substance use has moved beyond experimentation. Regretfully, no one sign or even combination of signs reliably indicates a growing problem. This is because most of the pre-

To the list of typical signs of adolescent addiction, I would add one other: getting caught. Getting caught is a common theme expressed by those who have written autobiographies about their addictions. Toren Volkmann was thrown off several varsity teams in high school because of his drinking (Volkmann and Volkmann, 2006). The Moyers family knows that drinking is the reason their normally law-abiding son was arrested for breaking and entering. Although the adolescent is likely to protest that this is the "first time," the more likely scenario is that he or she has become increasingly comfortable using larger and larger amounts of substances. The resulting impaired judgment leads to more apparent adverse consequences that result in getting caught.

vious seven changes in behavior can be due to an adolescent's normal development of identity and independence. The best rule of thumb is that, as signs consistent with addiction accumulate, the more likely the observed changes are substance related.

For the adolescent who is caught using, there is one sure sign that substance use is a problem: using alone. Adolescent experimentation with substances is part of their social life. Substance use outside a social context (e.g., when alone) is a significant warning sign that substance use is problematic.

Screening Tools for Adolescents

An adolescent who shows signs of dependence drinks smaller quantities of alcohol and less frequently than an alcohol-dependent adult. Adolescents diagnosed with alcohol dependence rarely drink every day but, on average, every other day (Hasin et al., 2003). For these reasons, special scales are developed to screen for adolescent substance use problems.

In reality, few adolescents with substance use problems will agree to a screening and if they do, they are unlikely to respond honestly. Despite these limitations, I am providing one screening tool—the CRAFFT—that is designed specifically for children and adolescents (Knight et al., 1999). It is brief and assesses for both drugs and alcohol. Even if the adolescent does not provide the answers, the six CRAFFT questions (the name is created by combining the first letter of the italicized word in each question) provide parents and other concerned adults with a framework for understanding the major signs of adolescent addiction.

CRAFFT Screen

Answer each of the following questions.

1. Have you ever ridden in a *car* driven by someone (including your-self) who was high or had been using alcohol or drugs? Yes No
2. Do you ever use alcohol or drugs to *relax*, feel better about your-self, or fit in? Yes No
3. Do you ever use alcohol or drugs while you are by yourself (*alone*)? Yes No
4. Do you ever *forget* things you did while using alcohol or drugs? Yes No
5. Do your family or *friends* tell you that you should cut down on your drinking or drug use? Yes No
6. Have you ever gotten into *trouble* while you were using alcohol or drugs? Yes No

SCORING: Score 1 point for each "yes." A score of 2 or more is evi-dence of problematic or addictive levels of substance use.

An affirmative response to any one of the first three questions means that substance use is at risk of creating harm and steps need to be taken to lessen this risk.

1. Have you ever ridden in a car driven by someone (including yourself) who was high or had been using alcohol or drugs?

This question provides two pieces of information: if the adolescent is involved with close peers who are substance users and if he or she has driven under the influence. More importantly, the question is asked out of concern for the adolescent's ultimate well-being. Knowing that an adolescent is driv-ing under the influence or with others who are requires alternative means of transportation. Alternatives include calling a friend who is not at the party or a parent.

2. Do you ever use alcohol or drugs to relax, feel better about yourself, or fit in?

Most adolescent experimentation is driven by peer pressure or curios-ity; adolescents drink and use drugs to fit in or be "normal" rather than to *feel* normal. Others are drawn to experimentation for the adventure or excitement of doing something illicit or illegal—one of many ways adoles-cents test the boundaries of adult authority. These motivations are common and quite different from using substances for their psychological effects: to relax, alleviate boredom, overcome loneliness, or alleviate anxiety or depres-

The intention of the CRAFFT is transparent. There is no doubt about what it is measuring. An adolescent who wishes to keep an addiction hidden can simply respond "no" to each question. For this group, the adolescent version of the Substance Abuse Subtle Screening Inventory, or SASSI-A2, is ideal. Questions on the SASSI-A2 have no explicit connection to substance use, thus making it difficult to fake responses. This screening tool can only be administered by a health care provider, psychotherapist, or counselor who has the instrument and is trained to interpret the outcome (www.sassi.com/sassi/index.shtml).

sion. An adolescent using substances for their mood-altering effects is at risk of developing substance use problems and needs help developing alternative methods of coping.

3. Do you ever use alcohol or drugs while you are by yourself (alone)?

An adolescent who uses drugs outside the context of his or her peer group is certainly not using drugs in a normative fashion. A "yes" answer suggests a more serious problem is developing and requires attention from a professional.

The next three CRAFFT questions focus on the kinds of problems that emerge once substance use reaches a problematic or addictive level. Failure to remember what happened when high (i.e., blacking out) indicates that large quantities are being used. Getting into trouble and having friends or family ask you to cut back means that addictive behaviors are creating consequences that are readily observable to others. A "yes" response to any one of these three CRAFFT questions is a sign that a more formal addiction assessment is warranted.

Toxicology Screenings: Are They Valuable?

The American Academy of Pediatrics recommends that parents and schools do not conduct toxicology screenings. The benefits are limited and the cost potentially large if, in order to avoid detection, a child or adolescent shifts use to more dangerous drugs that are less likely to be included in a routine toxicology screen (Committee on Substance Abuse and Counsel on School Health, 2007). However, this section is provided for those who insist on using this method.

Sometimes the only way to know for certain if an adolescent is using substances is to perform urine testing or another type of toxicology screening. Toxicology screens provide an objective and reliable—but not foolproof—method for assessing substance use. The breathalyzer, used for measuring blood alcohol levels (BAL) resulting from recent alcohol consumption, was discussed in chapter 8.

Toxicology screens test bodily fluids such as urine, blood, and sweat for minute traces of drugs left after recent substance use. Hair samples, another source for toxicology screening, assess for substance use months after the fact. Of these, urine testing is most popular because it is easy to administer. Kits purchased at drugs stores test for a variety of substances including marijuana, cocaine, opiates, and methamphetamines. Urine screens are not available for alcohol, given the rapidity with which alcohol is metabolized. Because polysubstance use is common among adolescents, it is best to purchase kits that screen for a variety of substances.

The value of drug testing depends on it being administered correctly. Those who know about an upcoming drug test can secretly substitute a friend's "clean" urine or water down their own sample. Thus direct observation of urine collection is necessary. Accuracy also depends on the amount of time since a substance was used. Cocaine, amphetamines, and heroin are metabolized relatively quickly, but trace amounts are available as long as samples are collected within twenty-four to seventy-two hours after use.

Toxicology screenings can identify whether an adolescent is using substances but rarely are they an effective deterrent. Warnings that there will be random screens may lead to a temporary reduction in use or a shift to substances that are not identified by such screens (e.g., alcohol or inhalants).

However, if a parent or school program still wishes to employ a toxicology screen, a positive outcome must be followed by a visit to a health care professional in order to assess the degree of use and need for treatment. If treatment ensues and, as a parent, you want to continue random screenings, they ideally should be conducted at home or by a physician and not the treatment provider. When the therapist is given this responsibility, it can damage the therapeutic relationship, which is a critical component of effective treatment.

Late Adolescence, Early Adulthood, and Beyond: Binge Drinking

Twenty- to thirty-five-year-olds consume the most alcohol, although alcohol is not their only substance. "Club drugs," such as oxycodone, LSD, and

MDMA or Ecstasy, are a few of the more popular drugs. Binge drinking is a special form of alcohol consumption most common in a college-age population but not unique to this age group. Twenty-nine percent of highly educated employees report binge drinking in the previous three months (Matano et al., 2003).

Binging on alcohol involves heavy consumption of alcohol in a short period.

> Binge Drinking Criteria
> *Men:* Five standard drinks in a row
> *Women:* Four standard drinks in a row
> Drinking according to the previous pattern at least once in the previous two weeks
> *Frequent binge drinking:* Drinking in a binge manner three or more times in the previous two weeks. (Wechsler and Nelson, 2001)

Binge drinking is always risky because negative effects emerge from BALs that quickly rise to .08 and higher. Because binge drinking is so common in college settings, the specific negative effects are most often studied in college students. Forty to sixty percent of binge drinkers report missing classes, falling behind in schoolwork, acting in a regretful way, forgetting what happened, arguing with friends, engaging in unplanned sex, and driving under the influence. I wonder how often alcohol-related automobile deaths are the result of a non- or moderate drinkers consuming excessive amounts of alcohol when among a group of binge drinkers.

Frequent binge drinking creates additional adverse effects including unintended property damage, personal injury, and unprotected sex while intoxicated (Wechsler and Nelson, 2001). The full gamut of adverse consequences of binge drinking during high school and college years is described in *Smashed: A Story of a Drunken Girlhood* (Zailckas, 2005).

Binge drinking is easy to identify if you are there to observe it. Otherwise, this form of risky drinking often remains hidden. Harmful consequences are confined to the time of the binge, and given the intermittent nature of binges, it can take time for harmful effects to accumulate and become apparent. In between binges, a person functions well and drinks moderately or not at all.

Binge drinking, although a major concern on college campuses, is not confined to this setting. The hidden nature of binge drinking became apparent to me while treating Kevin, a successful classic music promoter in his mid-thirties.

Kevin came to therapy due to depressed feelings that appeared shortly after his wife completed her MBA and began a financially lucrative job. We were making progress addressing his depression when he came in late for a morning session. When asked what happened, he simply reported having overslept. We usually met in the afternoon so I didn't know if he was prone to sleeping late or not. However, given that he rarely responded to my questions with short answers, I became curious about why he overslept. Further questioning revealed that after his wife went to sleep the previous evening, he had taken a bottle of scotch to his study and drank six or seven shots until he fell asleep. As best he could tell, he drank in this manner at least once or twice a week. This clearly qualified as binge drinking. In between binges, he drank normally (a glass of wine with dinner) and functioned effectively.

Only after becoming aware of his binge drinking were we able to track its full range of negative effects. In addition to coming late to our session, he usually missed morning meetings after a binge and on several occasions this meant lost work. He also began to recognize how much more depressed he felt the morning after. Kevin's binge drinking was worrisome. He routinely drank alone and was using alcohol as a way to manage difficult feelings (i.e., jealousy and anger related to his wife's work).

Assessment of Binge Drinking

The three questions from the Quantity/Frequency Questionnaire mentioned in chapter 8 assess whether drinking fits a binge pattern.

1. On average, how many days per week do you drink alcohol?
2. On a typical day when you drink how many drinks do you have?
3. What is the maximum number of drinks you have had on a specific occasion during the past month?

If the maximum consumed is four or five drinks in a row, then the next question is: how often does this kind of drinking occur? Binging does not necessarily make a person a binge drinker. It depends how often drinking in this manner occurs. A binge drinker binges at least once in a two-week period. Or if, like Kevin, binging occurs three or more times in a two-week period, the problem is described as frequent binge drinking.

Some professionals recommend that instead of focusing on the quantity consumed, binge drinkers need to pay attention to the negative effects created by alcohol (DeJong, 2001). I believe that attention needs to be paid to both quantity and consequences. Consuming alcohol in quantities that represent binge drinking places most people at greater risk of alcohol-induced harm. A focus on negative consequences is of value for those who are more susceptible to alcohol's effects and thus reach dangerous BALs after consuming lesser amounts of alcohol not normally defined as binging.

What's a Parent to Do?

The best advice to parents is to present a consistent and firm antidrug message to your children. Talking about drugs in an open and warm manner is more effective than an angry or punitive approach (Pomery et al., 2005). This is not always easy to do when worried about a child's involvement with drugs and alcohol. At these times it is helpful to remember that use is not abuse, experimentation is the norm, and that talking can influence how children think about substance use—even when you feel you have not been heard.

Let Your Child Do the Talking

The doorway into a discussion of substance use will remain shut if you begin with a lecture or insist your child reveal his or her substance use. Instead, begin with a more benign, less personal approach.

When spontaneous mention is made of another's substance use, remain neutral and listen carefully, even though the tendency is to rush into action, warning of the dangers and insisting the child avoid drug-using peers. Being an attentive listener and letting a child talk about a taboo topic sends the message that such topics can be broached with a parent.

Conversations initiated by your child are best, but if none are forthcoming, try asking some questions. Begin by asking questions that are directed at eliciting a child's knowledge about substances. Ask, in a neutral manner, "What kinds of drugs are at your school?" Another knowledge-based approach is to explore an adolescent's beliefs about the prevalence of drug use among peers. The more specific the question, the better: "How much drinking was there at that party on Saturday?" or "I hated going to the bathroom in high school; it was always so smoky. How often do you find that?"

Another valuable question addresses a child's belief about how common substance use is among peers: "How many kids in your class drink alcohol?" Social norms research shows that beliefs about the frequency of substance use among school peers are usually exaggerated. Believing substance use is widespread means that experimentation is more likely (Reis and Riley, 2000). If your school can provide you with accurate information about the frequency of substance use, you can help your child develop a more realistic picture.

Asking questions that help adolescents talk about their beliefs and attitudes about substances is another way to start a conversation. "What do you think it's like to get drunk/get high?" "How much do you think you would need to drink in order to get drunk?" A child who is misinformed can be given accurate information. If your questions only yield "I don't know," then your child has provided you with the perfect opportunity to talk about specific substances and their effects.

In answering these questions, a child reveals his or her general attitude toward substance use. The belief that substances have only positive effects increases the likelihood of experimentation. As a parent you can help create a more balanced view by adding in the negatives while not dismissing what your child sees as the positives (see part III for further discussion about how to approach these conversations).

An adolescent who never mentions anything about substance use can be encouraged to read an autobiography about addiction. The one most likely to resonate is *Smashed: A Story of a Drunken Girlhood* by Koren Zail-

When asking about substance use, follow the approach advocated by good interviewers. Avoid questions that can be answered with a simple "yes" or "no." Instead, take a risk, assume the answer is "yes," and pose a question that requires a response that provides some information. Good interviewers do not ask, "Do you drink?" Assuming most people drink, they ask, "How much do you drink?" Similarly, you can assume that your child has tried alcohol, cigarettes, or marijuana or knows people who have. Ask questions that elicit your child's knowledge and beliefs about substances.

ckas (2005). This book follows Zailckas, a good student at a suburban high school, on her path from drinking to fit in, to forgotten days and nights in college. Marian Keyes (1998) provides an engaging yet humorous fictional account of alcohol and drug use in *Rachel's Holiday.* Other autobiographies written by adults describe their substance use as adolescents (see p. 237).

Avoid Judgments and Help Make Connections

A parent's first goal is to create a nonjudgmental atmosphere where a child can talk about substance use. Once this is accomplished, there is a more active role to play. Adolescents do not readily connect their substance use to its consequences. Thus, instead of chastising or moralizing about drug use, one point of leverage for this age group is to create connections that link negative consequences to the adolescent's own experience with substances.

Repeating the approach of grade school prevention programs—emphasizing the generic negative effects of drug use—is ineffective. Instead, parents gain leverage by creating links between specific behaviors and their consequences. If your child refers to someone they know who is using substances and having problems, do not assume the adolescent links the problems to substance use. This is your opportunity to make a connection. However, you don't need to jump in right away.

Establishing an atmosphere of open communication takes precedence. The first few times your child initiates a discussion of substances, it is best to just listen or ask for his or her impressions about what happened. At a later time, you can always refer back to this conversation in order to connect substance use to its consequences. Always take care to avoid moralizing.

"I have been thinking about what you told me yesterday—about Brett's drinking and how he began joking around, throwing things at Meg's car, and Meg's car was damaged. His behavior seems to have surprised you. Why do you think he did that?" Even if your comments are dismissed at that moment, this communication is the beginning of a process intended to help an adolescent link the abstract notions of risk learned in school to the actual effects of alcohol and drugs among peers. Reports in the local news about a drunk-driving accident or accidental overdose provide another opportunity to link up the abstract notion of "negative consequences" to something meaningful in an adolescent's life. An adolescent whose family discusses the effects of drug use has less frequent substance use and dependence (Pomery et al., 2005).

Make Safety a Priority

Talking about substance use is just one way parents lessen use and decrease the likelihood of harmful effects. A parent's other role is more active: creating a safe environment. Two important contributions to a safe environment involve (1) limiting access to alcohol and other substances and (2) containing negative outcomes when substances are used.

Having access to psychoactive substances is necessary for an addiction to develop. Parents will want to limit access not only to alcohol, but to prescription medications, household products such as airplane glue, paint solvents, and over-the-counter medications.

Over-the-counter cough and cold medications that contain the cough suppressant dextromethorphan (DXM) have become a hugely popular substance to abuse. Increasing the normal dose of DXM tenfold creates psychedelic-like out-of-body experiences, hallucinations, poor judgment, and decreased motor control. When taken in such large dosages, the other active ingredients in medications containing DXM (e.g., antihistamines, expectorants) have resulted in life-threatening effects, such as high blood pressure, seizures, irregular heart beat, and even death. Limiting the number of products in the home with DXM is important but not foolproof. DXM, distilled from over-the-counter medications, can be purchased in powder form on the Internet.

While no parent wants to advocate experimenting with drugs and alcohol, realistically, the chances are good that your child will experiment. Whether substances have been used yet or not, it is critical that you and your child discuss what he or she can do in order to avoid being in a car with anyone who is intoxicated, whether as driver or passenger. The dangers of an intoxicated driver are well documented, but even an intoxicated passenger poses a threat. Lowered impulse control can lead to behaviors that endanger everyone in the car. To ensure your child's safety, the rule should be that the adolescent can call home for a ride, no matter where he or she is or what has happened. That ride will be provided with no questions asked.

Another contribution parents make to reducing harm is to remind adolescents about safe drinking. Hopefully, this topic has been addressed in a school prevention program, but parents can take it a step further. Those who are new to drinking have little sense of the effects different amounts of alcohol will have. The effect of alcohol is largely determined by blood alcohol levels discussed in the previous chapter. Websites such as www.intox.com/wheel/drinkwheel.asp provide a way to demonstrate how much alcohol can be consumed without impaired judgment and control. A parent will want to make this kind of information available to support the importance of safe drinking.

When Experimentation Opens the Gateway to Addiction

According to the "gateway" theory, prior drug use predicts future drug use. Ingesting readily available substance like alcohol can become a gateway to using illegal and/or more physically addictive substances (Kandel, 1982). Adolescents try what is available. Usually, this is alcohol and cigarettes, although recently marijuana has become one of the first drugs of experimentation. Given that availability determines what substance will be used, polysubstance use is the norm. Last Saturday, a group of teens drank alcohol because a friend was able to steal liquor from home. They also smoked because another friend had a pack of cigarettes. This Saturday, they smoked cigarettes and then drank cough syrup because they heard that this was a good way to get high.

Once high school and college students begin to drink or smoke, they are more likely to be exposed to peers who do the same. Exposure to substance-using peers provides further opportunities to accept the offer to use. Most adolescent experimentation with drugs goes no further. But for some, experimentation with legal substances becomes the gateway for using illegal drugs and more addictive substances, such as crack or heroin.

On the continuum of addiction, true adolescent experimentation is similar to adult recreational use in the sense that it is normative for this age group, occurs with peers, and is done primarily for social reasons (to be like one's peers) and not to manage psychological states. Adolescent experimentation takes on a larger meaning when certain risk factors are present. The transition from experimentation to abuse and dependence is strongly influenced by genetics, family environment, and psychological factors. The characteristics of adolescents who are most likely to become addicted are as follows.

1. *Drinking begins at a young age, usually between twelve to fourteen, although earlier is possible.*
   Those who write about their personal experiences with addiction uniformly refer to starting to drink during this period. Such was the case for Pete Hamill (1994), the journalist, who grew up with a frequently unemployed, alcoholic father and a mother who struggled to keep the family together. As he entered his teens, he began sneaking beers while his father got drunk with friends in the living room.

2. *There is a history of addiction in the family.*
   Autobiographies about addiction support what research documents: genetics and family environment play a significant role in addiction development. A child growing up in a family where a parent, usually the father, has an addiction and/or an antisocial personality is at greater risk (Cadoret, Troughton, O'Gorman, and Heywood, 1995). What a child receives from addicted family members is not a specific addiction but the proclivity to become addicted. A child with an alcoholic father may become an alcoholic, a pathological gambler, or develop a work addiction.

3. *Psychological risk factors are present.*
   Adolescents at greatest risk for developing substance-related problems have low religious participation and/or low levels of conventionality. Low educational achievement and expectations are also common (Wills, McNamara, Vaccaro, and Hirky, 1996). Other risk factors include problems controlling emotions, especially anger and aggression, and sensation-seeking behaviors. Sensation seeking is in evidence when a child constantly seeks out new forms of entertainment, becomes easily bored, and is mesmerized by highly stimulating and often risky activities like car racing or bungee jumping. Adolescents with untreated depression and attention deficit hyperactivity disorder are also more prone to substance use; substances become a way to self-medicate the discomfort created by these disorders. Having few alternative modes of coping (other than turning to substance use) is another risk factor. Signs of inadequate coping include responding to challenges with anger, helplessness, or loafing (Weinberg, Rahdert, Colliver, and Glantz, 1998).

4. *Situational factors contribute to increased substance use.*
   Not surprisingly, adolescents whose substance use is most likely to escalate are experiencing numerous life stressors. They live in a dangerous neighborhood, are exposed to a contentious divorce, or are emotionally and physically abused. When combined with limited coping skills, the only way to deal with these stressors is to escape through substances.

Risk factors do not guarantee an addiction but they do indicate a greater likelihood that experimentation will evolve into some form of problematic use.

Should a problem develop, it is critical that parents do not ignore the early signs. Too often the shame and stigma of having a child with an addiction lead parents to see past the problem. William Cope Moyers reflects on how his parents managed to not see his addiction as an adolescent: "It's so much easier and more socially acceptable to talk about a 'problem' than an 'addiction,' a 'mistake' rather than pattern of out-of-control behavior, a 'defiant act' rather than conduct that defies rationalization" (2006, p. 73). Any parent who believes this cannot happen to them must read the Volkmanns' work: *Our Drink: Detoxing the Perfect Family* (2004) or *From Binge to Blackout: A Mother and Son Struggle with Teen Drinking* (2006). These books chronicle how easily even the most vigilant family can look past a child's addiction. See chapter 17 for a more developed discussion of how personal factors impede accurate recognition of addiction.

Resources

School systems, along with middle school and high school counseling departments, are an excellent resource for information and treatment options. Some schools will accept "anonymous" referrals and have a counselor speak to a student without indicating who provided the student's name.

In larger metropolitan areas, contact the local Intergroup to see if there are twelve-step programs available for adolescents.
    www.alcoholics-anonymous.org/en_find_meeting.cfm?PageID=29
Talking tips for parents:
    http://ncadistore.samhsa.gov/catalog/referrals.aspx?topic=83&h=
    resources
Also refer to the resource list at the end of chapter 8.

CHAPTER 10

The Unseen Faces of Addiction

Older Adults and Women

Substance-Use Problems in Older Adults: Alcohol and Medication

Older adults, variously defined as over sixty or sixty-five, drink less, but less drinking does not necessarily reduce the risk of harm. Reduced consumption is offset by the fact that as one ages, it takes less alcohol to become intoxicated. Although alcohol is the substance most commonly associated with abuse, the biggest area of concern for older adults is misuse of prescription medications (National Center on Addiction and Substance Abuse at Columbia University, 1998).

Alcohol-Related Problems

The amount of alcohol that qualifies as normal drinking in midlife becomes problematic when over the age of sixty-five. The safe drinking level for older men and women is one standard drink (0.5 ounces alcohol) per day (Menninger, 2002). Even this amount poses dangers for those whose health is compromised, those who are taking prescription medications, or those who are using over-the-counter medications that contain alcohol.

The incidence of heavy drinking is relatively small in this age group. Only 7 percent of men and 2 percent of women are considered heavy users. However, the figure increases to 24 percent for older adults with serious medical and psychiatric conditions (Menninger, 2002).

I suspect these figures underestimate the true extent of alcohol problems, which are easily hidden in this age group. The typical social, occupational, and legal consequences that are necessary for a diagnosis are inconsistent with the lifestyle of many older adults. A retiree's drinking will not have work-related consequences. Negative interpersonal consequences are fewer if an older person is living alone. There is no spouse with whom to argue about too much drinking. Arguments, if they occur, will be with extended family members.

The physical effects of an older adult's alcoholism frequently are mistaken for routine signs of aging. Alcohol facilitates bone loss, a major concern for women, and hastens age-related decreased muscle mass. These physical changes, combined with alcohol's numbing effects, lead to increased accidents and falls that result in more severe injuries. Other alcohol-induced symptoms—such as time that cannot be accounted for, sleep disturbances, and falling asleep outside of bed—are easily brushed aside as typical to the normal aging process.

Given that alcoholism manifests itself in physical symptoms, one might expect a physician to take notice. Regretfully, medical providers are no more adept at recognizing addiction in the elderly than in other adults. When physicians were asked to diagnose an older woman whose presenting concerns contained classic signs of alcoholism (e.g., irritability, weight loss, reduced energy), less than 1 percent of the doctors considered that the diagnosis might be alcoholism (National Center on Addiction and Substance Abuse at Columbia University, 1998).

I have seen the effects of physicians' failures to identify excessive alcohol use in the elderly. A seventy-two-year-old man came to therapy because his family thought that he was depressed. Not surprisingly, a careful assessment revealed that he was drinking too much for his age: depression was simply a side effect. He had been drinking two to four drinks daily for more

Relatives may hesitate to define an elderly family member's substance use as a problem. Drinking can even be condoned as adaptive. "Mother has some right to relief." "Dad's drinking doesn't bother anyone; it's the only pleasure he has left." Relatives can even collude in supporting an elderly parent's addiction. A senile family member who becomes upset with her struggles to remember is easier if she passes out early in the evening.

than six years. His physician, whom he saw at least twice a year, had never raised this as an concern.

When alcoholism remains hidden, its symptoms may be misdiagnosed as depression, anxiety, or a physical ailment. A physician may prescribe medication to treat these disorders that interact negatively with alcohol. Sedating medications that treat sleep problems or reduce anxiety and pain enhance alcohol's effects. One drink when taking such medications can be dangerous. Medications for hypertension and arthritis also interact negatively with alcohol (Moore, Beck, and Babor, 2002). As discussed later, keeping close tabs on prescribed medications helps prevent such harmful outcomes.

For some older adults, current alcohol problems are a continuation of a substance use disorder that has plagued them all their life. More often, older adults with alcohol problems have been drinking moderately throughout life but begin drinking more in response to the losses that come with aging (retirement, death of a spouse). Increased alcohol consumption, initially used to manage grief, can transform normal, time-limited grieving into a prolonged depression. Early recognition is key in ensuring that health status is maintained (Menninger, 2002).

Assessment of Alcoholism in Older Adults

Items on the Michigan Alcoholism Screening Test (MAST) have been modified and shortened to address unique aspects of alcohol use among older adults (Blow et al., 1992).

Short Michigan Alcoholism Screening Test— Geriatric Version (S-MAST-G)

© The Regents of the University of Michigan

1. When talking with others, do you ever underestimate how much you actually drink? Yes No
2. After a few drinks, have you sometimes not eaten or been able to skip a meal because you didn't feel hungry? Yes No
3. Does having a few drinks help decrease your shakiness or tremors? Yes No
4. Does alcohol sometimes make it hard for you to remember parts of the day or night? Yes No
5. Do you usually take a drink to relax or calm your nerves? Yes No

6. Do you drink to take your mind off your problems? Yes No
7. Have you ever increased your drinking after Yes No
   experiencing a loss in your life?
8. Has a doctor or nurse ever said they were worried Yes No
   or concerned about your drinking?
9. Have you ever made rules to manage your drinking? Yes No
10. When you feel lonely, does having a drink help? Yes No

TOTAL S-MAST-G SCORE (0–10) _____

SCORING: Two or more "yes" responses is indicative of an alcohol problem. For further information, contact Frederic Blow, Ph.D., at University of Michigan Alcohol Research Center, 4250 Plymouth Road, SPC 5765, Ann Arbor, MI 48109-5765.

Because medications interact with alcohol, a screening for alcohol problems with an older person should include completion of the Alcohol Related Problems Survey (ARPS), which provides a simple means for keeping track of current medications (see p. 134).

Medication Abuse in Older Adults

Older adults are more likely to abuse prescription medications than alcohol and this problem is more prevalent among older women than men (National Center on Addiction and Substance Abuse at Columbia University, 1998). Medication abuse, whether the result of prescribed or over-the-counter drugs, usually involves (1) taking more medication than prescribed and/or (2) using alcohol along with the medication when the interaction of the two is dangerous. The two drug groups most likely to be abused are sedatives for

Adults over the age of fifty-nine receive, on average, nineteen prescriptions a year with five medications being taken at any one time (National Center on Addiction and Substance Abuse at Columbia University, 1998). An aging adult sees numerous physicians, each of whom may be unaware of the patient's full range of medications, because they fail to do an adequate assessment or the patient has limited recall. Often patients neglect to mention over-the-counter medications because they assume that any drug that is not prescribed must be less potent and not worthy of concern.

sleep and anxiety, and analgesics for pain. Common adverse effects include drowsiness, memory loss, confusion, and accidents, especially falls.

Keeping track of dosages and medications when many are being taken and changed frequently is difficult at any age. To keep an accounting of current medications, there is a section from the ARPS, a relatively new instrument designed specifically for older adults (Moore, Beck, and Babor, 2002; Fink et al., 2002). When used to assess alcohol problems, a professional must administer the full ARPS. However, the section on medication can be used by anyone. This comprehensive checklist helps to keep track of medications and can be provided to doctors and pharmacists. Along with the ARPS, older adults should give health care providers their answers to the Quantity/Frequency Questionnaire from chapter 8 as a way to avoid negative interactions between medications and alcohol.

ARPS Medication Checklist

1. How many different medications do you use at least once a week? (Count all medications, even if you get them without a doctor's prescription. Do not count eye drops, vitamins, minerals, or ointments.)
2. Do you now take two or more regular or extra strength (325 mg or more) aspirin every day or almost every day?
3. Do you now take any of these medications at least *once a week?*
   a. Sedatives or sleeping medicines such as Ambien, Soneta, Restoril (tenazapam),Valium, Dalmane, Librium, Xanax, Ativan, Halcion
   b. Tranquilizers or antianxiety medicines such as Olanazapine, Zyprexa, Risperdal, Thorazine, Mellaril, Haldol
   c. Narcotic medications such as Darvon, Demerol, codeine, morphine, Percocet, Vicodin, oxycodone, Oxycontin, Tramadol, Tylenol #3
   d. Muscle relaxants such as Flexeril, Soma
   e. Erectile Dysfunction medicines such as Viagra, Cialis, Levitra
4. Do you now take any of these medications every day or almost every day?
   a. Ulcer and stomach medicines such as Zantac, Tagamet, Prilosec, Pepcid
   b. Arthritis and pain medicines such as Celebrex, Motrin (ibuprofen), Voltaren, Relafine, Lodine, Clinoril, Aleve (naprosyn), Tylenol, Advil, Bextra

c. Diabetes medicines such as glyburide, glipizide, metformin, Glucophage, Avandia, Actos
d. Blood pressure medicines such as Cardizem, Vasotec, Lotensin, Atenolol, Cozaar, Novasc, water pills, Hyzaar, Lopressor, Captopril, Zestril, Alstace, Atacan
e. Nitrates such as Isordil, Nitropatch, Imdur
f. Other medicines for the heart such as digoxin, Lasix, Aldoctone (spironlactone)
g. Coumadin (warfarin)
h. Seizure medicines such as Tegretol, Dilantin, phenobarbital, Depakoite, Keppra, Lamictal
i. Depression medicines such as Elavil (amitriptyline), Pamelor (nortriptyline), Paxil, Prozac, Zoloft, Celexa, Lexapro
j. Nonsedating, non-drowsy antihistamines such as Claritin, Zyrtec, Allegra
k. Sedating, sleep-inducing antihistamines such as TylenolPM, Benadryl, Chlortrimeton
l. Cholesterol-lowering medicines such as Lipitor, Zocor, Pravachol, Crestor
m. Bladder medicines such as Terazosin, Flomax, Hytrin

(© Dr. Arlene Fink. Used with permission.)

Are Women Really Less Prone to Substance Addictions?

Alcoholism is known as a man's problem. Across all age groups and nationalities, more men than women experience alcohol-related problems. In the United States, men are two to three times more likely to receive a diagnosis of alcoholism. When it comes to drug use, women also make up a smaller percentage (Wilsnack, Vogeltanz, Wilsnack, and Harris, 2000).

Gender differences in substance-related disorders originally were assumed to be due to women being inherently less addiction prone. Research failed to support this idea. Instead of biological explanations, gender differences in addiction have more to do with early exposure to substances (Hansen, 2002). Adolescent boys are exposed to drugs and alcohol much more often than girls. Exposure increases access, and with access comes the opportunity to develop problematic use. By controlling for differences in early exposure to substances, gender differences disappear. This means that once a girl accepts an offer to use drugs, she is as likely as a boy to become dependent.

Given the significant role access to substances plays in development of an addiction, gender differences are expected to disappear in the near future. Recent statistics indicate that young girls are as likely as boys to experiment with alcohol (Wilsnack, Vogeltanz, Wilsnack, and Harris, 2000). The equal rate of experimentation is a relatively new phenomenon that is just beginning to influence the incidence of abuse and dependence among adult women. As the incidence of women's substance use problems increases, there is good reason to believe that their addictions will go unrecognized.

Unmasking Women's Substance Addictions

That more men are addicted to substances than women may be a self-perpetuating tradition. Once we believe there is a gender difference, we are more apt to recognize addictions in men than women. This is already happening with medical and mental health providers who are more likely to ask a man about substance use (Weisner and Matzger, 2003). Research also shows that signs of alcoholism are more readily identified in men than women. When physicians suggested a diagnosis for a case history containing signs of alcohol abuse, a substance-related diagnosis was five times more likely when the case was said to describe a man than a woman. Similar but less dramatic gender differences in diagnosis were observed with pediatricians (National Center on Addiction and Substance Abuse at Columbia University, 2000). The current male bias in identifying alcoholism may mean that the gender gap already is much smaller than it appears.

Even in the absence of this bias, many women's addictions remain hidden because assessment practices are better suited to recognizing if a man

Not all people are aware that safe drinking limits differ by gender. Low-risk drinking is one standard drink a day for women and two for men. Relative to men, women have a lower ratio of water to blood. Because alcohol is water soluble, a woman will have a higher blood alcohol level (BAL) after consuming the same amount of alcohol as a man. thus she will reach a dangerous BAL more quickly with fewer drinks (L. Becker and Walton-Moss, 2001). Following male safe drinking limits adversely affects a woman's health. Routinely consuming as little as two drinks a day increases the risk of an early death, liver disease, and breast cancer (Bradley, Boyd-Wickizer, Powell, and Burman, 1998).

has a substance-related disorder. The negative consequences contained in screening tool questions are more consistent with the male experience. Women are less likely than men to have adverse legal and financial consequences as a result of substance abuse. In the case of alcohol, men are much more likely to be arrested for driving under the influence (DUI) and, through the ensuing encounter with the legal system, have their substance use problem identified. Women have fewer DUIs because they are less likely to drink and drive. They often drink alone at home or, if socializing as a couple, the man is usually behind the wheel. The negative consequences of women's substance use are primarily interpersonal in nature, involving conflicts with family and friends. Screening tools that focus on behavioral consequences outside the interpersonal realm or that define safe drinking based on male norms will underestimate the severity of a woman's problem or miss it altogether.

Another factor that masks a woman's addiction is her interpretation of the problem. When men acknowledge they have a drinking problem, they seek specialized addiction treatment. Women whose lives are being adversely affected by drinking are more likely to believe they are suffering from emotional problems, so they seek help from a mental health provider (Wasilow-Mueller and Erickson, 2001). From a woman's perspective, seeking therapy makes sense. Compared to men, women more frequently suffer from co-occurring addiction and mental illness, especially depression. Drinking becomes a form of self-medication to alleviate uncomfortable moods. Thus, when thinking about getting help, a woman's psychological symptoms will be more longstanding and have greater salience than her drinking. From this vantage point, seeking help in a mental health care setting makes sense.

Mental health providers, when presented with the classic signs of depression, will see the problem they are best trained to see—depression—and the addiction will remain masked. To see how easy it is to miss a woman's addiction take the case of Milly.

Milly came to therapy expressing concerns consistent with the classic signs of depression: sleep problems, decreased appetite, unhappiness. She had been depressed before and taken medication once. The onset of her current depression was rather sudden. This was easily explained by a major change in her daily routine. Her husband had begun outpatient treatment for alcoholism after being arrested for his second DUI. He went to his program every evening, which meant Milly had responsibility for caring for their two children, ages two and four, both day and night. She complained bitterly about having little time for herself.

I asked Milly questions directed at better understanding how her husband's alcoholism treatment affected her and the family. Did she drink with him? She did. What was it like to have a husband who no longer drank? She acknowledged missing their time together but was adamant about not missing their fights. When asked how she coped with the extra stress that came with not having a break from caring for their children, Milly didn't have much to say. The only specific thing she mentioned was that getting together with friends helped, although she qualified this by saying she rarely had the free time to do so. When asked what she missed about these get-togethers, she said she enjoyed talking and then hesitated. When I noted her pause, she added that she also liked having a few glass of wine or some sherry.

Questions from this point on were directed at getting a sense of how much Milly was drinking. Until asked, she did not realize that she had been drinking more. She kept small bottles of flavored vodka in her dresser and would drink one as a way to relax while the children napped. In the evenings, she would sneak a drink or two in order to be able to fall asleep. (It is surprising how often people drink in order to help them sleep when, over time, alcohol creates sleeping problems.) She was careful not to let her husband know she was drinking out of fear that he would start again. Milly's attempt to self-medicate her depression with alcohol was backfiring.

Without asking the right questions, Milly's potentially dangerous use of alcohol would have been missed. A knowledgeable professional would want to ask about substance use, given the presence of a subtle sign of addiction in Milly's life: she is married to an alcoholic. Alcoholics tend to be married to other alcoholics. Sometimes, two people with similar drinking patterns meet, share other interests, and get married. For others, marriage is the catalyst for a couple developing similar drinking pattern—usually the partner who drinks less begins to drink more.

Early Detection Saves Lives

Marriage more profoundly affects a woman's drinking than a man's. In marriage, a wife's alcohol consumption mimics her husband's, but a wife's consumption level does not influence her husband's (Leonard and Mudar, 2003). This was true for Milly. She began drinking more after getting married as way to spend "quality" time with her husband, who was more willing to come home right after work if she would drink with him.

Men's alcohol consumption is shaped more by friendships than marriage (Leonard and Mudar, 2003). Frequent socializing where heavy drinking is central can turn a moderate drinker into an alcoholic. This danger is great-

As part of my intake with Milly, I asked if there was any kind of sexual or emotional abuse in her background. There had not been. I asked this question because 70 percent of women treated for an addiction have a history of abuse. In mental health settings, among women diagnosed with posttraumatic stress disorder (a frequent outcome of sexual abuse), 30 to 40 percent have a coexisting addiction (Brems and Johnson, 1997; Wasilow-Mueller and Erikson, 2001). A woman who drinks, who is married to an alcoholic, or who has a personal history of sexual abuse needs to be aware of her alcohol consumption, as she is at high risk of developing an addiction.

est for men who have a genetic proclivity to addiction. Having a father who is an alcoholic places a man at a much higher risk for developing alcoholism. Men who are most likely to follow their fathers' path have a history of drinking at a young age and evidence of antisocial behavior in adolescence. They drink for alcohol's mood-altering and stimulating effects. Early detection of substance-related problems for this group has life-altering implications. If left untreated, early drinking almost invariably leads to severe and difficult-to-treat substance dependence. Abstinence is the best solution for them, and this is easier to achieve earlier in the addiction process. For women of childbearing age, alcohol consumption can lead to fetal alcohol syndrome. Addressing drinking problems before becoming pregnant prevents this sad outcome. Early detection is important for women of any age, because the progression from normal drinking to substance dependence occurs at an accelerated rate. Early detection and intervention can derail this process.

Alcohol Screens for Women

Because negative consequences and safe quantities are different for women, it's no surprise that screening tools are most accurate in identifying men's problematic substance use (Cherpital, 1997). To compensate, cutoff scores on popular scales are modified for optimal identification of a woman's alcohol problem. A cutoff of 4 points is recommended for the AUDIT and 1 point for the CAGE (Bradley, Boyd-Wickizer, Powell, and Mitchell, 1998).

A better alternative is the 5P's screen (the critical word in each question begins with a *p*), which is designed specifically for women. Its questions reflect the unique aspects of a woman's alcohol problem, which is shaped by close relationships and negative consequences in the interpersonal realm

Although not included on the 5P's screen, the question "Have you used drugs or alcohol during pregnancy?" needs to be answered by anyone who is pregnant. If the answer is "yes," it is essential to bring this information to a doctor's attention. For some women, even small amounts of alcohol on an intermittent basis can contribute to the pervasive physical and mental effects associated with fetal alcohol syndrome. For this reason, abstaining from alcohol is recommended.

(Center for Substance Abuse Treatment, 2004; Washington State Department of Health, 2002).

5P's Screening Tool

1. Do your *parents* have a problem with alcohol? Yes No
2. Have you had a *partner* who had a problem with alcohol? Yes No
3. Do you have *peers* (friends) who have problems with alcohol? Yes No
4. Have you used alcohol in the *past*? Yes No
5. Has anyone ever told you that you had a *problem* with alcohol? Yes No

SCORING: Responding "yes" to three or more items is indicative of a fully developed alcohol problem. However, any "yes" response merits further reflection, because each question identifies a risk factor for developing alcohol problems.

Resources

Women for Sobriety is a nonprofit organization, distinct from Alcoholics Anonymous, that provides help for women with alcoholism and other addictions.

www.womenforsobriety.org

Also refer to the resources listed at the end of chapter 9.

CHAPTER 11

Gambling Addiction

Gambling has had a complete makeover in the last thirty to forty years. It is no longer an illegal activity confined to smoke-filled rooms hidden in the back of bars and private clubs. Legalized casinos along with lotteries and racetrack betting are available across the country. Legalization has brought with it a much improved image for gambling and the gambler. Gambling is a new type of competitive sporting event. Tournaments are televised with commentators, like sports announcers, making note of the high stakes, mounting tensions, and elation of a good play. Its acceptability is further enhanced by state-run lotteries that are endorsed and operated by government agencies. Once gambling was legalized, transformed into entertainment, and government sponsored, people who previously avoided it because of its stigma, their moral values, or sensitivity to social pressures had fewer reasons to avoid this activity (Shaffer, Hall, and VanderBilt, 1999).

Gambling problems are burgeoning because along with legalization has come an increase in the number of places to gamble. As the "gateway" theory of substance use emphasizes, addiction is not possible without access to the potentially addictive behavior. Increased access ultimately leads to an increased incidence of an addiction. Neighborhoods with more liquor stores have a higher overall consumption of alcohol. Similarly, the closer one lives to a casino, the higher the rate of gambling problems. Within a fifty-mile radius of a casino, you will find double the usual rate of problematic gambling (National Gambling Impact Study Commission, 1999).

What Is Gambling?

Gambling involves taking a risk or relying on chance when the outcome is uncertain. Something of value, usually money, is wagered in the hope of winning a desired outcome—more money or a prize. Gambling comes in many forms. You can place a bet at a race track or contact a bookmaker to put money on the outcome of a sporting event. There are lotteries, scratch cards, and numerous casino card and dice games. "Games of chance" like bingo and raffles raise money for charities. Playing the stock market, especially day trading, meets the definition of gambling. Usually the act of gambling is visible: you place a bet, you buy a ticket. Gambling also can be covert; private wagers are made and a careful tally of wins and losses is kept in one's mind (see "Gambling's Masks," p. 150).

Today, anyone with a computer lives close to gambling. The Internet is the new casino. The distinctive nature of Internet gambling has the potential to increase gambling problems in a far more dramatic way than legalization. Internet gambling will be more difficult to control because it is usually done alone in the absence of social pressure to stop or limit one's losses. Electronic cash, which has no material existence (there is no plastic card or green paper), can be experienced as if it were play money, so losing it has less significance. Internet gambling parlors have the potential to be even more lucrative than land-based casinos.

Of all the behavioral addictions, gambling is the best known and the only one included in diagnostic manuals. Between 1 and 2 percent of the adult population qualifies for a diagnosis (Shaffer, Hall, and VanderBilt, 1999), although the figure doubles for young adults and adolescents. These percentages appear small, but when translated into actual numbers, there are more than five million adults in the United States addicted to gambling. Assuming that each gambler's addiction adversely affects three people, all together, gambling touches the daily lives of twenty million people. These figures do not take into account less severe forms of gambling addiction, which are more likely to remain hidden.

DSM-IV Criteria for Pathological Gambling

Pathological gambling is not defined by how often one gambles or how much money is lost. An addiction may be present even when financial losses are minimal.

A pathological gambler

1. is preoccupied with gambling (e.g, reliving past gambling experiences, handicapping or planning the next venture, or thinking of ways to get money with which to gamble).
2. needs to gamble with increasing amounts of money in order to achieve the desired excitement.
3. has repeated unsuccessful efforts to control, cut back, or stop gambling.
4. is restless or irritable when attempting to cut down or stop gambling.
5. gambles as a way of escaping from problems or of relieving a dysphoric mood (e.g., feelings of helplessness, guilt, anxiety, depression).
6. often returns another day to get even ("chasing one's losses") after losing money gambling.
7. lies to family members, therapist, or others to conceal the extent of his or her involvement in gambling.
8. has committed illegal acts such as forgery, fraud, theft, or embezzlement to finance gambling.
9. has jeopardized or lost a significant relationship, job, or educational or career opportunity because of gambling.
10. relies on others to provide money to relieve a desperate financial situation caused by gambling. (American Psychiatric Association, 2000, p. 674)

Persistent and recurrent maladaptive gambling behavior is indicated by five or more of the above.

What Gambling Teaches about Other Addictions

These criteria overlap with those for substance-related disorders but pathological gambling has a number of distinct attributes that I find useful when it comes to recognizing other addictions.

Criterion 1 states that an addicted gambler is mentally preoccupied with this activity. The pathological gambler wonders which race to bet on and how much to wager. There are fantasies about what winning will mean and worries about the cost of a loss. Obsessive ruminations accompany many kinds of addictions and should not be mistaken for an obsessive-compulsive disorder, as discussed in chapter 2.

Criterion 5 highlights a distinguishing feature of addictive behaviors that is omitted from the diagnostic criteria for substance addiction: the

The complex relationship between addiction and psychological distress is capably illustrated in Bill Lee's (2005) memoir about his gambling addiction. Lee was an unhappy little boy who never felt safe at home with his father, an alcoholic gambler who could be abusive and sexually provocative. He managed the chaos of his internal and external worlds by being compulsively neat. Later, he found that the excitement of gambling provided an escape. Gambling also served another function. As a child watching his family struggle for money, he concluded that becoming rich was the only road to happiness. Initially, gambling had a self-medicating effect; it helped Lee leave behind his psychological distress. But over time, gambling returned him to his original feelings of uncertainty and self-loathing (i.e., the paradox of addiction). He rarely stopped when winning big or losing little. He gambled to the point that he hated himself for his losses. Even when he had money, it did not bring the happiness he imagined. He never spent money on personal comforts; he saved it to gamble more. He neglected his health and his appearance. He wore the same tennis shoes until the sidewalk tore up his socks. Even when loathing himself for gambling, he could not stop; to stop meant unburying the pervasive and frightening sense of chaos and self-hatred he felt as a child.

behavior's motivation. A gambler's motivation falls into two general categories: stimulation or escape (McCormick, 1987). Stimulation- or action-seeking gamblers are prone to feeling understimulated; brief moments of excitement punctuate a chronic sense of boredom. Gambling provides needed arousal, variety, and stimulation. Other gamblers are attracted to this activity for its escape value. Depression, stress, or loneliness temporarily vanish while following a horse race or playing cards. Criterion 5 serves as a reminder that any behavior that occurs primarily because of its mood- or self-altering effects is at risk of becoming addictive.

I find criterion 7 to be the most interesting: the pathological gambler lies to conceal the extent of his or her involvement in gambling. Gamblers lie about where they get their money and how much is lost. They minimize gambling's adverse effects. Lying is common to all addictions. What puzzles me is why a gambler is simply said to be lying, but when a substance addict does not tell the truth, it is called "denial." This distinction is significant because it affects how we approach a problem: you try to encourage and support a liar to tell the truth and face reality. The approach for those "in denial" is more aggressive: you confront them with reality until they admit to having a problem.

Addictive Gambling Screen

South Oaks Gambling Screen (SOGS)

The South Oaks Gambling Screen (SOGS) is the most widely used gambling assessment tool. The SOGS assesses lifetime prevalence of gambling, associated problems, and preferred gambling activities (Lesieur and Blume, 1987). Because of its length and scoring procedure it is not the best screen to self-administer. An online version is available at www.gov.ns.ca/health/gambling/IsThereAProblem/SouthOaks/.

Canadian Problem Gambling Index

The screening tool I prefer was developed in Canada as part of a nationwide study of gambling. The Canadian Problem Gambling Index classifies gambling behavior along a continuum from casual or no-risk to severe problem gambling (Ferris and Wynne, 2001).

Before you answer these questions, think about your gambling in the last year. Gambling includes lotteries, scratch tickets, bingo, raffles, slot machines, any kind of casino or Internet gambling, betting on sporting events, and personal investing in stocks, options, or commodities (but not mutual funds).

Canadian Problem Gambling Index

Use the following letters to answer the questions:

A = Never   B = Sometimes   C = Most of the Time
D = Almost Always

In the past twelve months:

1. How often have you bet more than you really could afford to lose?
2. How often have you needed to gamble with larger amounts of money to get the same feeling of excitement?
3. How often have you borrowed money or sold anything to get money to try to win back the money you lost?
4. How often have you borrowed money or sold anything to get money to gamble?

5. How often have you felt that you might have a problem with gambling?
6. How often have people criticized your betting or told you that you had a gambling problem, regardless of whether or not you thought it was true?
7. How often have you felt guilty about the way you gamble or what happens when you gamble?
8. How often has gambling caused you any health problems, including stress or anxiety?
9. How often has your gambling caused any financial problems for you or hour household?

SCORING: A = 0, B = 1, C = 2, D = 3
Add up your total score.
Total score = 0: Casual gambler
Total score = 1–2: At-risk gambler
Total score = 3–7: Problem gambler
Total score = 8+: Severe problem/pathological gambler

The Gambling Continuum

Casual Gambling

The casual gambler plays for fun or when socializing with friends who are gambling. Winning money is part of the enjoyment but not the central motivation. Being a casual gambler does not preclude gambling frequently and for high stakes. However, the casual gambler is in full control and rarely if ever experiences negative consequences such as losing more than intended. The successful professional gambler who knows the odds, weighs the risk, and is always in control of his or her game would be considered a casual gambler.

At-Risk Gambling

Where the casual gambler rarely experiences negative consequences, the at-risk gambler intermittently experiences adverse effects. Usually these consequences are relatively minor and are a direct result of the behavior itself (NC 1): the person is tired from staying out too late, has sore legs from sitting too long, or is disappointed about not winning. These negative consequences come as a surprise and steps are taken to avoid them in the future. When not gambling, the game is put aside; there is not the kind of obsessive thinking common to problematic forms of gambling.

Frequent gambling and large bets are not necessarily evidence of addictive gambling. This may be professional gambling. Katy Lederer's *Poker Face* (2003) is an introduction to what it means to have family members in the gambling business. Her brother and sister are professional poker players in Las Vegas. Her sister, Annie Duke, one of the best female professional players, has written her own book, *Annie Duke: How I Raised, Folded, Bluffed, Flirted, Cursed, and Won Millions at the World Series of Poker* (2005). The description of the comfortable and controlled life as a professional poker player contrasts starkly with the chaotic, dramatic, secretive life of Bill Lee (2005), who writes from the perspective of a pathological gambler. These three books make it amply apparent that the addicted gambler is a very different breed than the professional gambler. The former plays with a lot of ego and hopes for luck. The addicted gambler is prone to distorted thinking: losing is attributed to bad luck while winning is connected to one's skill as a gambler and a sense of power arising from the belief in one's ability to control the uncontrollable. For the professional player, gambling is a skill involving careful study of the odds and disciplined assessment of each hand.

While numbers do not define a behavior as addictive, a recent study looked into how often and how much is lost by gamblers at different points along this continuum. At-risk gamblers gamble no more than three times a month and over the course of year spend less than $500 or 1 percent of a family's gross income (Currie et al., 2006). They are in control of the activity, set a limit, and stick to it. As a result they are less likely to do what turns a low-risk gambler into a problem gambler: chasing one's losses (Nova Scotia Office of Health Promotion, 2004).

Problem Gambling

The problem gambler finds gambling fun and enjoys its social elements, but these pleasures are secondary to gambling's mood-altering effects. Problem gamblers are experiencing more severe negative consequences on a more regular basis. NC 2 or secondary negative consequences—those involving reactions to direct negative consequences (NC 1)—are becoming common. A late night gambling leaves you exhausted, angering your boss or spouse. You feel remorseful about losing so much money, but the loss does not threaten financial well-being. There is enough money for daily necessities, but the family cannot go on vacation. By the time a person becomes a problematic gambler, he or she spends more time and/or money on gambling than was intended, but there is still some control. Functional consequences are beginning to emerge as gambling begins to threaten the capacity to fulfill life roles and responsibilities. Guilty feelings about how much money goes into gambling are growing; a depressed mood is setting in. Lying about how much is lost occurs but no stealing or lying to get money has occurred.

Severe Problem Gambler

As a gambling addiction moves from moderate to severe, functional consequences emerge and become more numerous (Ladd and Petry, 2002b; Shaffer, Hall, and VanderBilt, 1999). Constant arguments, in response to financial strain, result in an emotionally distant marriage or divorce. Personal items are sold to get money to gamble. Legal problems arise due to stealing and unpaid bills. Distorted thinking sets in as the gambler chases losses, believing that a string of losses means a win is just around the corner.

The pathological gambler has a very different relationship to betting than the casual or at-risk gambler. Gambling is no longer about fun or money. If asked, pathological gamblers will say the goal is to win money or be entertained. Yet their behavior suggests otherwise. They continue to gamble despite having accumulated large winnings. As Lee (2005) describes it, once addicted, the goal is not win money but to keep playing the game.

In *Double Down: Reflections on Gambling and Loss* (Barthelme and Barthelme, 1999), two brothers chronicle the downward spiral in quality of life as they move together along the continuum of gambling. After the death of their parents, the brothers move to the South, taking teaching jobs in nearby towns. Accustomed to greater variety and stimulation than their new lives provide (and as way to avoid dealing with the loss of both parents), they turn to gambling at the boat casinos docked in a nearby city. On their first visit, they are big winners—a common occurrence for those who later develop a gambling addiction. But by the end, they are losers whose lives are dominated by adverse consequences of pathological gambling.

Steps along the Continuum of
Addictive Gambling

Casual Gambling

Motivation: Casual gambling is a social activity or form of entertainment; enjoyment comes both from winning money and the social experience.

Consequences: Negative consequences are rare and minor.

Degree of Control: The casual gambler is in full control, knows the odds, and weighs the risks; he or she rarely, if ever, loses "too much."

At-Risk Gambling

Motivation: Gambling is an enjoyable activity but not necessarily a social activity; the at-risk individual usually sticks to preset limits and doesn't think about gambling when not engaged in it.

Consequences: Intermittent negative effects, if they occur, are a direct result of gambling (e.g., staying up too late, losing too much money).

Degree of Control: Generally, the gambler is in control, sets limits, and sticks to them. Rarely is more money lost than he or she can afford. Discovering that gambling creates desirable changes in experience is a risk factor for becoming a problematic gambler.

Problematic Gambling

Motivation: Gambling is enjoyed for its mood-altering effects, as a source of stimulation, or as a way to escape.

Consequences: Problematic gambling results in more frequent and severe negative consequences, many of which affect other people (i.e., problems meeting role obligations). The gambler lies about or minimizes how much is lost but doesn't engage in criminal activities to obtain money to gamble. Financial well-being is affected (e.g., there is money for necessities but little more).

Degree of Control: The gambler feels guilt about money spent gambling but continues to regularly spend more time and money gambling than was intended.

(Contnued)

> ## Steps along the Continuum of
> ## Addictive Gambling (Continued)
>
> **Severe Problem Gambling**
> *Motivation:* No longer about enjoyment or winning money, gambling
> may alter mood but what is most important is a felt need to keep
> playing even after achieving the desired wins, mood, or level of
> stimulation.
> *Consequences:* Negative consequences are increasingly severe; mounting
> threats to financial well-being are common.
> *Degree of Control:* The gambling addict finds it difficult to stop think-
> ing about gambling. Distorted thinking emerges regarding his or
> her ability to control luck/chance. Losses become the reason to con-
> tinue gambling (i.e., chasing losses), but when (or if) wins accu-
> mulate, the addicted gambler does not stop.

Gambling's Masks

Knowing the ways gambling problems can be masked facilitates identification of gambling problems before they reach the pathological level. There is
ample opportunity to do this. The path from recreational gambling to
pathological gambling is long; the average time to full addiction is eight to
twelve years, with this time frame being somewhat more rapid for women
(Derevensky, Gupta, and Winters, 2003). Recognizing problems early, at the
at-risk or problem level, limits the devastating effects on self, family, and
finances that occur when gambling reaches its pathological form.

> Common correlates of gambling, such as substance abuse, depression,
> and anxiety, like resulting physical problems, draw attention away from
> the primary problem. The co-occurrence of substance addictions, espe-
> cially alcoholism, is not surprising in light of the practice in casinos of
> providing active gamblers with free liquor. Depression can be lethal
> when mixed with gambling. As losses mount, suicide is often contem-
> plated; 15 to 20 percent of those diagnosed with pathological gambling
> actually make a suicidal attempt (Petry and Kiluk, 2002).

The Mask Created by Shame and Illegal Acts

The financial burdens that usually accompany pathological gambling would seem difficult to hide. Yet long before the mortgage goes unpaid, before there is no money for food, or the automobile is repossessed, the addicted gambler resorts to lying and even stealing to get additional funds. Gamblers are very resourceful—and deceitful—when it comes to getting money. Relatives are asked to help defray a spouse's medical expenses for an illness that does not exist. Money is taken from business accounts at work. As the big win continues to elude the gambler, losses and lies continue to accrue along with debt. With mounting debt comes mounting shame; shame for having gotten into debt, shame for not being able to get another big win, shame at having hurt the family. Shame is a powerful motivator that prevents self-identification of a gambling addiction. In addition, the immoral and illegal acts driven by the hope that there will be another big win like the first big win becomes even more reason to keep the addiction hidden.

The Mask of Covert Gambling

Gambling is an overt activity: card playing, betting on sports, buying lottery tickets. Richard Rosenthal from the UCLA Gambling Studies Program reports how his treatment of gambling disorders led to the discovery of covert gambling.

Rosenthal was treating a man—I'll call him Zack—whose recovery from an overt gambling addiction appeared successful until he admitted to having begun visiting prostitutes. Rosenthal knew that if sex was all that his patient wanted, this very attractive and charming man knew women who would be happy to have sexual relations with him. Why would Zack visit prostitutes, in light of his acknowledged fear of getting HIV and other diseases? Even more curious was his behavior when he found a prostitute who seemed "safe." Instead of returning to her, Zack looked for someone else. Not surprisingly, the answer had something to do with gambling. Despite feeling anxious about his risky sexual behavior, this man took great pleasure in winning the bet—in this case, winning meant avoiding HIV and sexually transmitted diseases. Winning this covert bet created a rush like the rush Zack experienced when overtly gambling. Despite giving up gambling, Zack had found a way to stay in the game.

Rosenthal refers to the wager of covert gambling as the "mind bet." This is a private bet made with oneself. Like overt gambling, covert gamblers flirt with luck: luck is with me or against me. The covert gambler will park illegally and feel elated when, upon returning, he or she sees that

Covert gambling extends outside the treatment setting. You don't need to be a problematic gambler to resort to covert betting. A woman drives without a license and bets on not getting caught. A man leaves home for an appointment with no time to spare. The bet is that the bus or subway will arrive within seconds of his arrival at the stop or that he'll avoid traffic, hit all of the green lights, and find a parking place right in front of the meeting place.

there is no ticket. Bill Lee (2005), long before casinos consumed his life, talks about the thrill of betting on insignificant happenings. In school, he would bet on which raindrop sliding down the window would be the first to reach the sill.

The good news is that covert gambling is cheap. However, this does not mean it is without adverse consequences. Most are minor, like running out of gas, getting a parking ticket, or taking time away from the family. However, some consequences are dangerous. Covert gamblers put themselves in positions of danger (e.g., engaging in extreme sports, provoking a fight, stealing, practicing unsafe sex), all the time making mental bets that luck will be on their side. If luck abandons them, the outcomes of lost bets can be severe: injury, incarceration, or death. Covert gambling can also become a problem when it begins to structure one's day or is combined with overt gambling where, much like cross-tolerance for substances, two similar behaviors combine to create symptoms consistent with an addiction.

The Mask of Demographics: Women

A woman's gambling is at risk of being overlooked because gambling is assumed to be a man's addiction. The gamblers portrayed in books and on television are most often men. Gambling venues tend to be male friendly: casinos are filled with sexily clad waitresses, there is betting on sports and skill-related games that men primarily play, such as basketball or pool. But as Annie Duke (2005) and the occasional women on televised Texas Holdem tournaments remind us, gambling is not just a man's game. Although the number of men diagnosed as pathological gamblers outnumber women two to one, this still means one third of problem gamblers are women.

A woman's initial exposure to gambling is social in nature. She accompanies friends or a partner to the racetrack or casino. A strong predictor of problematic gambling in women is having a spouse or close friend who enjoys gambling. A wife may follow her husband in developing a gambling problem. But the opposite is not true; a husband's gambling level is relatively unaffected by his wife's gambling (Ladd and Petry, 2002a).

Men are attracted to gambling for its stimulating effects. They prefer public and more hands-on gambling such as high-stakes card games, betting on sports or animal races, or betting on activities that test their skill (e.g., golf).

The transition from casual to problem gambler is most likely when a woman finds that gambling helps her escape from daily problems. While gambling initially is social, once it becomes problematic, a woman prefers solitary games of chance such as slot machines and lotteries. Lotteries, as well as bingo, are often overlooked as forms of gambling, given that they have achieved a kind of social legitimacy. The solitary nature and social acceptability of women's gambling contribute to its invisibility.

Further adding to the invisibility of women's gambling is the amount wagered. Financial devastation created by uncontrolled gambling is its most salient adverse effect and the one most often looked for when assessing for this addiction. Men are more likely to lose big. Because men gamble more frequently and bet larger amounts than women, their mounting financial losses come to a family's attention. A woman's preference for slots and lottery tickets takes a less severe financial toll that is more easily hidden. This may change if women become involved in a new form of solitary gambling with higher stakes: Internet casinos.

While financial losses may be contained, women gamblers are not immune to other problems. They have high rates of concomitant psychiatric disturbances (Petry, 2003), especially depression. A health care provider is apt to recognize the depression but not the underlying gambling problem.

The Mask of Demographics: Adolescent Gambling

Casinos, lottery ticket purchases, and racetrack betting are off-limits to adolescents, but this has not deterred the growth of gambling addictions among adolescents at a rate that equals or exceeds that of adults. The vast majority of high school students have gambled at least once. Up to 6 percent of these recreational gamblers will develop problems controlling this behavior (Derevensky, Gupta, and Winters, 2003). Betting on sports is the preferred activity of adolescents, although playing cards is becoming increasingly popular, as poker gains in popularity on television and is portrayed as an easy and fun way to get rich quickly.

Adolescent gambling, like drinking, occurs outside adult supervision. Usually the stakes are small and the main point is to have fun. Internet gambling

Is Online Gaming a Form of Gambling?

Videogames and gambling have common features (Griffiths and Wood, 2000). The goal of gambling is to win as much money as possible while the goal of videogames is to acquire as many points as possible or to achieve the next higher level. Both outcomes reinforce behavior on an intermittent basis (see chapter 3). You lose most of the time and every now and then you win money or make it to the game's next level. Each time, the number of attempts it takes to "win" differs. Sometimes you win twice in row; other times it takes ten, twenty, or more tries before winning. With intermittent reinforcement, a person continues playing in the absence of immediate rewards in the hopes that success will come on the next try. There is a big difference between the two; gambling is controlled by chance, and video games involve an element of skill. So far, there is no evidence that videogame playing is correlated with increased gambling risk, but this does not rule out the possibility that videogames are addictive in their own right (see chapter 12).

may present an added risk for this group by significantly increasing access to gambling and providing opportunities to lose larger sums. Computer-savvy teenagers may be drawn to this form of gambling where age limits are not easily imposed despite warnings that underage players are not allowed.

Adolescents' gambling is rarely self-identified and usually remains unseen by family and friends. Worrisome effects of problematic gambling overlap with those for substance addictions (e.g., grades drop, time unaccounted for, change in social group) and can be mistaken for a substance addiction or typical adolescent growing pains (Derevenksy, Gupta, and Winters, 2003; Griffiths and Wood, 2000). Risk taking, moody and sulky behavior, and evasiveness about one's whereabouts could reflect an adolescent's individuation or it could be a sign of an addiction. Because adolescents feel that they know it all, can manage all, and are invincible, the adverse effects of gambling are minimized and assumed to be temporary.

Further masking gambling problems during adolescence is the fact that financial losses have less impact relative to the adult gambler. Adolescents do not have a family to feed or mortgage to pay. While adolescents can incur large gambling debts, more often, gambling losses lead to an inability to buy lunch or a new CD. A subtle sign of problematic gambling is when an adolescent begins selling his or her possessions or when money inexplicably goes missing from the home.

An adolescent's early experiences with gambling predict whether a problem is likely to develop. Family members should pay special attention if a child begins gambling at a young age (by age ten), has had a "big" win early on, and has close family members who gamble. A behavior with the ability to create positive feelings is much more likely to become addictive. A child or adolescent who appears depressed before gambling but upbeat and animated while gambling is at risk of becoming addicted (Griffiths and Wood, 2000).

More often than not, parents remain unaware of the problem until their child runs into trouble with the law. The health and social consequences of an unrecognized gambling addiction can be serious. As with adult gamblers, suicide and attempted suicide is common, education and family life are disrupted, and there are arrests and high rates of other addictive and psychiatric disorders (Larimer and Neighbors, 2003).

Resources

Online trading addiction quiz:
   www.healthyplace.com/Communities/Addictions/netaddiction/resources/
   online_trading.htm
Compulsive online gamblers quiz:
   www.netaddiction.com/resources/online_gambling.htm
Online auction addiction quiz:
   www.netaddiction.com/resources/auction_houses.htm
Gamblers Anonymous twenty questions self-screening test:
   www.gamblersanonymous.org/20questions.html
Gamblers Anonymous:
   www.gamblersanonymous.org/
Gam-Anon, for the family members, friends, and loved ones of problematic and addicted gamblers:
   www.gam-anon.org/
South Oaks Gambling Screen (SOGS):
   www.gov.ns.ca/health/gambling/IsThereAProblem/SouthOaks/

CHAPTER 12

Computer Addiction

The computer has become a multipurpose communication device that does much more than the original function after which it is named. Computers are used to socialize, bank, gamble, listen to music, access information, shop, watch movies, trade stocks, read newspapers, convey information, attend classes, play games, and write books. It is a resource for medical knowledge, self-help, and psychotherapy for all kinds of problems including computer addiction. For those who prefer less traditional forms of guidance, there are computer psychics.

Budding actress Sarah Lassez managed the uncertainties of her challenging career by having her future read in tarot cards, the minds of clairvoyants, and even coffee sediment. Paying a set fee for each visit, she was able to afford the cost of having another person reaffirm her hopes of a successful future. This changed once she discovered Internet psychics. She began to consult them on a daily basis. Reassured by their reassurances, her anxiety would abate temporarily but once it returned, Sarah would click on the Internet again, often up to six times a day, at a cost of $1,000 each month. Finding it increasingly difficult to control her contact with online psychics, she sought help from a therapist who recommended a twelve-step program. Upon finding no program for her type of addiction, she began her own website (www.psychicjunkie.net) where others, too ashamed to get help, can find support in overcoming their reliance on psychic predictions (Williams, 2006).

Sarah's experience with Internet psychics raises the central question about computer addictions: What exactly is it that you are addicted to when addicted to a computer? An addiction's name usually reflects the activity or object creating the problem, such as exercise addiction or alcohol addiction. I doubt that the machine itself—the keyboard or screen—is the source of a computer addiction.

For most, the addictive nature of the computer primarily rests with the Internet. Certainly this was true for Sarah Lassez, who was able to keep her contact with psychics under control until she discovered them online. A similar story of how the Internet contributes to loss of control over once-moderate behaviors is told in the next chapter on sexual addictions. A person with no history of sexual addiction becomes a cybersex addict after discovering online pornography.

Understanding the source of a computer addiction requires an exploration of the ways this form of entertainment, communicating, and accessing information is reinforcing and mood-altering. A variety of answers have been proposed:

Virtual relationships can be more comfortable than face-to-face interactions. The computer provides opportunities for interaction that were not available with older forms of technology. Most time spent online is interactive in nature; the two most preferred activities are participating in chat rooms and multiple-player games (Young, 1998). Chat rooms provide a way to make friends, share common interests, and find social support. If these kinds of reinforcement are not readily available in a person's life,

Humans have a habit of developing intense relationships with their newest technology. Computer addiction is the latest in a series of technology addictions. It began with radio—the first technological form of mass communication and entertainment—and was followed by television and now computers. Marie Winn (2002) has captured the allure of these technologies in the title of her book, *The Plug-In Drug*. Initially published in 1985 to examine the population's romance with television, the most recent 2002 edition includes computers.

then more and more time will be spent on the computer. One study of computer-addicted college students showed them to be computer-savvy males who were relatively shy and inhibited in face-to-face interactions. Once on the computer, they became socially outgoing and engaging. For them, the computer serves as a way to cope with social problems (Mora-han-Martin and Schumacher, 2000; Nichols and Nicki, 2004).

The computer provides intense and novel stimulation that facilitates coping. Persons with addictions often score high on tests that measure enjoyment taken from sensation seeking. The various sources of information, social interactions, and gaming accessed through the computer provide the stimulation seeker with the "rush" of novelty and a way to avoid boredom. This stimulation also facilitates coping through escape. Online activities provide distraction from daily problems. Certainly, online fantasy games are a perfect form of escape.

The computer provides the opportunity to reap the benefits of anonymity. Anonymity on the Internet is more a feeling than a fact, given that programs exist for tracking our every activity. However, the sense of anonymity allows some people to feel safe to act in new, often less-inhibited ways. We have all heard about the computer being a place to take on a different persona, one that is considered more attractive and appealing. The sexually awkward become flirtatious. The chronically "nice" guy becomes more challenging. While much is made of people faking their gender, the most common form of deceit is lowering one's age (A. Cooper, Schere, Boles, and Gordon, 1999). These new personal attributes and resulting interactions are reinforcing and potentially mood altering.

Immersion in the medium provides an alternative sense of reality or altered consciousness. As with a drug, an altered sense of reality (e.g., loss of self, sense of boundlessness) can be rewarding (Griffiths, 1995). This is probably one component in the strong appeal of fantasy-based interactive online games. But similar feelings can arise from intense concentration when answering e-mails, searching for information, or otherwise being engaged in computer activities.

The computer provides instant gratification. We all have desires and wishes. Some of us are better than others at delaying gratification. One form of control is to put some time between the desire and access to gratification. While walking to the store to buy a bottle of liquor, the budding alcoholic can talk himself out of the need for a drink. With the computer's speed, a desire—whether to make a purchase, find a sexual

What's Your Motivation?

Give as many answers as possible to the following question: what are your expectations when you turn on the computer?

When this question was posed as part of a research study, there was a wide array of answers. Most answers referred to the content that can be accessed through the computer (e.g., product comparisons, information about medical conditions, resources such as encyclopedias). Others emphasized internal experiences arising from computing. Many of these responses suggested that computer use had a self-medicating effect. The computer was a way to relax, relieve boredom, to be distracted from worry, or to feel good. Similar to what has been observed with substance-based addictions, computer addiction was more common for the group whose answers indicated that they expected the computer to help them regulate or manage inner (often unpleasant) experiences (LaRose, Lin, and Eastin, 2003).

Another way to determine if the computer creates mood-altering effects is simply to keep a log of how you feel an hour before using the computer, while on the computer, and an hour after logging off.

liaison, or access information—can be gratified within seconds, and over time we can lose control over these impulses.

Computer addictions have been said to affect the lives of 12 to 15 percent of the population. This would make computer addiction second only to substance addiction. Even more conservative estimates, which suggest that 6 percent of the population has a computer addiction, still seem high (Collins, Skinner, and Toneatto, 2006). A more realistic estimate is probably between 1 and 2 percent of the population. But these percentages will grow in number if development of computer addictions follows the gateway theory, and ease of access makes addiction more common. Indeed, computers are much more accessible than they were just a few years ago, given the significant decline in price, increased speed, ease of use, and ability to use them almost anywhere.

At this time, race and gender do not affect the incidence of computer addictions, although they are more common among younger and well-educated persons, especially college students (upward of 10 percent) (Hall and Parsons, 2001). While both men and women use computers to the same degree, they use them for different purposes. E-mail and the Web are used equally by both genders. Men prefer games, gambling, and pornography, while women use the computer more to find and maintain relationships through chat rooms and instant messaging.

Computer Addiction Criteria

The criteria for computer addiction are modeled after those for pathological gambling.

A person with problematic computer use

1. experiences pleasure, gratification, or relief while engaged in computer activities.
2. is preoccupied with computer activity, including thinking about the experience, making plans to return to the computer, surfing the Web, owning the newest and fastest hardware, or returning to these activities to escape problems or relieve dysphoric moods.
3. needs to spend increasingly more time or money on computer activities to change mood.
4. fails repeated efforts to control these activities.
5. is restless, irritable, or experiences other dysphoric moods, such as increased tension, when not engaged in computer activities.
6. needs to return to these activities to escape problems or relieve dysphoric mood.
7. neglects social, familial, educational, or work obligations.
8. lies to family members, therapists, and others about the extent of time spent on the computer.
9. threatens or loses significant relationships, job, financial stability, or educational opportunity because of computer usage.
10. exhibits physical signs, such as carpal tunnel syndrome, backaches, dry eyes, migraines, headaches, neglect of personal hygiene, or eating irregularities.
11. experiences changes in sleep patterns. (Orzack and Ross, 2000, p. 114)

Meeting five or more of the above criteria is taken as evidence of problematic computer use.

Those who are computer addicted according to the above criteria use the computer, on average, forty hours per week (Hall and Parsons, 2001).

Long hours online cut into sleep, which in turn, create their own negative consequences. Not only does sleepiness lower effectiveness the next day, but repetitive late-night hours on the computer disrupts the natural sleep cycle and insomnia occurs (Rotunda, Kass, Sutton, and Leon, 2003). Increasing sleep disturbances subsequently contribute to the social and occupational problems represented in criterion 9. Perhaps only second to substance-related addictions, computer addictions have their most devastating effects in the workplace as illustrated by the "Butterfly Effect" later in the chapter.

Further negative consequences of computer use emerge in relationships and at school. More than 50 percent of those whose computer use is problematic report serious interpersonal consequences. Likewise, close to 60 percent of students blame the computer for a decline in school grades and less time put into study (Young, 1998).

Distinguishing Addiction and High Engagement

In everyday language, a fondness for doing something repeatedly is often equated with addiction—you're addicted to eating bread, you're a television addict. A behavior done with intensity also is considered an addiction. Teens talk on the phone or communicate by instant message for hours on end. Adults ignore family and friends while spending hours immersed in a good book. Do these teenagers have an instant-messaging addiction? Have these adults come down with a book-reading addiction?

While any behavior is potentially addictive, Dr. John Grohol (2003), who runs one of the oldest online mental health resources, reminds us that it is a mistake to describe a behavior as an addiction when all that is known is that a significant amount of time is spent on the behavior or it occurs in an overzealous manner. Think of the committed Olympic athlete who, in order to maintain and improve skills, exercises hours every day. This athlete may lift weights as often as the person addicted to exercising, but it would be an error to conclude that this Olympic-bound weightlifter has an exercise addiction—devotion to an activity, by itself, is not a good measure of addiction.

A behavior's high frequency or intensity may simply be part of a phase. Long hours on the computer may be required for work or a school project. Even without special tasks, intense computer use can be phasic (Grohol, 2003). Initially, the computer is an enchanting way to get information and socialize. This is the period of heaviest use. Over time, disillusionment or loss of interest sets in along with decreased use. This may be followed by a combination of periods of no use, moderate use, and intense use.

The idea that behaviors go through phases has implications for evaluating whether any behavior is addictive. Adolescents "discover" alcohol and drink frequently, but only a few go on to become addicted. Poker playing has risen in popularity in response to televised tournaments; some adolescents fill their weekends with poker playing. For the vast majority, frequent card playing is part of a phase. While being highly involved with an activity is not the same as an addiction, high engagement can be a risk factor depending on the person's background, emotional well-being, and coping skills.

Computer Addiction Screen

The following screening for computer addiction is designed specifically to distinguish addiction from high engagement (Charlton, 2002).

Respond yes or no to each.

1. I often experience a buzz of excitement while computing.
2. I rarely think about computing when I am not using a computer.
3. I tend to want to spend increasing amounts of time using computers.
4. When I am not using a computer, I often feel agitated.
5. I never miss meals because of my computer activities.
6. I often fail to get enough sleep because of my computing activities.
7. Arguments have sometimes arisen at home because of the time I spend on computing activities.
8. My social life has sometimes suffered because of my computing activities.
9. Computing activities have sometimes interfered with my work.
10. I have made unsuccessful attempts to reduce the time I spend on the computers.

SCORING: One point is scored for a "no" response to questions 2 and 5. Each "yes" to the remaining eight questions is scored as 1 point. A score of 5 or more is taken as evidence of addiction.

The first three questions measure computer engagement. A highly engaged person gets pleasure from the computer, thinks about it a lot, and wants to spend more time computing. If your total score is 3, consider yourself highly engaged. Please be aware that high engagement is not without risk. A high level of engagement may be phasic, or it can easily turn into problematic computer use if the reinforcement provided by computer use is not available elsewhere or has the capacity to reliably shift subjective experience (e.g., taking on a new, more valued identity, alleviating boredom).

The content of questions 4 through 10 represent symptoms of computer addiction. Addiction is characterized by an onset of negative consequences that result in self-neglect (missing meals, loss of sleep) and conflicts at work and with others. A loss of control is evident when repeated efforts to cut back on time spent on the computer fail. Withdrawal is reflected in uncomfortable feelings (agitation) when the computer is unavailable. While the cutoff for a problem is a score of 5, any positive response to these seven symptoms of computer addiction should be examined.

The Continuum of Computer Addiction

Recreational Computer Use

The computer serves as a resource to meet defined goals for the recreational user. The computer is a tool for achieving certain ends: completing a work assignment, reading a newspaper online, returning e-mails, playing a game, finding a romantic partner. The recreational user gets off the computer once the task or goal is accomplished. Rarely does he or she stay on longer than intended, but, like the social drinker who occasionally has a few too many, the recreational user occasionally spends more time on the computer than intended.

At-Risk Computer Use

The at-risk user becomes immersed in the computer, loses track of time, and ends up using the computer for longer periods than intended. Often the machine is turned on with no well-defined goal in mind. Being highly engaged puts a user at risk because it exposes him or her to the reinforcing effects of computers that come in the form of stimulation provided by online information, anonymity, or immersion in the cyberworld. At this point, the computer is not always used as a tool for accomplishing specific tasks; the various reinforcing effects of computer use are beginning to take control. Negative consequences are limited in scope for the at-risk user and a direct result of computer use (NC 1). The most common negative effect is spending too much time on the computer so that other responsibilities go unmet. Physical consequences like dry eyes, a sore behind, and leg, back, and neck pain come with extended time online.

Secondary consequences (NC 2) emerge intermittently for the at-risk user. Secondary consequences involve physical, personal, and interpersonal reactions in response to the direct effects of computer use. Spending more time than intended often forms the basis for secondary negative effects. A school assignment is handed in late after instant messaging late into the evening. A wife is angry that her husband—who spends the after-dinner hours at the computer—no longer goes to bed when she does.

Problematic Computer Use

Problematic computer use brings an increasing intensity and frequency of secondary negative consequence. The problematic user goes online as a way to escape or manage mood. He or she has begun to suffer negative social, emotional, and financial consequences associated with addiction. The behavior is becoming difficult to control. Despite stated intent to cut back, time online increases. Functional consequences begin to emerge in the form of problems meeting role obligations and responsibilities. A marriage is sorely strained as a wife's anger becomes an everyday occurrence, and the kids complain about Dad's lack of availability. Lack of sleep due to late nights online, combined with personal use of the computer at work, erodes work performance to the point that the boss has noticed.

Fully Addicted Computer Use

As functional consequences persist and become more severe, computing behavior has become fully addictive. Thoughts of using the computer preoccupy the user during time away from the computer. These thoughts, combined with a sense of jitteriness or agitation when a computer is not readily

---

Steps along the Continuum of Computer Addiction

Recreational Computer Use

Motivation: Computer use is appropriate and goal oriented (e.g., to get information, communicate with others).

Consequences: None.

Degree of Control: Recreational users stop using the computer once their goals are achieved. They rarely if ever stay on longer than intended.

At-Risk Computer Use or Highly Engaged Use

Motivation: At-risk computer users have no specific goal in mind. The computer is used for enjoyment and its reinforcing effects (e.g., novelty, stimulation, feeling anonymous).

Consequences: Consequences are limited and mild (e.g., dry eyes, sore neck). More serious consequences (e.g., failure to meet responsibilities, others get angry) are rare occurrences and come as a surprise.

Degree of Control: The at-risk user stays on longer than intended and loses track of time. For the highly engaged user, this kind of use is temporary or phasic. If the reinforcing effects of computer use are of psychological value (i.e., as a way to cope or create potent subjective experiences), then problematic use is more likely to develop.

Problematic Computer Use

Motivation: Computer use still provides some enjoyment, but it stops being enjoyable as the user begins spending more time on the computer than intended or feels compelled to visit certain online sites and has difficulty stopping. Computer use provides an escape or way to manage mood.

Consequences: Serious negative consequences are beginning to multiply; the person feels guilty about how much time is spent on the computer and is becoming less effective in meeting major responsibilities.

Degree of Control: Computer use is difficult to control, and despite the desire to cut back, use increases.

Fully Addicted Computer Use

Motivation: The computer is used for its mood-altering effects and/or as a way to counteract withdrawal (obsessive thinking, jitteriness, agitation) when away from the computer. Tolerance is apparent as more time with the computer is required in order to achieve a sense of satisfaction or mood change.

Consequences: Negative effects are difficult to hide and affecting general quality of life.

Degree of Control: Thoughts frequently turn to the activities done with the computer and more time is spent than intended when using the computer, despite intentions to cut back.

available, can be a sign of withdrawal. Tolerance is apparent when more time with the computer is required in order to achieve a sense of satisfaction or mood change. The negative effects on functioning are explicit: a wife has sought therapy to address her dissolving marriage or a final warning has been issued at work.

Computer Addiction's Masks

The Mask of the Nerd

Computer addiction is more common among men with strong technological skills who are somewhat more lonely than their college peers (Morahan-Martin and Schumacher, 2000). This person is very similar to the stereotypic image of the computer nerd: a technically adept but shy young man with pens and pencils in his pocket protector.

With more user-friendly computers and the burgeoning of the Internet and "virtual" relationships, women and older adults are increasingly involved with computers. Today men and women are equally likely to access the Internet. The stereotype of a young male computer geek can mask a developing computer addiction in women and older people.

The Mask of Emotional Distress

Depression and loneliness are the most common correlates of computer addiction. Following the pattern set by other addictions, the relationship between emotional problems and computer use varies from person to person. For some, depression and loneliness precede addictive involvement and the computer provides mood-altering relief from these negative states. These beneficial effects are only temporary and, over the long run, high levels of Internet use bring a decline in social involvement and an increase in depressive feelings (Kraut et al., 1998; LaRose, Lin, and Eastin, 2003). The danger here is that the more apparent depressive symptoms will be identified as only emotional in origin and the link to computer use will go unrecognized.

Computer Addiction Masks Other Addictions

What appears to be a computer addiction can actually be another addiction that is gratified partly by online activities. Typical examples are accessing cyberporn as part of a sexual addiction, online shopping as part of shopping addiction, or playing blackjack online as part of a gambling addiction. In each of these examples, there is a primary addiction—to sex, shopping, gambling—

in which the computer merely serves as a conduit to a behavior that is already addictive offline.

Other times what appears to be a computer addiction is actually an addiction to a particular online activity. A recreational shopper who has no problem controlling her impulses in a store becomes addicted to online bargains and auctions. The addiction would not exist without the computer and except for this specific online activity, computer use is not a problem. In this example, the addiction would be most accurately described as an addiction to online shopping.

From the very first time, Glenda said she got a "real kick" out of gambling—especially blackjack. Poker required too much thinking and she liked the fast-paced nature of blackjack. Before going to a casino, Glenda set a financial limit for herself. She never had a problem leaving a casino after losing or winning a preset amount. Then she discovered online gambling. The ease of access, immersion in the online world, and a sense of anonymity resulted in developing gambling-related debts and spending significantly less time with her children.

Glenda has an online gambling addiction in much the same way Lassez is addicted to online psychics.

The Butterfly Effect Mask

A butterfly moves its wings and the course of the world changes. The image is meant to suggest that small events can have significant consequences. This describes how employees' use of the Internet affects a business.

This mask is unlike the others that keep an addiction hidden. That is because the negative effects are not at the individual or interpersonal level. An employee who uses the computer for personal purposes simply creates a minor decrease in productivity. For some, it may simply be a diversion, much like a trip to the water fountain. For others, the workplace is used to access sites that they fear could be tracked from home (i.e., sexual material). As longer working hours leave little time to socialize, an employee can begin visiting chat rooms while finishing off the day's work (Griffiths, 2003). Taking a few moments for personal use of the computer seems minor. For the company, the effect is major: when many employees take a little time out of the workday for personal tasks, a company's overall productivity declines.

For some employees, time spent online will not be so confined. For those who are addicted, cravings that develop during the day are managed by going online. Signs of addiction in the workplace include loss of productivity, increased mistakes, decreased interaction with coworkers as online interactions replace real-time interactions, and quickly changing screens when someone approaches the employee's desk.

Resources

Access to a variety of screening tools for computer-related addictions, including tests that partners and parents can use to decide if a partner or child has a computer addiction:

www.netaddiction.com/resources/iaindex.htm

Online meeting room for computer addicts:

www.turnintostone.org/Wikka_hm/Wikka/HomePage

You can also locate local treatment resources by searching "computer addition."

CHAPTER 13

Sex and Cybersex
Addictions

Despite the stereotype of a sex addict as someone who is aroused by women's underwear, stalks children, or exhibits himself, most sexual addictions do not involve unconventional sexual behaviors. In fact, most sexual addictions involve common forms of sexual expression. Even sexual intercourse within a monogamous relationship can represent an addiction.

One man in treatment for sexual addiction described having sex four or more times a day with his girlfriend. Initially a willing partner, over time she began to resent that their relationship involved little more than sex. He was chronically late for work and despite warnings from his manager, he could not leave the house without having an orgasm several times, either through intercourse or masturbation. Sex cost him his job. Other sexual behaviors that can compose a sexual addiction include viewing pornography, visiting an adult bookstore or sex club, flirting, cruising for a new sexual partner, engaging in multiple love/sexual relationships, having phone sex, and seeking out prostitutes.

As with any other addiction, frequency alone does not make a sex addiction. Despite derogatory labels like nymphomaniac or satyriasis (the male version of nymphomania), frequent sex is not necessarily evidence of addiction. Frequent sexual urges and intercourse can simply mean that a person is highly sexual (Blumberg, 2003). The approach to defining sexual addictions is identical to other addictions. No specific type of sexual behavior in itself is addictive.

When it comes to sex, it is easy to fall into a moralizing stance. If you are in a committed relationship, any sex, pornography viewing, or flirting, can be considered immoral. While there are sexual behaviors that are immoral and illegal, neither of these attributes makes a behavior addictive. A member of a couple who seeks a sexual liason online may be unfaithful to the relationship (and may have problems with intimacy), but this act does not make for an addiction. To underscore the point that sexual addictions usually involve sexual urges and behavior that are more common than unconventional in nature, Peele (1999) half seriously and half humorously suggests we all are familiar with sexual addiction. "Many (perhaps most) people give a good rendition of sexual addiction in their youth. But a substantial majority overcome this tendency with growing maturity, responsibility and self-knowledge" (p. 155).

Instead, addiction rests with how the sexual behavior relates to the rest of a person's life. If sexual behavior is difficult to control, associated with cravings, and creates predicaments in the financial, legal, occupational and/or social arenas, then addiction is likely (Coleman, Raymond, and McBean, 2003).

The personal costs of a sexual addiction include depression, anxiety about getting caught, and guilt or shame when sexual acts contradict moral values. Social costs include arrests, job loss, damage to meaningful personal relationships, and harm to children, if they come across a parent's sexually explicit material. Having multiple sexual partners, a common side effect of sexual addiction, markedly increases the risk of compromised health including sexually transmitted diseases or unplanned pregnancy. The increased exposure to HIV infection means that substance addiction is not the only addiction that can kill.

In *Love Sick* (2001) Sue William Silverman writes about her inability to control her need for serial sexual affairs. What begins as an intensely passionate sexual union becomes, before long, little more than a quick sex act in a local motel. Outside her home, she appears to function well. No matter where she has been the night before, she appears promptly each day at a job that means little to her. "I'm friendly and industrious. Seemingly sober and normal, I work hard all day, get the job done. . . . I live the day world only because I know night is coming (p. 198)."

Life at home is not so functional. She no longer has sex with her husband; they don't even sleep in the same room. The most intimate act with her spouse is making him a good dinner each night—except for Thursdays when dinner is rushed because of late afternoon meetings with her current addictive object. Silverman's husband is well aware that his marriage is in trouble. However, he has no idea that the root of the problem is his wife's sexual addiction, despite her remark, "I might have a few sexual issues to work out" (p. 123), and seeing the "addict clothes" in her closet. Common to many who live with an addicted person, "he doesn't see what he sees . . . or know what he knows" (p. 123). He attributes their failing marriage to his wife's depression and possible eating disorder.

The health care professionals Silverman seeks out for her emotional distress are typical in their failure to identify the real problem. Her first ten therapists, like her husband, miss the addiction. Despite talking to them about sex and seduction, "all they see is a woman who's depressed. They feed me antidepressants and don't understand a pill won't fix me" (p. 206). Only the eleventh recognizes the "addictwoman" she really is.

Determining who is most likely to have sex addictions and their prevalence poses a challenge. When researchers want to know how many people in a community have a certain kind of problem, they conduct door-to-door interviews. Information about drinking patterns in the general population is gathered this way. Imagine using this door-to-door approach to collect data on sexual behavior! As a creative alternative, two researchers advertised for persons who were concerned that their sexual behavior might be addictive (Kafka and Prentky, 1992).

They found that our image of a typical sex addict is probably as distorted as our image of an alcoholic. The sex addict is often assumed to be a man who is either a sexual offender or socially isolated, living a marginal existence. Except for gender, none of these images fit the profile of those who responded to the researchers' advertisement. The typical respondent was a thirty-four-year-old man who came from a Catholic background. He was married, a college graduate, and earned a middle-class income. Sexually addictive behaviors first emerged in adolescence or early adulthood and peaked in frequency during his late twenties and thirties.

Three to six percent of the U.S. population is estimated to have a sexual addiction (A. Cooper, Scherer, Boies, and Gordon, 1999; Coleman, Raymond, and McBean, 2003). Most of these estimates were made before the burgeoning of sexual content on the Internet, which has brought with it a new form of sexual addiction: cybersex addiction.

A Special Form of Sexual Addiction: Cybersex Addiction

Sexually oriented subject matter has always been available, but the Internet has made it available in a new way. Al Cooper, one of the foremost researchers on sexual addictions, describes what makes cybersex different: the triple A's of accessibility, affordability, and anonymity (A. Cooper, 2000).

Accessibility: Online sexual content is readily accessible. Access to pornography no longer requires a special trip to the store or a three-day wait until it arrives in the mail wrapped in plain brown paper. Whether at home or work, as long as a computer is in the room, sexually oriented content is there with a mouse click.

The most frequently searched content on the Internet is sexual in nature. Most people, at least men, have accessed some form of online pornography. While most of this occurs on a home computer, close to 20 percent of people have accessed sexual material from their office computer.

The sexual content on the Internet is boundless: sadomasochism, sex acts with children or animals, voyeuristic live-camera feeds. Much of this material has always been available offline, but only to a select few who knew where to get it and could afford it. Now, by entering a few words into a search engine, most any kind of sexual content is available instantaneously. As an interactive form of communication, the Internet allows access to sexual material that moves beyond seeing and listening to previously recorded material. Chat rooms are a place to share sexual fantasies in real time. Web cams allow observation of real-time sexual acts in faraway places.

Affordability: A great deal of cybersex material is available without cost. More unconventional, highly erotic material is readily available at low cost.

Anonymity: Perhaps most importantly, cybersex is anonymous. You can have a sexual liaison without going to a public place to meet the person. Your local retailer will not know you have viewed a sadomasochistic video. Although sophisticated miniprograms may track online activity, it is still true that a person can remain anonymous to whomever she or he is interacting with online. This sense of anonymity may allow for stronger involvement with sexual material than occurs in the presence of another person.

To discover who seeks cybersex and the nature of the materials accessed, more than nine thousand people responded to a survey on Internet use that included completing the Sexual Compulsivity Scale presented below (A. Cooper, Delmonico, and Burg, 2000; A. Cooper, Scherer, Boies, and Gordon, 1999). Most respondents had used the Internet for sexual pur-

Online sexual material can be highly provocative and engaging, and while millions access this content and most find it stimulating, surprisingly few people seek this material for the purposes of sexual gratification (A. Cooper, Schere, Boies, and Gordon, 1999). Many who access cybersex are simply curious or looking for entertainment. Others are purchasing sexual items to be used with a partner. For others, the Web is a sex education classroom filled with information that otherwise is not readily available. Observing certain sexual acts online can be informative, normalize sexuality, and lessen anxiety.

poses but did so less than one hour per week. The identified cybersex addicts, like sex addicts, were predominantly male. Whereas sex addicts tend to be married, men whose sexual involvements primarily occur online tend to be single or dating.

Women are not immune to sexual or cybersex addiction. In this large-scale study, women composed 12 percent of the sexual addict group. Women accounted for an even larger percentage of the cybersex addicts (21 percent). Among gay/lesbian or bisexual respondents, 6 and 9 percent, respectively, were sexually addicted. These figures increased to 16 and 21 percent in the cybersex addiction group.

Chat rooms were by far the most frequently used source for sexual encounters for women. This is not surprising, given that woman are relationship-focused. Men were more drawn to visually erotic material on the Web, although the men who were becoming addicted leaned toward chat rooms. Chat rooms became a place to meet people for online sexual encounters or to arrange offline meetings.

Sexual Addiction Criteria

Patrick Carnes has been active in bringing sexual addictions to public awareness with the goal of decreasing shame and enhancing the availability of treatment. Carnes's website can be found at http://sexhelp.com/.

These ten criteria for sexual addiction are adapted from Carnes (2005):

1. Inability to resist urges, desires, or cravings to engage in a specific type of sexual behavior.
2. Engaging in these sexual behaviors more frequently or for longer periods of time than realized or intended.

3. Efforts to stop or reduce these behaviors are unsuccessful.
4. The time spent thinking about sex, obtaining sex, being sexual, and recovering from sex feels like it is more than what is normal.
5. Preoccupied with thinking about, preparing for, and having sex.
6. Sexual behavior frequently replaces or gets in the way of meeting expected obligations at work, home, school, or in one's social life.
7. The preoccupation with sex and sexual behavior continues despite the knowledge that they create recurrent negative consequences or exacerbate other problems.
8. Tolerance: the sexual behavior is having diminished effects or the behavior is increasing in frequency, intensity, or done with increased risk in order to achieve the desired effect.
9. Sexual behavior replaces or limits social, occupational, or recreational activities.
10. Withdrawal: Feelings of discomfort, irritability, restlessness, or not quite feeling right when unable to enact the sexual behavior.

Meeting one or two criteria places you at risk. Evidence for three criteria indicates that sexual behavior has become problematic and potentially fully addictive. Five to seven criteria are endorsed by those formally diagnosed with a sexual addiction.

Sexual and Cybersex Addiction Screens

The Sexual Compulsivity Scale (SCS) (Kalichman et al., 1994; Kalichman and Rompa, 2001) assesses how closely current sexual behavior approaches a fully developed addiction. Before answering, remember that sexual behavior is broader than activities that lead to sexual gratification and include routine flirting, visiting adult bookstores, and viewing pornography.

Sexual Compulsivity Scale (SCS)

For each question, indicate how well the sentence describes you. Use the following scale:

Not at all like me   1.....2.....3.....4   Very much like me

1. My sexual appetite has gotten in the way of my relationships.
2. My sexual thoughts and behaviors are causing problems in my life.
3. My desires to have sex have disrupted my daily life.

4. I sometimes fail to meet my commitments and responsibilities because of my sexual behaviors.
5. I sometimes get so horny I could lose control.
6. I find myself thinking about sex while at work.
7. I feel that my sexual thoughts and feelings are stronger than I am.
8. I have to struggle to control my sexual thoughts and behavior.
9. I think about sex more than I would like to.
10. It has been difficult for me to find sex partners who desire having sex as much as I want to.

SCORING: Add the numbers for each question to get a total score.
Not problematic: Less than 24
Moderate sexual addiction: 24–30
Sexually addicted: More than 30

Cybersex addiction is determined based on time spent online pursuing sexual material. Sex addicts (scoring more than 30 on SCS) who spend eleven or more hours online each week in sexual pursuits are considered to be cybersex addicted (A. Cooper, Delmonico, and Burg, 2000). Quantity is rarely the best way to define addiction and, thus, less than eleven hours online can represent problematic or addictive cybersex, depending on the nature of negative consequences. An online screening tool specific to cybersex is available in the "Resources" section at the end of this chapter.

Cybersex addicts fall into two types. There are those who have no sexual addiction history and would probably not have developed one if sexual material were not readily available on the Internet. For this group, Cooper's "triple A's"—accessibility, affordability, and anonymity—create the conditions that set in motion the development of a sexual addiction (A. Cooper, Delmonico, and Burg 2000). The other type of cybersex addict is prone to sexual addiction independent of the Internet. For this group, which is predominantly men, the Internet is merely one forum for their addictive sexual behavior (Griffiths, 2001).

The Continuum of Sexual Behavior

"Regular" Sexual Behavior

The first point on the addiction continuum describes a behavior as "social" or "recreational." These descriptors don't work well for sexual behavior. Not all forms of sexual behavior are social in nature (i.e., masturbation) or for recreational pleasure (e.g., having sex to have a baby). Thus I refer to this first step on the sexual addiction continuum as "regular" sex. Regular sex is done safely without any exposure to adverse effects or unexpected consequences. All parties involved—even if only oneself—are consenting. (Masturbation that is compulsive and out of control is not considered "consenting.") Regular sex is enjoyable. When sex occurs with another person, it is usually one part of a larger relationship—a way of being intimate, giving and getting pleasure, and not primarily a means to escape or manage psychological well-being.

Having described the common attributes of regular sex, it is important to say that not every regular sex act will have these qualities. Sometimes sex won't be enjoyable. Likewise, sex in a relationship is still regular sex even if it does not always have the goal of enhancing intimacy. Sometimes people have sexual intercourse just for self-gratification or as a way to forget their troubles. These experiences do not make sexual behavior wrong or addictive. However, when sex is routinely separated from intimacy, sexual activity increases despite lack of enjoyment, sex is devoid of feelings, or the primary motivation for sex is to cope or escape, then sex is at risk of becoming addictive.

At-Risk Sexual Behavior

At-risk sexual behavior is any kind of sexual activity that has the potential to create negative consequences. This would include accessing information or participating in sexual acts that are illegal or induce guilt, having unsafe sex, or routinely spending more time than expected in the pursuit of sexually related activities.

Legal sexual activities such as seeking out multiple sexual partners or cybersex qualify as addictive only if they meet the sexual addiction criteria listed earlier. However, these kinds of sexual pursuits are risky for some people. Frequent use of pornography is at high risk of becoming addictive for a person who is socially isolated or having difficulty establishing close relationships. A history of childhood emotional, physical, and especially sexual abuse increases the risk of developing any addiction, and sexual addiction is no exception. As many as 83 percent of people with sexual addictions report a history of some kind of abuse (Carnes, 2001).

The highly explicit, erotic material available online poses a danger for adolescents who are just beginning to explore their sexuality or anyone who has yet to be sexual within a caring relationship. The intensely arousing nature of this explicit visual material can set unrealistic standards of arousal and excitement that are not met in "real" sexual relationships. In addition, exclusively gratifying intense sexual desires, independent of the limitations

Exposure to highly explicit forms of erotica available online is in itself a risk factor for sexual addiction. These are not the images of breasts or hints of pubic hair found in pornographic magazines. These are bare-all images and videos of fully exposed male and female bodies doing any and all kinds of sexual acts with other humans, objects, and animals. The intensely stimulating and arousing nature of this material can far exceed what is available with a "real" partner. Continued pursuit of this "high" can end in addiction.

and boundaries created when two people interact, generates a very unrealistic sense of sexuality and intimate relationships.

If you or someone you know is involved with cybersex, there are subtle signs when recreational use becomes something more. A man who shifts from the visual erotica on the Web to visiting chat rooms needs to be wary of a budding addiction. This transition can mark a shift from pornography as source of arousal and entertainment to the use of the Internet for sexual liaisons online or offline. Another sign that online sexual behaviors or fantasies are becoming risky is doing or imagining things one would never consider offline (A. Cooper, Galbreath, and Becker, 2004). The anonymity of the Internet can facilitate behavior that counters moral values and leaves a person feeling ashamed and guilty.

Another sign that sexual behavior is at risk of becoming addictive is the pursuit of more stimulating, exciting, and provocative material despite disappointment and/or lack of gratification from the experience. This experience parallels the experience of a drug addict who has developed tolerance for a drug. Like the drug, sexual material is pursued in increasing quantity and frequency but the desired "high" is never achieved.

Problematic Sexual Behavior

Sexual behavior reaches the problematic level of addiction when risky sexual behaviors continue despite full recognition of their potential for danger. Negative consequences are no longer unexpected. Distress, in the form of guilt, arises when sexual activities are inconsistent with one's sense of acceptable sexual behavior or more time is devoted to sexual behavior than seems appropriate. Direct negative consequences are intermittent in the at-risk stage but once they become routine, the sexual behavior qualifies as problematic. Secondary negative consequences (NC 2) emerge. A partner is

Mood-altering substances and behaviors are a way to cope with unpleasant feelings when other means of coping are unavailable. Depression is one such unpleasant feeling. The connection between depression and sex addiction is an interesting one. One sign of clinical depression is a decline in sexual interest, and yet for some people, sex is a way to overcome depression. Research suggests that people for whom exposure to highly stimulating sexual acts or erotic material provides a temporary relief from low moods are more vulnerable to sexual addiction (Bancroft and Vukadinovic, 2004).

angry and feels betrayed upon discovering that her partner has been viewing pornography, having phone sex, or visiting prostitutes.

Sexually addictive behaviors, like other addictions, are often motivated by a need to manage some aspect of psychological life. Silverman's autobiography, *Love Sick* (2001), chronicles how she and other men and women manage their emotional life through sex. Many insist that they are looking for intimacy and love, but over and over again they end up with only sex. "I just 'use' him like a distraction to numb out. To avoid dealing with the fact that my marriage and my life are a mess" (p. 142). "I know I use this flirting to keep men away from me, you know, to prevent them from knowing the *real* me" (p. 252). Sex for the sex addict is rarely about sexual pleasure and never about intimacy.

Fully Addictive Sexual Behavior

For the sex addict, interpersonal relationships are secondary to sex, and sex is less about pleasure and more about altering one's psychological state (e.g., to avoid anxiety or escape depression) or sense of self (e.g., to feel loved or worthwhile). Anyone interested in a better understanding of how sex addiction is not about the joys of sexual pleasure can read Chuck Palahniuk's *Choke* (2001), a rather brutal novel about how the main character, Victor Mancini, relies on sex to blot out the bitter realities of his past and present.

A sexual addiction self-medicates the same kinds of feelings as other addictions. It temporarily helps to overcome depression, to decrease anxiety, to avoid feelings of low self-esteem, to soothe oneself, or to escape feeling empty. Sexual addictions seem uniquely suited to alleviate one particular feeling: powerlessness and lack of control. A woman gets a rush—not just a good feeling—from her ability to arouse a man's sexual desire. She enters the room feeling weak and vulnerable but is transformed once she senses that the man next to her has noticed and has been aroused by her glance. Now she is invulnerable.

The equation of sex with power is best explained by the fact that many women with a sexual addiction like Silverman have a history of sexual abuse. Silverman's father was her sexual abuser and from him she learned that sex (and love) were about one person having power over another. As an adult, attracting the sexual interest of strangers temporarily erased the sense of powerlessness created from years of experiencing her father's unpredictable late-night visits. Each new affair brought renewed hope that she was loveable and had some control over her life.

A fully developed sexual addiction is in evidence as thoughts of sex begin to permeate waking time. Sexual feelings and thoughts about possible sex acts impede working effectively. Daily life becomes organized around obtaining the desired sexual experience. Before, sex only interfered with meeting specific responsibilities; now, sexual thoughts, feelings, and activities hinder fulfilling role obligations as employee, boss, spouse, or parent.

A young gay man I treated spent a portion of each workday plotting his route home from work. Should he walk down this street and run into X or go down that street and have a good chance of seeing Y? Or maybe he should hang outside one of the gay sex clubs and meet someone new. Typical of a fully developed addiction, his sexual urges and thoughts were as difficult to keep in check as was his sexual behavior once he found a willing partner. Even when a partner was suspected of being HIV positive, he did not always take appropriate precaution. His lack of control was also evidenced by the inability to stick to the rules he set for himself to only have safe sex and limit his cruising for sexual partners to three times a week.

Sexual Addition's Masks

The Mask of Relationship Problems

Often the partner of a sexually addicted person feels the adverse effects of the addiction, but the addiction itself remains unidentified.

Like most people, Larry had no intent of becoming addicted to cybersex. One night when he could not sleep after having another fight with his wife about finances, he got up and went to the computer. By the time he came for treatment, he had no recall of how he happened to come across a sexually oriented chat room that night. He and a woman shared sexual fantasies into the

Steps along the Continuum of Sexual Addiction

Regular Sexual Behavior
Motivation: The primary goal is pleasure and/or intimacy and not escape.
Consequences: No adverse consequences.
Frequency/Control: Sexual behavior occurs as often as is mutually acceptable to the consenting partners.

At-Risk Sexual Behavior
Motivation: Intended goal of pleasure or intimacy is not achieved due to a history of abuse, limited coping skills, or substance abuse. More provocative sexual material or activities inconsistent with personal values is pursued. If online, there is a shift from visual erotica to sexually oriented chat rooms.
Consequences: The nature of sexual activities has the potential to create negative consequences, but these are limited in scope (e.g., guilt) and intermittent. Steps are taken to avoid these outcomes in the future.
Frequency/Control: Sex often lacks in pleasure or intimacy but continues at the same frequency or becomes more frequent.

Problematic Sexual Behavior
Motivation: Sexual behaviors are motivated by the need to manage psychological well-being.
Consequences: Direct negative consequences are no longer unexpected (e.g., guilt), and secondary negative consequences have emerged (e.g., guilt about one's sexual behavior is creating depression). Sexual behavior continues despite recognized adverse consequences.
Frequency/Control: What used to be gratifying is no longer as gratifying. Tolerance is developing, and in response, more frequent or provocative sexual material or activities are sought. The time devoted to sexual pursuits disrupts effectiveness of daily functioning.

Fully Developed Sexual Addiction
Motivation: Sex is primarily about managing emotional life and not about pleasure or intimacy.
Consequences: Negative consequences are salient and pervasive.
Frequency/Control: Sexual thoughts, feelings, and activities hinder fulfilling role obligations. A sex addict's daily life becomes organized around sex.

early morning. He totally forgot about his financial worries, and although tired, he awoke the next morning feeling better than he had in a long time. Five months later, Larry was spending four or more hours a day cruising the Internet for sexual material; some of these hours were accrued at work and he had stopped having sex with his wife.

Relationship problems, especially reduced sexual intimacy, can mask a sex or cybersex addiction. The sex addict's partner, like Silverman's husband, is aware that something has changed. The sex addict seems less engaged in the relationship, wants more private time, and brushes aside requests for more intimate time together as a couple. When Larry's wife approached him, she was told, "Honey, I'm too busy. I need to get some work done on the computer." It is easy to see how consequences of sexual addiction become disguised as a relationship problem.

The effect of sexual addiction extends beyond one's primary relationship. Children suffer when a parent is lost to his or her sexual preoccupations or when a child accidentally comes across sexual materials in the home. In *Love Sick* (2001), it is surprising how often the sex addicts Silverman meets on her path to change mention premature exposure to a parent's sexuality. One man reported that as a young boy, he saw his father masturbating. He secretly returned many times to observe his father masturbate to pornography and then steal it to use himself. This man's early exposure to this kind of sexuality left him feeling like he never learned what normal sex or relationships with women were meant to be.

Regretfully, unmasking a sexual addiction rarely eliminates relationship problems. Even minor relational problems are made more complex by the hurt and anger created by actual or virtual sexual betrayals. Relationship problems arising from a sexual addiction usually run deeper. Sexual addiction is just one more arena—like fights over money or housework—for giving expression to a limited ability to communicate and to be intimate. The couple must ultimately address these issues.

The Mask of a Partner's Blinders: "I Must Not Be Sexy Enough"

A male sex addict will tell his partner, "All men have affairs" or " All men like to watch pornography." It is not true that *all* men have affairs, and while it is probably true that the majority of men access pornography at some time in their lives, *all* men do not. More importantly, of the men who do access pornography, few do it in an addictive manner.

Another common rationalization for sexual interests outside of a primary relationship involves blaming the partner: "You need to do something about your body." If only "your breasts were larger," "you weren't heavy," "you wore sexier clothes," "you would have anal sex." While Freud was wrong about a lot of things, he was right about one thing: people are prone to feeling vulnerable about their sexuality. Having a significant other who is sexually unfaithful shakes one to the core. Am I attractive? Am I desirable? Sexy? Loveable?

Once these self-doubts are aroused, the sex addict's partner becomes more amenable to accepting blame. Suddenly the addiction is *not* the problem, the partner is the problem. This kind of dynamic is not unique to sex addictions. Alcoholics often blame family members for their addiction. However, the idea that a sex addict's partner is to blame for the sex addiction seems harder to shake. The truth is that one's partner can be disappointed about what sex acts are preferred or the size of body parts, but disappointment is never an explanation for a sexual addiction.

Resources

Cybersex addiction quiz:
   www.netaddiction.com/resources/cybersexual_addiction_test.htm
Sex Addicts Anonymous:
   www.sexaa.org/
Sexaholics Anonymous:
   www.sa.org/
Patrick Carne's website:
   http://sexhelp.com/
This website has compiled an extensive set of resources for sexual addicts, their friends, and family:
   www.sarr.org/
For those whose lives are affected by sexual addictions:
   www.codeps.com/joomla/

CHAPTER 14

Buying Addiction

Throughout most of human history, material goods were few and survival was the center point of daily existence. Peter Whybrow (2005), in his book *American Mania: When More Is Not Enough*, explores the consequences of our current affluence. His observations are relevant to understanding addictions, in general, and buying addictions, in particular.

> After generations of frugality and adjustment to scanty conditions, we are poorly equipped . . . to handle an overload of anything, be that the information we are fed, the choices we are offered, or the food we eat. While few individuals have trouble identifying when they are hungry, defining that point during a meal at which one becomes satiated is a more difficult task. And so is the task even greater, we are learning, when it comes to material prosperity. When is enough, enough? And when does enough become excess? (p. 106)

People who never seem to have enough material goods are referred to as "shopaholics" or buying addicts. They are not necessarily the same. People who shop do not always buy, and those who buy excessively do not always shop. I will refer to the problem as a buying addiction because it is the money spent on purchases that creates negative consequences. The emphasis on buying does not rule out the possibility of a shopping addiction. Recall that most any behavior can become addictive. Thus there are

183

people whose shopping is so extensive that even without making a purchase, their behavior creates the kinds of problems associated with addiction.

There are many routes to a buying addiction. Some routinely purchase luxury items, although a buying addiction most often involves acquiring inexpensive items. There are those for whom negative effects arise as a result of purchasing gifts rather than personal items. Sometimes a buying addiction is hidden behind a hobby; collecting a specific object becomes a justification for shopping and buying.

Save Karyn: One Shopaholic's Journey to Debt and Back (2003) is Karyn Bosnak's humorous autobiographical account of her buying addiction. Bosnak moves from Chicago to New York City to work in television. Once there she begins shopping for designer clothes to fit the part. Weekly manicures, stylish haircuts, and personal training sessions add to her debt. This is not the first time Karyn has been careless with money; during college she once spent her tuition money on clothing. Karyn expresses some concern as her credit card debt approaches $25,000. Concern grows into a major worry

Easy access to a behavior plays an important part in how prevalent an addiction becomes (i.e., the gateway theory). The closer you live to a casino, the more prevalent are gambling addictions. Most everyone has ample opportunities to make a purchase. The "malling" of America means there are stores within easy driving distance. Catalogues arrive in the mail daily. A television network is devoted solely to shopping. And if these options are insufficient, there is the twenty-four-hour-a-day shopping mall in one's computer. The Internet provides a unique approach to buying that melds gambling and shopping—the merchandise auctions of eBay.

Social attitudes and expectations also contribute to addiction by defining which behaviors "should" occur frequently. For example, adolescents are more likely to experiment with alcohol if they believe drinking is common in their school. When hallucinogens were made popular in the 1960s by rock stars and seekers of enlightenment, there was a marked increase in use of such substances in the general population. Today we live in a consumer culture where shopping and buying are valued activities (see "The Mask of Consumer Culture" on p. 190). Both have become forms of leisure, as is amply evident in the number of stores in any tourist area.

when Karyn loses her job. This turning point forces her to face how emotionally significant buying has become; the items she acquires are central to her identity. "Without a job, and without being able to pamper myself like I was used to, I slowly started to lose grasp of who I was. It might sound stupid, but I began to realize how much I identified who I was with where I worked and what I looked like" (p. 285).

She realizes that not all is lost: if she sells her purchases and has fewer "things," she can get a better sense of who she is and, at the same time, pay off a portion of her debt. Shortly after launching her first eBay auction, she decides, as a lark, to develop a website entitled SaveKaryn. Here she confesses her sin of overspending and asks people to make small donations to help pay off her debt. (This is a true story!) News of her website spreads through cyberspace, and within weeks thousands of people are visiting it. Money slowly trickles in, along with e-mails supporting her spunkiness and chastising her for bad behavior. In the end, Bosnak becomes a bit of a celebrity and is free of debt.

Bosnak's profile is typical for a buying addict. This behavioral addiction is more common to women. As with Bosnak, problematic buying usually begins in late adolescence. Bosnak's job loss helped her to face the problem sooner rather than later. In most cases, the buying addiction goes unrecognized and unabated for years. On average, a woman does not seek treatment until her mid-thirties.

Most buying addicts like Bosnak purchase items that are wearable and intended to enhance appearance, such as clothing, shoes, jewelry, and makeup. Because more things are acquired than can be used, most go unused. It is common for a buying addict to find outdated clothes in her closet with price tags still attached (Christenson et al., 1994).

The motivation behind Bosnak's addictive buying is also characteristic: to manage unpleasant emotional states. The negative feelings that shopping and buying alleviate include anxiety, worry, depression, or, as for Bosnak, low self-esteem (Faber and O'Guinn, 1992; Edwards, 1993). For Bosnak, self-worth depends on what she owns.

Bosnak is the kind of addicted buyer who is selective about her purchases. She feels better about herself and has a better sense of who she is by owning items indicative of social status (e.g., designer handbags, expensive creams). Buying products associated with famous people brings Bosnak psychologically closer to such people, which in turn makes her feel more worthwhile. Bosnak shares with other women whose identities rest with acquiring things, the belief that complete realization is just one purchase away (Yurchisin and Johnson, 2004). All of us are exposed to this belief through

> The feelings that occur while shopping distinguish the normal from the
> addictive buyer. After making a purchase, the buying addict shifts from
> feeling negative to more positive, while normal buyers' feelings go from
> positive to slightly negative. The mood-altering effects are apparent
> when addicted buyers describe a high or a rush when making a purchase
> (Faber and Christenson, 1996).

advertising, where products are sold based not on merit but on the status,
sex, or glamour it will bring to our lives. The addicted buyer believes this
message wholeheartedly.

Unlike Bosnak, some addicted buyers don't care what they purchase.
This excessive buyer is much like the alcoholic who does not care whether
it is good or bad liquor, just that there is liquor available to be consumed
(Kohut, 1987). Likewise, this kind of addicted buyer does not care if the purchase is a lipstick or a pair of shoes; the act of acquiring something is more
important than what is bought.

As with other behaviors, defining what qualities make buying problematic can be difficult. Impulsive purchases or having an excess of material goods are common to buying addictions but are not necessarily signs
of addiction. How many of us, at one time or another, have made a purchase on a whim or had more of an item than is necessary or could be
used in a reasonable amount of time? The difference between these normal behaviors and an addiction resides in whether such behaviors give
rise to adverse effects. The most salient adverse effect of buying comes
from the cumulative effect of multiple purchases: credit card debt beyond
one's economic means. Attempts to manage this financial crisis can give
rise to legal troubles when the solution to debt is writing bad checks or
shoplifting.

Estimates of buying addiction range from 1 to 6 percent of the population (Faber and O'Guinn, 1992). Surprisingly, the latter figure may be the
most accurate. When a random selection of people were interviewed over
the telephone regarding their buying and shopping patterns, 5.7 percent
qualified for a buying addiction (Koran, Farber, Aboujaoude, Large, and
Serpe, 2006). While most knowledge of buying addictions comes from treatment of women, this survey revealed that rates were almost equal for men
(5.5 percent) and women (6 percent). Compared to those without problem
buying, this addicted group was younger and had lower incomes.

For those with extensive financial resources, excessive purchases do not necessarily create hardship. Michael Jackson is known for his multimillion dollar shopping sprees in Las Vegas. Imelda Marcos's expansive shoe collection had little impact on her capacity to keep buying. Addictive buying is harder to recognize when money is not an issue or when less expensive items are purchased. Those seeking status and identity through acquiring items with certain designer logos can avoid debt by purchasing cheap designer knockoffs. In the absence of adverse financial effects, other clues to addictive buying include

- excess clutter when there is no more room to store purchases;
- time spent shopping gets in the way of social and work life;
- hiding purchases and not being able to find them later;
- getting caught in lies about what one was doing (e.g., a stop at the dry cleaner's serves as a cover to go shopping at the mall).

Addictive Buying Criteria

The following criteria that incorporate both buying and shopping are modeled after the diagnostic criteria for substance-related disorders (Goldsmith and McElroy, 2000).

1. Maladaptive preoccupation with buying or shopping, or maladaptive buying or shopping impulses or behavior, as indicated by at least one of the following:
   a. Frequent preoccupation with buying or impulses to buy that is/are experienced as irresistible, intrusive, and/or senseless
   b. Frequent buying of more than can be afforded, frequent buying of items that are not needed, or shopping for longer periods of time than intended
2. The buying preoccupations, impulses, or behaviors cause marked distress, are time-consuming, significantly interfere with social or occupational functioning, or result in financial problems (e.g., indebtedness or bankruptcy).

The first criterion emphasizes intensity and drive-like qualities of both thoughts and behaviors related to shopping and buying. Note that to meet this criterion it is possible to simply think a lot about buying without actually having to make a purchase. Criterion 2 turns to negative consequences. While meeting both is evidence of an addiction, meeting either suggests a problematic relationship to buying and/or shopping

Addictive Buying Screen

Elizabeth Edwards (1993) developed the following scale to measure addictive buying behaviors.

Rate how much each statement applies to you using the following scale.

1 = never 2 = rarely 3 = sometimes 4 = often 5 = always

1. I feel driven to shop and spend even when I don't have the time or money.
2. I get little or no pleasure from shopping.
3. I hate to go shopping.
4. I go on buying binges.
5. I feel "high" when I go on a buying spree.
6. I buy things even when I don't need anything.
7. I go on a buying binge when I'm upset, disappointed, depressed, or angry.
8. I worry about my spending habits but still go out and shop and spend money.
9. I feel anxious after I go on a shopping binge.
10. I buy things even though I cannot afford them.
11. I feel guilty or ashamed after I go on a buying binge.
12. I buy things I don't need or won't use.
13. I sometimes feel compelled to go shopping.

SCORING: Step 1: Reverse the scores of questions 2 and 3: score of 1 becomes 5, 2 becomes 4, 4 becomes 2, and 5 becomes 1. Step 2: Add together all numbers to get a total score.
Recreational buyer: 27 or less
At-risk buyer: 28–43
Problem buyer: 44–58
Addicted buyer: 58 or more

You can break down your total score on this scale to see which aspects of buying behaviors are most problematic:

Tendency to shop: add questions 4, 5, 6, 7, and 12, then divide
   by 5
Drive to spend: add items 1 and 13, then divide by 2
Feelings about spending/shopping: add items 2 and 3, then divide
   by 2
Dysfunctional spending: add items 8 and 10, then divide by 2
Post-purchase guilt: add items 9 and 11, then divide by 2

Consider making changes for those questions where the average
score is four or above.

The Continuum of Buying

Buying addiction, like all addictions, typically is thought of as dichotomous—
one is addicted or not—and yet it makes sense that this addiction occurs
along a continuum. More moderate problems arise before more serious ones
emerge. There is debt before there is unmanageable debt. There is a sense of
embarrassment about how much is in one's closet before embarrassment
becomes shame and lying to hide purchases becomes routine.

Recreational Buying

There are people who make only planned purchases and acquire only things
that are needed. There are no strong feelings associated with this activity.
This pragmatic purchaser is a bane to the advertisement industry. Not so the
recreational buyer. The recreational buyer enjoys shopping and buys many
kinds of items: those that are necessary, have entertainment value, and/or
contribute to personal development (e.g., for learning). An occasional
impulsive or unplanned purchase is made. Some purchases may even be
motivated to moderate a bad mood. But there are few negative consequences; when there are, these are intermittent and unexpected (e.g., the
credit card bill is higher than expected).

At-Risk Buying

The more frequently a purchase is associated with improved mood or self-
esteem, the more this behavior is at risk of becoming an addiction. The at-
risk buyer is similar to the recreational buyer, but he or she has begun to
experience some direct negative consequences, such as guilt for making too
many unnecessary purchases or knowingly overspending. Negative outcomes
are limited and have yet to become apparent to others.

The impulsive buyer can be considered to be at risk. The impulsive buyer makes spontaneous purchases based on seeing an item. The motivation for the purchase comes from the person's attraction to the item rather than an attempt to manage internal states (DeSarbo and Edwards, 1996). The impulsive buyer is at risk of becoming a problematic buyer if constantly exposed to attractive objects and unable to control the impulse to acquire them.

Problematic Buying

The problematic buyer shops and makes purchases to manage mood, often feels guilty, and has begun to suffer the negative social, emotional, and financial consequences associated with addiction. At this level, buying is more likely to occur alone due to a growing sense of shame. While the acts of shopping and buying are hidden, the negative effects are no longer easily disguised. A husband confronts his wife about the extent of the credit card bill. A roommate is angry because her closet is filled with her roommate's possessions.

Addictive Buying

The addicted buyer experiences the full range of negative consequences as the need to buy takes precedence over other activities. Daily responsibilities and obligations are neglected. The addicted buyer experiences strong urges to shop, has difficulty keeping the behavior in check, and thinks often about shopping and buying. Ruminative thinking can disrupt relationships and performance at work. As lunch approaches, a woman begins to think not about what to eat but where to go shopping. Should she go to the store or stay at her desk and go online? Once in the store, should she get the knock-off Gucci bag? Or maybe Prada would be better? Buying brings temporary relief from negative moods. Tolerance has developed if more money must be spent or more items purchased in order to bring the good feelings that come from completing a purchase.

Shopping Addiction's Masks

The Mask of Consumer Culture

Once upon a time, wealthy people confined their display of wealth to other wealthy people. The 1980s saw a shift in attitude. On a weekly basis, Robin Leach would bring wealthy people into our homes in the television series *Lifestyles of the Rich and Famous.* Paris Hilton continues to remind us of just

Steps along the Continuum of Buying Addiction

Recreational Buying

Motivation: Most purchases are made for practical reasons or for the pleasure of owning an item.

Consequences: Negative consequences, if any, are intermittent, minor, and unexpected (e.g., surprise at the amount of a credit card bill), and steps are taken to minimize such surprises.

Frequency/Control: There is an occasional impulsive purchase, but most purchases are planned and needed.

At-Risk Buying

Motivation: Shopping and buying are enjoyable activities. Buying becomes risky when this behavior is discovered to be a way to improve mood or self-esteem.

Consequences: Negative consequences are contained (e.g., guilt about spending too much or having too many things) and rarely severe enough to be recognized by others.

Frequency/Control: There is some recognition that buying feels driven and/or impulsive.

Problematic Buying

Motivation: Buying and shopping occur primarily for their mood-altering effects. The behavior is much more likely to occur alone. Once a desired item is owned, it is often forgotten about.

Consequences: Adverse social, emotional, and financial consequences are becoming more apparent. Problematic buyers lie about and/or hide purchases.

Frequency/Control: More is acquired than can possibly be used. Despite recognizing that buying is creating problems, the activity continues.

Addictive Buying

Motivation: There is a "need" to shop and/or buy. The act of buying is more important than what is bought.

Consequences: Shopping and buying get in the way of meeting daily responsibilities.

Frequency/Control: There is limited or no control over the behavior. Despite short-lived pleasure from purchases, the buying addict believes that the next purchase will be "the one" to bring the desired effect.

what a wealthy girl can do. Although its strength is beginning to wane, conspicuous consumption remains a cultural value.

Acquiring material goods has little to do with meeting basic needs and more to do with demonstrating one's status in society. Luxury goods, expensive vacations, and elegant homes set the standard for the less affluent. One result is the highest-ever consumer debt. Another result is a sense of inner emptiness in response to feeling that one never has enough because someone else always has more (Kasser and Kanner, 2003). A few respond to this inner emptiness with a quest for meaning and self-development but more often attempts to fill the void turn to acquiring more things. Within this cultural context, it can be difficult to tell at what point being a good consumer becomes an addiction.

The Mask of "She's Just a Woman"

Women are socialized to believe that a large part of their value rests with their appearance. This includes not only body size but what she wears. It is not considered out of the ordinary for a woman to buy too many shoes or have more blouses than she could possibly wear. This apparent "normal" female behavior can mask a shopping addiction.

Changes in the demographics of buying addiction are already apparent. While statistics from treatment centers indicate that this is a woman's problem, a general population survey shows an equal distribution across genders (Koran, Farber, Aboujaoude, Large, and Serpe, 2006). A new form of masculinity has begun to emerge that incorporates concerns about personal appearance: the "metrosexual." This heterosexual man cares about being fashionably dressed; he gets facials, buys skin care products, and shops for designer apparel. The assumption that buying addiction is solely a woman's problem can mask this addiction in men.

The Mask of Emotional Disorders

Women with buying addictions have a high incidence of anxiety, substance use problems, and eating disorders such as binge eating and bulimia (Christenson et al., 1994). Excessive buying is also prevalent in women diagnosed with depressive disorders (Lejoyeux, Tassain, Solomon, and Ades, 1997). Family members, as well as the addicted buyer, are more likely to recognize the problem as anxiety, depression, or substance dependence than a buying disorder. While the good news is that recognizing a problem can lead one to seek help, health care providers may be fooled by the presenting problem, and the buying addiction may remain masked.

Resources

Website with treatment options created by April Lane Benson, editor of *I Shop, Therefore I Am* (2000), which contains seminal articles on buying and shopping addiction, treatment, and assessment:
  www.stoppingovershopping.com/
Debtors Anonymous:
  www.debtorsanonymous.org/
Shopping Addicts Support (SAS) online help group:
  http://health.groups.yahoo.com/group/shopping_addicts

CHAPTER 15

Exercise Addiction

Less than 10 percent of the population exercises regularly. Up to 3 percent of this group exercises in a way that can be considered addictive (Terry, Szabo, and Griffiths, 2004; Hausenblas and Symons Downs, 2002).

When not done in an addictive manner, exercise provides the physical benefits that come with increased muscle strength, flexibility, and endurance. Most forms of exercise—be it running, swimming, yoga, or biking—provide gains in at least two of these three areas. Promoting fitness and improving health are the two most common reasons for regular exercise. Another reason is to become more skilled by improving performance and technique. This is the driving force behind the intensive physical workouts of elite and Olympic athletes. The benefits of exercise extend beyond the physical. Exercise is a way to meet new people, socialize, and share common interests (e.g., joining a nature hike club). Exercising for the previous reasons rarely becomes addictive.

It is odd to think that physical activity designed to keep you fit and healthy can become the basis for a self-destructive addiction. This outcome is most likely when exercise is motivated primarily by its capacity to improve appearance and enhance emotional well-being. By toning and building muscle, exercise creates a shapely appearance and controls weight. Exercise has psychological benefits as well: it increases self-esteem, raises positive feelings, and lowers negative ones (Steinberg, Nicholls, Sykes, and

> Physical activities done with great intensity and at high frequency have been referred to as "positive addictions." The reference to "positive" describes exercise's ability to promote health. As discussed in chapter 2, characterizing an addiction as positive is an oxymoron. Addiction, by its nature, is defined by negative consequences. Frequent regular exercise that does not create negative consequences is best described as a good habit.

LeBoutillier, 1998). These psychological benefits are not simply a response to exercise-induced changes in appearance. Increased endorphin levels arising from repetitive and intense physical activity also improve mood (Adams and Kirby, 2002). These effects are strongest when exercise has an aerobic component. Herein lies the addictive potential of exercise: any behavior with the capacity to create reliable changes in feeling, mood, or self-experience can become addictive, especially when there are few or no alternative means to generate these desirable outcomes.

Negative consequences of addictive exercise are both physical and psychological. Fatigue and physical injuries result from overtraining. Overtraining occurs when the intensity of the exercise routine is maintained despite muscle strains or sore joints. Recreational exercisers are not immune to overtraining. They do it out of ignorance and learn from the experience. Addicted exercisers overtrain out of an inability to control the behavior.

Exercise may be unique among the addictions, given that guilt, which is one of the first negative consequences for other addictive behaviors, is usually absent. Unlike the drug user or married sex addict engaging in sexual liaisons in a chat room, there seems to be nothing about exercise to feel bad about. To the contrary, addicted exercisers often feel virtuous about their pursuit. Instead, adverse psychological consequences are interpersonal in nature and arise as significant others realize that they take second place to exercising.

Men are more likely to have an exercise addiction than women. Men who become addicted to physical activity strive to feel better, mentally and physically. Exercise also changes a man's appearance, but this is not what drives his addiction. It will be no surprise to know that women who become overly involved in exercise value its ability to bring about good feelings and

The adverse physical consequences of addictive exercise are not limited to stress fractures, sore knees, or aching muscles. Once exercise becomes addictive it is difficult to stop even for a day. As a result, severe or recurring injuries never fully heal. One young woman with a genetically based weakness in her ankle joints was so insistent on keeping up her running that she ultimately wore down the bones in her ankles and was confined to a wheelchair.

to improve appearance, be it through reshaping the body or reducing its size (Hausenblas and Symons Downs, 2002).

Exercise Addiction Criteria

The criteria that define behavioral addictions most often draw from those for substance dependence or pathological gambling. As an alternative, Scottish researcher R. I. F. Brown developed a model of addiction designed to capture the essential qualities of all addictions independent of whether the problem originated with a behavior or substances. The following six italicized components of addiction reflect Brown's general model of addictions as manifest in an exercise addiction (Brown, 1997).

Six Components of Exercise Addiction

1. *Salience* refers to exercise becoming central to a person's life and thinking.
2. *Conflicts* arise between people and within oneself as a result of exercise. Exercise activity *conflicts* with doing other activities.
3. Exercise *modifies mood* and is a way of coping.
4. *Tolerance* is indicated with increasing amount of time devoted to exercise in order to achieve the desired effect.
5. *Withdrawal* appears in the form of unpleasant feelings that arise when exercise rate declines dramatically or ceases (e.g., due to injury).
6. Addictive disorders are prone to *relapse*. This means that they are difficult to stop or keep under control. Even after prolonged periods of time off, if one returns to exercise, the initial level of exercise is returned to in a relatively short period of time.

Exercise Addiction Screen

Exercise Addiction Inventory

Annabel Terry, Attila Szabo, and Terry Griffiths (2004) developed the following exercise screening tool.

How well do each of the following statements describe your experience with exercise? Use the following scale to rate how much each statement applies to you.

1 = strongly disagree 2 = disagree
3 = neither agree nor disagree 4= agree 5 = strongly agree

1. Exercise is the most important thing in my life.
2. Conflicts have arisen between me and my family and/or my partner about the amount of exercise I do.
3. I use exercise as a way to change my mood (e.g., to get a buzz, to escape, etc.).
4. Over time I have increased the amount of exercise I do in a day.
5. If I have to miss an exercise session I feel moody and irritable.
6. If I cut down the amount of exercise I do, and then start again, I always end up exercising as often as I did before.

SCORING: Add all responses.
Recreational exerciser: less than 12
Problematic exerciser: 13–23
Exercise addiction: 24 or more

The Continuum of Exercise Addiction

Recreational Exercise

The recreational exerciser strives for health and fitness. Improving or developing a physical skill may also be a desired outcome. The recreational exerciser is not immune to injury but when this occurs, the person learns from the experience and takes steps to avoid future injuries.

At-Risk Exercise

As an outside observer, it is probably impossible to distinguish recreational from at-risk exercisers. The difference rests with their motivation. Exercise is at risk of becoming addictive when the primary purposes for exercising (health, fitness, skill development) are subsumed to its appearance- and mood-altering effects. If exercise is intended to self-medicate depression, the quality of the workout is secondary to achieving the desired change in mood. Injuries are more likely because fitness is not the primary goal.

Being a highly committed or elite athlete, while not the same as an addiction, can put one at risk. The routine and intense nature of physical activity required to achieve this skill level increases the body's production of endorphins. This effect is often referred to as "runner's high." Despite skill development being the initial motivation, if the psychological benefits of training become a way to manage stress and other negative moods, the committed athlete may begin to lose control of this behavior. Not surprisingly, runners are at greatest risk of slipping from committed athlete to addicted athlete (Thornton and Scott, 1995).

Problematic Exercise

A typical sign that at-risk exercise is becoming problematic is when the original goals of an activity are achieved but the frequency or intensity of the exercise regimen continues to increase. This is exemplified by the woman who achieves her long sought-after goal of fitting into a size 8 but continues to up the number of exercise classes, because she has decided that 6 is really her ideal size.

For Tom, recreational running ultimately became a problem.

When Tom stopped smoking, he began running as a way to regain his stamina, to feel healthy, and to counter the potential weight gain that accompanies quitting nicotine. At first, he could barely run half a mile, but he persisted and marked his one-year anniversary of not smoking with a two-mile run. He looked and felt great. But he kept increasing the distance.

Upon reaching the five-mile mark, Tom noticed that the pleasure he took from running had began to elude him. He added another half mile. A sense of accomplishment and pleasure returned briefly only to disappear again. In response, he added another half mile, and so the cycle continued until he was running ten miles three or four times a week. He dismissed his wife's concern that he was looking gaunt. Although he complained periodically about knee pain, he stuck to his weekly schedule. Tom told friends that running had become the highlight of his day.

As the intensity of an exercise regimen grows beyond what is needed to achieve health, fitness, or improve skill, signs that exercise is becoming problematic surface. Exercise takes on great emotional significance. For

Tom, running is the highlight of his day. Exercise is central to nearly every conversation, and all conversational threads lead back to exercise. Much like the adolescent whose substance use is problematic, the problematic exerciser is known to change peer groups in order to be among those who share a similar commitment to physical activity.

At the problematic level, the negative effects of exercise are manifest at work and in interpersonal relationships. Not only was Tom's wife worried about his gaunt appearance, she was angry with him for not meeting his responsibilities at home. On the days she had early morning business meetings, they argued because she needed his help getting the kids ready for school and he insisted on running. If Tom finally agreed to help out, he would run during his lunch hour, even though this meant returning late and keeping the rest of his team waiting. These examples illustrate a more general sign of a growing problem: a person insists on exercising even when there are good reasons not to (e.g., inclement weather, a major family event, illness).

Fully Addictive Exercise

A behavior transitions into a fully developed addiction when it becomes difficult to control, and negative consequences become sufficiently pervasive and consistent, impairing daily functioning. The near-obsessive ruminations about the activity, combined with the time it takes to exercise and the resulting fatigue, are reflected in a failure to take care of the children, attend to household responsibilities, or meet deadlines at work.

The two classic signs of addiction—tolerance and withdrawal—frequently accompany exercise addiction (Adams and Kirby, 2002). Tolerance takes the form of increasing distance, repetitions, or time committed to physical activity in order to achieve a sense of completion or the good feelings that accompany exercise. It is important to distinguish tolerance from increased levels of exercise necessary for improved skill. As Tom's stamina and strength improved, his initial half-mile run gradually increased to four miles. This represented improved skill. Tolerance appears later as he keeps adding in miles in order to feel a sense of pleasure from running.

Tom's quest to regain the initial pleasure he achieved from running by adding more miles reminds me of what Ann Marlowe said about heroin's high in her addiction memoir: "And heroin is one of the indisputable cases where the good old days really are the good old days. The initial high did feel better than the drug will ever make you feel again" (1999, p. 9). The parallel

Experiences of withdrawal are not necessarily a sign of addiction. Suddenly ceasing any routine behavior is followed by withdrawal symptoms, albeit minor ones. The behavior does not even have to be mood altering. If after years of brushing your teeth in the morning, you should suddenly stop, you will have the sense that something is not quite right when you leave the house. Even a recreational exerciser can experience mild withdrawal when the behavior is stopped, a vague sense that something is missing or a sense of sadness or nervousness.

between heroin and exercise is more substantial than it appears. The "high" that accompanies an aerobic exercise, like running, is due to the increased production of endorphins, which act on the body in much the same way as heroin (Adams and Kirby, 2002).

For some people, intense exercise—like drinking alcohol daily—is maintained in order to avoid the discomfort of withdrawal. A reported "need" for daily exercise can disguise withdrawal symptoms. Exercise addicts who are forced to stop their preferred activity due to severe injury report feelings of emptiness, depression, and anxiety that far exceed what a recreational exerciser experiences when injured (Sachs and Pargman, 1984). Often these signs of withdrawal are not recognized for what they are; instead, the person looks to something in their immediate environment to explain their distress (e.g., emotionally upset about being injured, a spouse's lack of sympathy).

When Is the Committed
Athlete an Exercise Addict?

The degree of skill sought by elite athletes, like those who train for select teams or the Olympics, requires frequent and intense workouts that can be misinterpreted as addictive due to the time involved and strong emotional commitment. Just as the professional gambler differs from the pathological gambler, the highly committed athlete can be distinguished from the addicted athlete. The committed athlete is motivated primarily by external factors (e.g., improving a skill, social recognition). Addiction is more prevalent when the primary motivation is internal in nature (e.g., to raise self-esteem or to feel powerful). Both addicted and committed athletes feel that exercise is central in their lives, but for the committed athlete, exercise is just one of many of life's significant elements. While they look forward to breaks from their intense workout regimens to enjoy other things, addicted athletes have no interest in taking time off (Sachs and Pargman, 1984).

Response to injury is another way to distinguish elite athletes from exercise addicts. Elite athletes respect an injury as the body's way of communicating how much is enough. They rest the injury until it is fully recovered, learn from the experience, and take steps to avoid future injury. The addicted exerciser responds to an injury in strikingly different manner. The person is annoyed that the body has broken down and dismisses the injury's significance. Exercise is resumed before the body is fully healed. Routinely responding to an injury in this way explains why addicted exercisers rarely maximize their skills.

The intensity of withdrawal also distinguishes committed and addicted athletes. This is best illustrated with long-distance runners. Physiological benefits of the endorphins created by intense running are the same whether a

Steps along the Continuum of Exercise Addiction

Recreational Exercising
Motivation: The goal of exercise is health and fitness.
Consequences: None or few; an injury serves as a learning experience about what *not* to do.
Frequency/Control: Exercise has its place and does not interfere with other activities and responsibilities.

At-Risk Exercising
Motivation: At-risk exercise looks very much like recreational exercise. It is goal driven but the goal involves exercising more than what is needed for health. For some people, this level of exercise is intended to develop skill. For other people, quantity (e.g., number of laps, pounds lifted) takes precedence over skill (e.g., better to lift more, even if form suffers). Exercise is at risk of becoming problematic when it is done primarily for its effect on appearance and mood or when the highly committed athlete with limited coping skills discovers that the psychological benefits of exercise (e.g., runner's high) provide a way to cope.

(Continued)

Steps along the Continuum of Exercise Addiction (Continued)

Consequences: There is increased risk of injury. Other types of negative consequences are minor and limited in number.

Frequency/Control: Frequency and intensity of exercise leads to aches and pains. Routinely ignoring the body's messages to cut back or take a break is a sign that exercise is at risk of becoming problematic.

Problematic Exercising

Motivation: Exercise takes on emotional significance; the intensity level far surpasses what is required for health, fitness, or improved skill.

Consequences: Exercise interferes with meeting daily responsibilities and is a source of relationship conflicts (e.g., significant others complain about the time commitment to exercise; work deadlines are missed).

Frequency/Control: Despite achieving stated goals, frequency/intensity of exercise continues to increase. Exercise takes priority over other activities.

Addictive Exercising

Motivation: Exercise is a means to meet emotional needs or avoid withdrawal.

Consequences: Negative consequences are pervasive, consistent, and impair daily functioning.

Frequency/Control: The addicted exerciser thinks about exercise when not doing it and has difficulty cutting back or stopping despite good reasons to do so (e.g., injury, important obligations).

long-distance run is part of skill development or an addiction. Yet withdrawal symptoms seem to be moderated by motivation. Recall the story in chapter 2 of soldiers in Vietnam who managed the stresses of war by using heroin. Once stateside, they gave up the drug without experiencing intense withdrawal. So it seems that committed athletes, if required to stop running due to injury, experience much milder withdrawal symptoms than the addicted athlete (Sachs and Pargman, 1984).

Exercise's Masks

The Mask of Exercise as a Healthy Habit

Humans have muscles that were meant to move. Get off the couch and exercise! Regular exercise is the route to better health. Because exercising and being healthy are readily equated, it is not always apparent that too much of this good thing is damaging.

The person on the way to becoming addicted to exercise readily dismisses the initial negative consequences. Shins begin to ache or there is a vague pain behind the knee. A spouse comments on running taking too much time away from family. A manager questions why her employee is too fatigued to work effectively. The significance of these comments is downplayed in light of the salient notion that exercise is good for you. Well-intentioned friends and colleagues support this belief by complimenting the budding addict about weight loss, self-discipline, or improved body tone.

Even if negative consequences are self-identified, an exercise addiction is easily hidden from others. Only the addicted person knows that a long-loved hobby has been put aside to make available another hour at the gym. Lies to a boss and friends go undetected. Only the exercise addict knows that declining a friend's invitation with "I have a work obligation," is, in reality, an exercise workout.

Even physical injury is not always sufficient to reveal an addiction. Initially, injuries are dismissed as an accidental outcome of healthy exercise. But over time, the physical consequences accumulate. Performance declines as a well-exercised body becomes gaunt, injuries keep mounting, or the same injury reappears in more severe forms. Recurrent injuries to the same area should be a clue to a physician that exercise has become unhealthy. By the time an exercise addiction becomes fully developed, exercise is far from a health-promoting activity, and the physical damages can be permanent. As with all addictions, the earlier the problem is recognized, the less severe and long-lasting the consequences.

The Mask of Moderation

Long-distance running is the most common form of exercise addiction. One explanation is that the extensive use of leg muscles and increased heart rate that accompany running are the most effective ways to stimulate endorphins and create a "runner's high." In fact, most forms of exercise addiction involve a significant cardiovascular element. But an addiction can emerge even when exercise appears to be in moderation.

The mask of moderation can be understood using polysubstance abuse/dependence as an analogy. The polysubstance abuser's quality of life is compromised because of the combined effects of several different substances, each of which is used in a moderate fashion (e.g., drinking combined with smoking marijuana and snorting cocaine). Similarly, exercise addiction is possible even though no single form of exercise has adverse effects. An exercise addiction emerges because of the combined effects of different forms of exercise, where each is done in moderation. The following is an example of what could be called a poly-exercise addiction.

Georgia meets friends in the early morning for an exercise class, takes the dog for run in the afternoon when she gets home from work, and then goes to a yoga class in the evening. Her children complain when she leaves the house in the evening, her husband is angry that dinner is rushed, and she has been criticized at work for never staying later than 4:00 p.m. Georgia insists that all these activities are important for her health and that she cannot skip any one of them no matter what it means to her family or for her job.

An Eating Disorder Masking an Exercise Addiction, and Vise Versa

Not all who score as exercise addicted on a screening have a primary exercise addiction. Some women (and fewer men) who demonstrate an addictive relationship to exercise have a co-occurring eating disorder, usually anorexia or bulimia (Bamber, Cockerill, Rodgers, and Carroll, 2000). An anorexic controls her weight by severely limiting food intake *and* exercising whenever she does eat to ensure that not an ounce of food becomes fat. The eating disorder grabs the attention of family members and health care providers, and in response, only the eating disorder is treated. This treatment will be ineffective. As the anorexic is made to consume more calories, she will simply increase her exercise regimen to counter the effects.

While an eating disorder can mask an exercise addiction, it is worth mentioning that an exercise addiction can mask an eating disorder. Bulimia is an eating disorder that involves vomiting or taking laxatives to avoid weight gain. Relative to these extreme approaches to weight control, exercising to prevent weight gain can seem like a healthy alternative—but it is not if it is done excessively to offset excessive eating. This approach to weight control has been referred to as exercise bulimia. Instead of using laxatives or vomiting, exercise bulimics resort to excessive and often punishing exercise. Exercise bulimia is a form of weight control among men but remains more common among women and adolescent girls (O'Dea and Abraham, 2002).

Special attention should be paid to the relationship between eating and exercise for adolescent girls. Eating disorders commonly make their first appearance during this developmental period. For some girls, their disturbed relationship with food is masked by their involvement with exercise—a socially valued activity. An adolescent girl's participation in sports and exercise is dangerous when the primary motivation for this behavior is to control weight.

Sixteen-year-old Janie was a sports enthusiast. She was on the high school girl's basketball, volleyball, and dance teams. She went to her daily practices and after completing homework, would go to the gym for an hour. On weekends, she awoke early to lift weights and run. She worked out for two to three hours. Before bed, she completed at least twenty minutes of sit-ups followed by a stretching routine. Janie looked great.

Only Janie knew that her exercise was driven in large part by how much she ate. During the school week, she went to gym after doing homework to work off the cookies she ate. Similarly, her weekend regimen had little to do with staying in shape and everything to do with burning the calories she consumed eating ice cream and other sweets in secret. If Janie were to stop her extensive sports and exercise activities, chances are good she would turn to bulimia or anorexia to keep her weight under control.

Resources

There are currently no self-help groups specifically for exercise addiction. Contact any mental health care provider skilled in addiction treatment. If exercise addiction is secondary to weight control (as a way to burn off calories from overeating), seek help from an eating disorder specialist.

PART III

Getting Help for an Addiction

Of the many alternative ways to understand addiction, the best known is addiction as a disease. Viewed this way, an addiction is a chronic disorder that inevitably slides into self-destruction with little for family and friends to do except stand by helplessly. Treatment programs based on this model emphasize that change ultimately depends on the individual. Only when the addict "bottoms out" is there any hope of change. Bottoming out or "hitting bottom," as it is also called, happens when a crisis arises that is undeniably a consequence of the addiction. For the alcoholic, it might be a run in with the legal system or receipt of divorce papers. For the gambler, it could be repossession of the car or bank foreclosure. The exercise addict might hit bottom after a permanent injury due to excess exercise. When addiction is considered a disease, a significant other's primary role is to get out of the way of the addict's progressive decline so that the bottom is reached sooner and treatment can begin. Once addiction treatment is initiated, family and friends are brought in to help support the change process.

Addictions do appear to be very disease-like by the time a repetitive behavior or substance use has created the biological changes that underlie physical tolerance and withdrawal. These symptoms represent the more severe side of a fully developed addiction. The continuum of addictions highlights the fact that this extreme is but one of many levels of an addiction. Whether addiction is truly a disease or not, the disease model leaves the impression that family, friends, and coworkers have a relatively limited role to play in helping the addicted person. This impression is an error.

As a friend, partner, or family member, there is much you can do. You can help the addicted person recognize the problem and enter treatment. You can participate in the addiction treatment in order to support and maintain change. To effectively do these two things, a third task is required: you must be well aware of the effects that having a close relationship with an addicted person has had on you. This is the topic of chapter 17.

The prerequisite for changing any problem, including an addiction, is identifying the problem. This sounds simple but as parts I and II have shown, an addiction's masks and self-disguises keep the problem hidden from self and others. The task of recognizing an addiction—especially in the earlier stages—often falls to those closest to the addicted person because health care providers who are charged by society to recognize addictions too often fail to do so. Family members have ample opportunities to help in this way, given that the vast majority of addicted persons are in regular contact with their close relatives (Stanton, 1997).

To facilitate identification of addictions at all phases of development, part II provided screening tools along with criteria for deciding where the more common forms of addictive behaviors fall along the continuum of recreational behavior to fully addicted. Because any behavior has the potential to be addictive, two sections ensure that any kind of addiction can be identified: the subtle signs of addiction described in chapter 7 and the addictive disorder screen in the introduction to part II.

Once identified, decisions can be made about what happens next. Sometimes the problem remits simply by recognizing it and requires no formal help. Other times, changing the addiction requires assistance in the form of self-help networks, the church, or professional health care providers. Here is another way significant others help: supporting the person in getting the necessary help. One role family members do *not* have is to try to change

How others can help:

- Using the knowledge gained in parts I and II, unmask the addiction.
- Support the addicted person in getting ready to accept the need to change (chapter 16).
- Do not try to change the addiction yourself.
- Address your own ambivalence about change (chapter 17).

another's addiction—only the addicted person can do that. Rather than change an addiction, significant others help by taking the steps necessary to *support* the addicted person in getting ready to change.

Chapter 16 explores how to prepare to make a change. "Preparing to make a change" may sound like a novel idea, but you probably have done it before. Rarely is a problem recognized and immediately changed. Think about the last time you made a significant alteration to your routine—starting a new relationship, breaking one off, changing eating habits, beginning a hobby. First you think about whether change is necessary and how best to go about it. You may start to change and then stop or realize that you are going about it the wrong way. You may even decide that your initial decision was a mistake and there is no need to alter anything. Understanding the distinct steps involved in preparing for change optimizes the likelihood that change is ultimately successful. To this end, chapter 16 describes the six phases involved in preparing to change and the actions to be taken by the addicted person and significant others at each step. Chapter 17 is addressed specifically to friends, family members, and colleagues who want to help an addicted person prepare to change but find impediments get in the way of effective action.

Unmasking Addiction
and Preparing for Change

If you have a relationship with someone whose addiction is severe, it is useful to know that behind the apparent willful destructiveness of addictive behaviors, he or she feels helpless to change the downward spiral that life has taken. The addicted person knows that his or her behavior is getting out of control. Feelings of shame and helplessness are mounting but rarely expressed. There have been tentative and, perhaps, serious attempts to cut back or stop, but these were kept hidden in case they failed (which they often do). Instead, the addicted person resorts to hiding, lying, minimizing, or shrugging aside the problem. At this level, neuroadaptation has set in, as discussed in chapter 3. The person has come to depend on the addictive substance or behavior in order to feel normal. Life has become small; most thoughts and actions focus on maintaining the addiction. Failure to feed the addiction in a timely fashion leads to cravings. Cravings, if left unfed, transform into withdrawal symptoms.

If you are the person struggling with an addiction, remember that the people who live and work with you share your helpless feelings. It is difficult for them to stand by and watch you self-destruct: they want to bring you back, they want you to be the person you once were, but they feel helpless and powerless to make these changes happen. Instead of speaking calmly to you about their concerns, they react like anyone else who has been rendered ineffective: they withdraw, become angry, or try to control you. While it does not look like it, these ineffective attempts to help come from a place of concern and worry for your well-being.

What Significant Others Should Not Do

Once an addiction is suspected or recognized, it is normal to want to help the person. When it comes to helping someone with an addiction, surprisingly often the intent to help becomes converted into deals ("If you gamble less, I promise to never get angry again"), frustration ("I don't know what I am going to do if you keep drinking like this"), anger ("Get the hell out of here"), and threats that are rarely acted upon ("If you don't stop spending so much money, I am going to leave"). The more helpless you feel and the more severe the addiction, the more persistently you voice these ineffective reactions.

Anger at the addicted person for failing to take your good advice or follow through on plans to get help usually backfires: your anger becomes part of the addict's rationale for the problematic behavior ("I have to drink [gamble, go for a run, etc.] so I can put up with you"). Threats, whether to leave the relationship or cut off financial support, are renewed expressions of anger that are certain to fail if not backed with a preset plan for putting them into action.

When anger, threats, and deals fail to work, then comes withdrawal. Withdrawing from the addict can be effective, but only when you have truly accepted your inability to rid the person of his or her addiction. Most often withdrawal is just a disguised form of frustration and anger. Rarely does it last. The addicted person approaches you contritely, asks for forgiveness, and perhaps cuts back on the addictive behavior for a period of time. If the addicted person responds to your withdrawal by staying out of your way, then you become worried that something bad has happened without you, and you take steps to reconnect.

Withdrawal is usually followed by a period of renewed overinvolvement with the addicted person. When your attempts to change the addictive behavior again fail, anger returns, followed by another round of withdrawal. The result is endless cycling through these ineffective forms of helping.

The truth is that you cannot change another's addiction. Only the person with the problem can do that. However, you can create an environment that optimizes the chances that change will occur. In other words, you help the addicted person prepare to change.

Preparing to Change Is Not the Same as Making a Change

The first task when preparing to change any behavior is to realize that the immediate goal is *not* to change the behavior. This point, which seems self-evident, is too easily forgotten. So much emphasis is made on changing that you can forget that in order to make a change you first need to get ready to do so. Keeping this first step in mind is more difficult when faced with a behavior, like an addiction, that is creating harm.

As you read this chapter, periodically remind yourself of this critical point: *before making a change, you must prepare for it.* This point is relevant whether you have an addiction or want to help someone who has. The addict, who is pressured by others or from within to make a change, overlooks this preliminary step. Likewise, significant others overlook the fact that they, too, need to make preparations before their help can be effective.

Something You Never Do: Go It Alone

Addiction takes an emotional toll on all who are exposed to it. To manage this stress and to be most effective in bringing about change, you need to have sufficient support for yourself—whether you are addicted or helping someone who is. Informal sources of assistance are available through networks such as twelve-step programs and Alcoholics Anonymous. Support is also available through churches and friends. The more severe the addiction, the less likely change can occur without formal treatment—even with the necessary support systems in place.

Techniques for Effective Communication

It is easy to yell and express disappointment, but to be helpful requires planning. Never bring up observations on the spur of the moment, and never discuss the problem when the person is under the influence of the addiction. As you think about how best to approach someone, remember becoming angry, withdrawing, or trying to control the addictive behavior ultimately harms your relationship, and it is the strength of the relationship that gives you some leverage in supporting change.

An easy-to-learn alternative to unproductive forms of communication is provided by William R. Miller and Stephen Rollnick (2002), who developed a set of techniques known as "motivational interviewing." These addiction specialists realized that almost every addiction treatment was designed for people who already had acknowledged a problem and were ready to do something about it. Missing were ways of talking that could help prepare the way for change.

Avoid Arguments

Never argue about whether the problem is really an addiction. Don't get engaged in defending yourself if you find the addicted person is blaming you

Rules for good communication:

avoid arguments
be empathic
develop discrepancies
roll with resistances

("If only . . . you were more supportive; we had sex more often; you told me how good I looked . . . I wouldn't need to do [a given addictive behavior]"). Instead, keep the focus on the negative consequences created by the addiction. As I discuss later, emphasizing negative outcomes is the core of the first phase of change. When your observations about the addiction's adverse effects are dismissed, don't argue about them. Instead, ask the person to draw his or her own conclusions:

- What would need to happen for you to consider that you have a problem with [drinking, the Internet, etc.]?
- What concerns do you have about how you [gamble, run, smoke pot]?

Even if you don't get an answer in the moment, the question has been heard.

Be Empathic

Being empathic involves trying to understand the addicted person's point of view without judging it is as true or false, right or wrong. Empathy requires keeping an open mind as the person tells you things you don't want to hear (e.g., how she is not ready to change or how he sees the addictive behavior as a good thing). Being empathic is not easy when listening to a loved one describe harmful behaviors. By not intervening or insisting on change, it can feel as if you are condoning the behavior.

While being an empathic listener is not easy, it can be quite effective. The empathic listener models how to listen without criticizing or judging. Addicted persons often have conversations in their head about their "bad" behavior. These mental conversations get cut short as self-criticisms set in. If given the opportunity to speak openly to a person who accepts what is said, the addicted person can begin to listen more carefully to him- or herself. It was an empathic listener that brought Augustine Burroughs (2003) to a surprising realization. Burroughs, who was allergic to alcohol, would take numerous antihistamines before a binge to avoid swelling up. Telling this story to an empathic addiction counselor helped him realize the absurdity of his drinking. Although it still took time for Burroughs to fully admit to his alcoholism, this realization contributed to his ultimate recognition that he had a problem and change was needed.

Develop Discrepancies

If you know the addicted person well, think about his or her goals, aspirations, and life dreams. Point out how addictive behaviors and their consequences impede or conflict with these desires. Creating discrepancies helps make negative consequences feel more personally relevant and real. This is one way to overcome the addicted person's tendency to minimize the significant negative impact of addictive behavior. Developing discrepancies is a critical part of the change process. This technique is presented in greater detail on pages 228 to 230.

Roll with Resistance

As addiction moves along the continuum of severity, the addicted person's reasons for why the behavior is not really a problem grow exponentially. Staying evenhanded in the face of such resistance is a challenge. Of the four motivational interviewing techniques, rolling with resistances is likely to be the least familiar.

One way to roll with a resistance is to go along with what the person says without agreeing with the content of what is said. Instead of fighting back after being told that your way of seeing things is wrong, you can simply say, "I guess you see it differently than I do." Or, if the addicted person insists, "You can't make me change," you can simply say, "Yes, that's true." Other times, you may be able to reframe what is said so it takes on a different meaning. If your expression of concern is rebuffed angrily (e.g., "Stop meddling in my business"; "You are such a nag, there is nothing to worry about"), the first desire is to lash back. Instead, reframe your "nagging" or "meddling" as evidence of your concern for the person. "Well, I really care about you, but I guess my constant hints and nudges about [addictive behavior] are not the best way to show it."

When the conversation is filled with anger or going nowhere, to roll with resistance involves taking a break. Let the other know that the conversation is getting too heated and you need to take five or ten minutes to cool down. This is different than withdrawing in anger when you suddenly stop speaking or leave the room.

Implementing these techniques for effective communication takes practice. As someone who is concerned about another's harmful behavior, you are likely to become frustrated and respond in a less-than-productive manner every once in a while. This is normal. However, if you find yourself routinely resorting to unproductive reactions, you will want to read chapter 17 to see what is interfering with implementing more effective modes of communication.

Phases of Change

Factors that support or impede the success of addiction treatment have been carefully studied. But what happens before a person is ready to make a change? "Stages of change" is a popular organizational scheme that outlines how people prepare to make significant life changes, be it to lose weight, stop smoking, begin exercising, or change an addiction (Prochaska, Norcross, and DiClemente, 1994; DiClemente, 2003).

There are six phases to the change process. The first three focus on preparing to change: precontemplation, contemplation, and preparation. Actual change occurs in the action phase, which is followed by the maintenance phase for sustaining the changes that have been accomplished. Because old behavior usually reappears, a sixth phase—relapse—is included as a normal part of the change process.

Reference to "stages of change" gives the impression that change occurs in a simple, linear fashion by smoothly moving from one stage to the next. Nothing could be further from the truth. A person who has decided to make a change may suddenly decide nothing is the matter (precontemplation phase). Or, before the first serious effort to change occurs (preparation phase), a person moves toward and away from making that change numerous times. Remaining aware of the nonlinear nature of change is essential. Otherwise, returning to an earlier phase will be too disheartening and become a reason to abandon your attempt to improve your own or another's life. I use the term "phases" rather than "stages" as a way to emphasize that a person travels back and forth through the change process before successfully incorporating a new behavior.

One part of getting ready to change involves understanding the kinds of events and experiences that get in the way of success. Chapter 17 focuses on impediments faced by those who want to help. Impediments the addicted person faces have been revealed in a study that asked alcoholics to describe

Phases of Change

Precontemplation: There is no problem or the problem is not clearly defined. No need for change is recognized.

Contemplation: A problem is recognized and need for change is acknowledged—some of the time. There is ambivalence about the addiction and the need for change.

Preparation: The person knows that change is needed. Some small changes may have occurred. Attention is focused on which approach to change will be best.

Action: Active steps to change are taken and continue despite setbacks.

Maintenance: The person consolidates change and adjusts to living without the problem.

Relapse: Temporarily returning to the old behavior is a common part of the change process.

These are not "stages" but phases; a person can move forward and backward many times before change can be maintained.

what got in the way of their seeking help sooner (To, 2006). Three answers stood out. Twenty-six percent said that they did not know where to go for help. Thus, one simple way to be helpful is to become familiar with the local resources in your community and to make this information readily available. However, making resources available does not mean constantly reminding the person that they need help! That is controlling. Resources lists are included throughout part II.

Another common reason for not seeking help sooner (cited by 34 percent of alcoholics in recovery) was fear of being shamed and embarrassed. The effective forms of communication described above will allow you to be helpful without shaming or embarrassing the addicted person. Working within the phases of the change framework also minimizes shame and embarrassment.

By far the greatest obstacle (73 percent) to getting treatment was a refusal to admit to the severity of the problem. Significant others have much to offer the addicted person in overcoming this tendency to minimize adverse consequences. The phases of change provide a step-by-step approach for increasing awareness of the scope and severity of an addiction.

Precontemplation Phase

Tasks for the Precontemplation Phase

Reevaluate behaviors that are taken for granted.
Emphasize self-reflection and understanding; there is no need for action yet.
Identify specific risks, harms, and adverse effects.
Emphasize negative consequences that create harm and are inconsistent with personal values and goals.

In the precontemplation phase, the problem has not yet been identified, or if it has, there is no sense that change is needed. From the addicted person's perspective, there is no problem. Perhaps the behavior has led to some difficulties, but these have not coalesced to the point that they are recognized as a problem warranting attention.

Typical Presentation Over the past six months, Sally has become disinterested in her work and her three-year relationship with her boyfriend, Jim. She smokes marijuana three or four times a week. On occasion she wonders if this might be a problem, but she never considers that her current lack of interest in her work and her boyfriend is connected to her drug use. Instead, Sally thinks she may be getting depressed.

The central task of the precontemplation phase is acknowledging that there is a problem. This task is accomplished by linking addictive behaviors to their adverse outcomes. As discussed below, this goal can be achieved without necessarily labeling the problem as "addiction."

The stages of change model assumes that failure to recognize a problem is a natural part of the change process. For addictions, failure to self-identify the problem is attributed to denial. Denial implies a strong unwillingness to acknowledge a problem. However, just because someone insists, "I am not addicted," does not mean that denial is in operation.

Denial is the strongest, the more fully developed the addiction. More often an addiction is not recognized because addiction's masks and self-disguises hide this problem. The myth that addictions are limited to substances masks identification of behavioral addictions. Other reasons that life problems are not linked to an addiction are (1) the addiction developed as a way to cope with psychological problems, which remain more salient than the addiction; (2) the adverse consequences of an addictive behavior are intermittent and thus not reliably connected to their origins; (3) the addictive behavior has created a limited number of adverse consequences, which are more apparent to others than the person with the addiction; and (4) what qualifies as an addictive behavior was defined as "normal" in the person's family of origin.

The tasks in the precontemplation phase are best accomplished by doing what screening tools do—focusing on negative consequences. When looking at an addiction's consequences, pay special attention to effects that are most likely to create harm or have already resulted in harm. Examples include physical effects of addiction, driving or working while intoxicated, having unsafe sex and risking exposure to HIV, damaging a marital relationship, or neglecting parental responsibilities. Developing discrepancies that show that addiction gets in the way of achieving life's goals personalizes the negative effects.

Becoming aware of negative consequences does not mean the person is ready to acknowledge the problem or give up the addictive behavior—nor is this necessary. Once dangerous consequences are identified, the harm-reduction approach described in the action phase can be used to lessen an addiction's adverse effects.

What Significant Others Can Do during the Precontemplation Phase Family and friends play a central role in the precontemplation phase; they bring a problem to awareness. This is accomplished by removing the masks and self-disguises that hide addiction either by explaining how certain behaviors could be part of an addiction or by encouraging the addicted person to respond to a screening tool.

When bringing your concerns to another person, refer to specific behaviors and consequences; general descriptions of a problem are rarely effective. Remember, the biggest obstacle to getting help is the addicted person's avoidance or minimization of an addiction's severity. Before saying anything, think carefully about the specific ways that family members, friends, and fellow employees are harmed by the behavior and how the addiction's adverse effects are inconsistent with the person's values and goals.

How you convey your observations makes an enormous difference. Screaming, pleading, or trying to induce guilt does not work. It is much less productive to announce, "You drink too much," than to say, "When you drink, we seem to have more arguments." The latter fits better with the goal of the precontemplation phase by pointing out how a certain behavior has an adverse effect.

Provide examples in a descriptive or neutral manner. Take care not to elicit another's shame and embarrassment; these feelings get in the way of being heard. Focus on what you have experienced. "I noticed that we got into a really big argument yesterday after you came home from the bar." Or describe what you have observed. "You had a huge argument with your friend John this past Saturday. Sunday, you woke up with a hangover. Do you think that your drinking had something to do with those arguments?" Framing observations in the form of questions feels less judgmental.

Here is what Sally's roommate had to say:

> Hey, Sal, I need to talk to you about something that's not so easy to talk about. You just don't seem to be yourself these days. I know you're pretty unhappy about work and your relationship with Jim, but I don't get it. You used to really like your job. There was a time a few months ago where you had hectic deadlines. That's when you started smoking more pot. But you told me that things are back to normal and everybody thinks you did a stellar job. Has something changed to explain why you're finding it so hard to go to work? And I'm really puzzled by what's happening between you and Jim. You both seemed to have been so in love; you were so excited to be talking about marriage and now, just as you start to hate work, you think you don't love him. Maybe you're depressed and ought to see somebody. Or maybe it's the pot. I can't help but notice that you've been smoking almost every day. It made sense when work was so hectic and you needed a way to chill out. But work has calmed down and you're still smoking. Do you think there's any connection? I mean, I know pot can make you less interested in doing things.

Sally's roommate points out the changes that have occurred during the past months (less interest in work and boyfriend; difficulty getting to work) and suggests that these are discrepant with her goals (e.g., enjoying work, getting married). Her approach is descriptive and not accusatory and ends with a question that asks Sally to think about whether smoking marijuana is creating problems.

Transitioning from the precontemplation to contemplation phase is easiest if the addiction is in the at-risk or early problematic stage. In such cases, a person may simply be ignorant and never considered that personal distress stems from a given pattern of behavior. Problems are mistakenly attributed to some other cause, such as depression or temporary situational stressors. As an addiction's severity increases, the addicted person is more likely to minimize expressions of concern and the problems addiction is creating. This is when you need to utilize the techniques for effective commu-

Intervention

Interventions are designed to remove the masks the addicted person has put in place to avoid fully recognizing the problem. Interventionists gather together friends, family, and others in the addicted person's life. Each person offers his or her experience of living with, loving, working with, and being friends with the addicted person. They speak of the changes they have observed and the negative consequences they have experienced. Many voices saying the same thing at the same time makes it harder for the addicted person to minimize the addiction's consequences. Resources for finding intervention programs are listed at the end of this chapter.

nication (see p. 213). For those with fully developed addictions, external support is often needed to move on to the next phase. In this case, an intervention may be necessary.

The precontemplation phase requires patience along with a clear understanding of what you are trying to accomplish. The goal is to create a more realistic picture of addiction's adverse effects. You will have experienced some of these effects directly and others you will have observed. Other times, adverse effects are inferred based on what you know about addictions. Sally's roommate made such an inference. Understanding that chronic marijuana use can result in an amotivational syndrome, she wondered if this drug was the reason for Sally's lack of interest in work and boyfriend. The appendixes at the end of this book present the psychological and physical effects created by different substances. Similar effects created by behavioral addictions have been noted in chapters 10 through 14.

A person need not accept having an addiction in order to move to the contemplation phase. All that is needed is acknowledgement that certain behaviors are harmful to self and others. Sometimes your observations will have apparent effects. As one woman put it, her comments about her son's drug use had him "stopping in his tracks to think more about the impact of his misuse" (Templeton, Zohhadi, and Velleman, 2004, p. 17). Be prepared to have your concerns ignored and attempts to talk about the problem dismissed when the addiction is at the more extreme end of the continuum. This is because the person you are trying to communicate with is filled with intense self-criticism about the addiction and his or her inability to change. Because of these internal self-attacks, your input tends to be experienced as judgmental and shaming, even if you use the techniques for effective communication mentioned earlier. But this does not mean you should say nothing. By talking in an empathic way (not yelling) about the perceived consequences of addiction, the individual is exposed to how his or her behavior is negatively affecting self and others. Even if your observations have no apparent impact, are negated, or ignored, they have been heard and can become an impetus for the person to begin thinking in a new way, be it now or in the future.

Increased awareness definitely has its value. Research has found that over the long run, family members' observations about the effects of substance use result in noticeable improvements in the relationships between themselves and the addicted relative, even if the addiction itself did not change (Templeton, Zohhadi, and Velleman, 2004). You may have hoped for more, but this is a first step and an essential component of the precontemplation phase.

What the Addicted Person Can Do during the Precontemplation Phase Take one of the screening tools. Look over the subtle signs of addiction. Do this privately and respond honestly. Try to be objective and put your self-critical voice to sleep. Spend some time developing clarity about the specific consequences of the behavior. Remember that recognizing an addiction does not require you to make any changes. Your task is just to reexamine your current behavior and its consequences without taking any action.

Is Admitting to Being Addicted Necessary? Moving from the precontemplation phase to the contemplation phase comes about when a problem is acknowledged; this transition does not require labeling the problem an addiction. Fully facing the negative consequences of certain behaviors is often sufficient. For others struggling with addiction, this transition only comes about when the problem is explicitly labeled as an addiction. Knowing she had an "addiction" transformed Carla's life. For her, the label brought together an array of worrisome and puzzling behaviors and made them seem more manageable. A married woman in her mid-thirties, Carla was referred to me after her addiction treatment for polysubstance abuse. Carla was a typical soccer mom, except that she had a history of trading sex for drugs, feeling chronically depressed if not high, and neglecting her children.

The following story describes how she got into addiction treatment.

Her husband demanded she get help or face losing the children after he found her passed out at the kitchen table next to a stash of painkillers and antianxiety drugs. At her hospital admissions, when the intake worker asked her to describe her problem, Carla faced her shame and confessed to all of her "bad" behaviors (e.g., abusing prescription medication, having sex with an old boyfriend in exchange for cocaine, leaving the children home alone so she could buy drugs). When the list was complete, the intake worker told her, "You are addicted." Carla immediately experienced great relief. Carla was deeply ashamed of her drug use but she did not consider this her primary problem. Drugs were simply a way to deal with an unhappy marriage and low self-esteem. She had never before fully realized how all her shameful activities— sex for drugs, lack of attention to her children—were drug related. When this array of behaviors was given the simple label "addiction," she felt less like a bad person, which she had felt helpless to change. As an "addiction," she experienced her problems as less diffuse and more manageable. She had her first inkling of hope that things could be different.

In the public's mind, addiction is most readily identified with problematic use of substances. Other than gambling, the behavioral addictions discussed in part II have received limited public attention. There is even less awareness of the fact that an exhaustive list of addictive behaviors is impossible because any behavior capable of altering experience has the potential to become addictive. Applying the term "addiction" to these kinds of behaviors has much the same benefit that Carla found in being told she was an addict. Identifying the problem as an addiction gives cohesion to behaviors that otherwise remain disconnected and provides a way to capture the inexplicable sense of "high" experienced when engaged in the activity. To realize the problem is an addiction helps make sense out of the out-of-control feelings and the inevitable sense of regret that arises later.

Ashley Judd, the daughter of country music singer Naomi Judd, was visiting her sister, Wynonna, who was in treatment for an eating disorder. When the counselors spoke to Ashley about her own problems, a number of behavioral addictions including codependency were revealed. Thinking of her problems as behavioral addictions allowed Ashley to feel like she could address her unhappiness. After treatment, she commented that "because my addictions were behavioral, not chemical, I wouldn't have known to seek treatment. . . . And those behaviors were killing me spiritually, the same as someone who is sitting on a corner with a bottle in a brown paper bag" (Associated Press, 2006).

Alcoholics Anonymous believes that accepting the label of alcoholic—
"Hi, I am Jon. I am an alcoholic"—is necessary for change. Adherents of
twelve-step approaches fear that refusing the label is a way to maintain the
status quo and minimize the problem. While true for some, for others it is
sufficient to acknowledge that a certain way of behaving is harmful to self
and others. Recognizing that a certain behavior pattern reliably creates
adverse effects, whether or not it is labeled as an addiction, marks movement
into the contemplation phase.

Contemplation Phase

Tasks of the Contemplation Phase

Recognize that there is no need to take action until ready.
Accept ambivalent feelings.
Do not focus solely on the negative.
Develop a full understanding of the benefits and costs of the addiction.
Develop a full understanding of the benefits and costs of change.
The benefits of change can only be imagined; remain hopeful.
Be patient, be patient, be patient.

The contemplation phase is ushered in when a problem is recognized and a
need for change acknowledged. However, the conviction that change is necessary waxes and wanes. Plans to cut back or stop completely are announced
but then nothing happens or attempts to change are ineffective because they
are ad hoc and not based on any well-thought-out plan.

Typical Presentation Ted knows he drinks too much. He has even
thought about cutting down or quitting. On three occasions he has told his
wife that he knows he should change his drinking habits. She has encouraged him to attend a twelve-step meeting with a mutual friend. He has not
gone. When she confronts him about his inaction he gets angry and says his
drinking is not a problem.

It may seem strange to have a person acknowledge the existence of a problem and do nothing about it—but we all do it. With mouths wide open in
the dentist chair we nod in agreement as the dentist warns of the dangers of
plaque between our teeth and insists we floss daily. How often have you
decided to cut back on eating bread or sweets before actually following
through? Why are such apparently simple changes so difficult to make? A
large part of the answer rests with ambivalence. Ambivalence arises because
making a change to our routine involves gains and losses.

Ambivalence is apparent when planning to make a major life change such as moving, changing jobs, ending a relationship, or changing an addiction. Ambivalence is characterized by complicated, conflicting feelings. There are pros and cons to maintaining the behavior, as well as pros and cons to changing. Whether you are addicted or in relationship with some one who is, understanding the complexity of ambivalence is the core task of the contemplation phase.

The origins of ambivalence are revealed by recalling how an addiction develops. Ted did not begin drinking with the intent of becoming a drunk. He began drinking as a way to relax when he came home from work. As the demands at work escalated and he became a father, he managed his stress effectively by drinking more. His consumption of alcohol increased gradually as did the severity of its consequences. Ted learned to manage hangovers with a few over-the-counter pain relievers and a drink at lunch. When drinking began to affect his work productivity, he began going in on Saturdays. He dearly missed being with his children, but he felt there was no choice; keeping up with work was a necessity. He drank more to manage the additional stress created by working on Saturdays. Herein lies the paradox of addiction: a behavior that originates for its enjoyment or to cope with what feel to be insurmountable stressors (benefits) ultimately makes life more unpleasant and less manageable (costs) (Donovan and Marlatt, 1988).

In the contemplation phase, all those involved with the addiction know about its negative effects. However, significant others and the addicted person experience these negative effects quite differently. Negative effects are all the significant other can see. The emotional situation is more complicated for the addicted person: yes, addictive behavior is creating problems, but at the same time, it is a part of life's routine and a primary way to cope or bring about desirable shifts in experience. Faced with the acute conflict created by recognizing the benefits and costs of addiction, the addicted person is caught in the web of ambivalence.

Significant others must be cautious not to make a typical mistake at this juncture: prematurely placing sole emphasis on the negative side of addiction. This mistake is common because the precontemplation phase focused on adverse consequences in order to facilitate acknowledgement of a problem. Continuing to emphasize the negative in the contemplation phase stalls the change process by raising defensiveness and cutting off a thorough exploration of both the positive and negative feelings about the addiction.

Ambivalence about the addiction is only one part of what needs to be addressed in the contemplation phase. There is a second side of ambivalence:

mixed feelings about change. We all have put off or hesitated to change something familiar in our lives. But why would someone not want to change an addiction that is obviously harmful? For many, an addictive behavior or substance, no matter how disruptive, has been a reliable and stable source of release and comfort, often for years. To give up the addiction feels much the same as losing a good friend or a part of oneself (Diamond, 2000).

Feelings of loss that come with giving up an addiction are familiar to the addicted person who has tried often to change but never succeeded. While the losses are known, the benefits of changing are merely promises. Work and relationships *might* be better or a spouse *may* be happier or self-esteem *may* improve. Learning to balance the sense of loss with hopefulness about the benefits of behavior change is the second task of the contemplation phase. Table 16.1 can be used to help give expression to the various components of ambivalence.

What Significant Others Can Do during the Contemplation Phase
Having recognized the scope of another's addiction, you have moved beyond

TABLE 16.1 Cost/Benefit Analysis for Changing a Behavior

	Benefits	Costs
Continue the Behavior		
Make a Change		

precontemplation to the contemplation phase. You feel that change is long overdue and the benefits of change are salient in your mind. However, much like the addicted person, you may have reasons to be ambivalent. Chapter 17 describes this ambivalence, discusses why it develops, and explores how to move past it. Once your ambivalence is resolved, you will be in the next phase of change: preparation. You need to be in the preparation phase in order to help the addicted person work through his or her ambivalence.

When your life is entangled with someone in the contemplation phase, it is easy to become intolerant because nothing seems to be different. Because you are prepared for change, you interpret the addicted person's recognition of a problem as a sign that he or she—like you—is prepared to change. It is difficult not to cajole, push, or demand that the addicted person get into treatment. Your recommendation may be obediently followed, but unless the treatment provider recognizes that the person is not ready to change and facilitates the move to the preparation phases, treatment is likely to fail.

Enormous patience is required when you are in a close relationship with someone in the contemplation phase. Developing it comes from reminding yourself that you are in a different phase of change (preparation vs. contemplation) and that the two sides of ambivalence block the addicted person from moving forward. To facilitate forward movement, your task is to accept ambivalence and support the person in expressing conflicting feelings about the addiction and the idea of changing it. A mental health provider who is familiar with the phases of change is best suited to accomplish these goals. But if this is not an option, there are ways for you to support the expression of ambivalence.

Ambivalence Part 1: Exploring the Benefits and Costs of the Addiction Faced with an addict's self-destructive behaviors, it is easy to forget the allure of an addictive behavior. Addiction has been understood as an attachment disorder where the addictive substance or behavior, not other people, becomes the most significant relationship. William Cope Moyers (2006) makes this point explicitly in relation to his substance use. "I was never lonely when I was using, even when I was separated from the people I loved most in the world, because my best friends were always with me. Cocaine was my running buddy, my soul mate, my faithful lover, my reliable colleague, my fun-loving playmate, who tagged along everywhere I went" (p. 185). Research backs up this connection between intimate relations and the good feelings created by an addiction. Cocaine's effect on the brain's reward system is the same one that is involved in the bonding of mother and infant (Insel, 2003).

Allow yourself to become curious and set out to learn about the benefits and rewards that come from the addiction. Some things you can ask are,

- Tell me about the pleasure you get from [drinking, gambling, working late, shopping, etc.]?
- Tell me what first attracted you to [being on the computer last night, smoking pot, going at the gym every afternoon]?

Initiating a discussion of the "positive" side of an addiction or even just listening to the other person talk about the benefits can feel as if, by simply listening, you are encouraging the addiction. The value of empathy rests with the ability to listen to and acknowledge feelings, but this does not mean you are condoning the behavior. Given the opportunity to talk about the positive side of addiction is an important step for both you and the addicted person in your life. You get to hear about its appeal, and the addicted person feels you are willing to acknowledge and understand his or her struggle. Your ability to listen to the positive side of addiction makes it easier for the addicted person to reveal the negatives more fully. This discussion can benefit all parties. You learn to respect an addiction's allure, and the addicted person feels more accepted and may gain a new perspective. Thinking back on its history, an addicted person can be jarred into realizing that a behavior initially done solely for its pleasure is more painful than realized. The initial allure is now more imagined than real.

Both outcomes occurred when I asked a man I was treating about what he enjoyed about his nightly drinking.

Gordon grew up in a large family but had no close friends as a boy. Drinking was the solution. In high school and later in college, getting drunk with the guys created a sense of camaraderie and made socializing easier. He met his wife in a bar, and although she drank moderately he continued drinking excessively nearly every day. When he drank, his wife insisted he sleep on the couch because his snoring kept her awake. Gordon resented being banned from their bedroom more than the arguments they had about his drinking. In light of these apparent costs, I asked him to tell me about the pleasures he took from drinking. He was truly stunned when after a few minutes' silence, he was unsure how to answer my question. The initial pleasures of alcohol—being able to feel like one of the guys—were no longer present.

The discussion of the positives is balanced by an exploration of the negative side of addiction. The negatives are made more meaningful by helping the person develop discrepancies between his or her aspirations or goals and addiction's adverse effects. You might ask the person the following questions or perhaps you know the person well enough to answer them yourself:

- What do you want to accomplish in life?
- What's really important to you? What really matters?
- What do you want your life to be like?

With this information, you can point out how the addiction gets in the way of meeting these goals. See how Ann helped Ted to develop discrepancies on page 230.

Ambivalence Part 2: Exploring the Benefits and Costs of Change
You no doubt find it easiest to express the advantages of changing; you have been voicing these benefits for quite some time. Work performance will improve; there will be money for things other than drugs, gambling, or shopping; health will improve; and of course, your relationship with the addicted person will improve. But change is not all positive from the addict's perspective: change means losing all the benefits of the addiction. Giving up an addiction also means that the addiction itself will be missed. In a halfway house after formal addiction treatment, Moyers (2006) reflected on his future without the "friendship" of his substances. "I missed them with a deep, aching longing that I hadn't felt in weeks. Would I ever get to see them again? Would I ever be able to experience the release they gave me?" (p. 185).
The discussion of mixed feelings about change can be approached in the following ways:

- "You know that I want you to stop [addictive behavior]. I think the change would be all for the good. But it's not all positive for you. Stopping [or cutting down] isn't easy. What would you miss about [addictive behavior]?"
- Ask the person to write a good-bye letter to his or her addiction. This is described further in the next section.

The emotional costs of losing an addiction are more acutely felt than the benefits. As someone close to the addicted person, it is important that you support expression of all feelings. However, if the negatives begin to far outweigh the positives of change, facilitate a more balanced discussion by helping the person find meaning and hope in change. Remind him or her of the positive outcomes that can be expected. When appropriate, show how these benefits will help the addicted person achieve life's goals and aspirations.

Ted is in the contemplation phase. He has acknowledged a drinking problem but has been unable to take any action. At first, Ann angrily insisted that he get help. When that failed, she stepped back and took stock of the situation. Instead of trying to get Ted to change, she tried to understand why he was stuck. With empathy came some willingness to understand his ambivalence. She knew how stressed he felt about being the best on his job (an aspiration) and that for as long as she had known him, drinking helped him relax. She had once used alcohol for similar reasons but having children put a stop to that. She also knew how guilty Ted felt about leaving the family to go to work on Saturdays. He always said he wanted to be more involved with his children than his own father was (an aspiration). Drinking had become Ted's habitual way of coping and he managed this guilt by drinking more.

With a better understanding of the value Ted found in drinking, Ann was less angry. When she approached Ted, she emphasized the discrepancies between his goals and the effects of drinking:

> I know how demanding work is for you and how much you hate to go in on Saturday to catch up on work. You would much rather stay here and be with the kids. When you come home and go to change your clothes, I always hope you will join us and we can all have fun together. But you feel so stressed out that instead you sit down in front of the television and open a beer. The next thing you know, it's dinner time and we haven't spent any time together. I know you just plan on having a beer or two in order to relax. How's that working?

Notice that Ann does not tell Ted to stop drinking although she does suggest an alternative to his current way of coping: instead of having a beer, join the family and have some fun. The main goal is to make Ted consider whether drinking really is helping him to cope, to suggest that drinking conflicts with one of his aspirations—to have time with the children (create a discrepancy)—and to show that not drinking or drinking less may have benefits, such as having time to enjoy the family.

Ann could bring another discrepancy to Ted's attention. His desire to be the best at work is undermined by his drinking during the week, hangovers, and occasional drinking during lunch. Without alcohol-induced deficits in his work performance, he would not need to go in on Saturdays.

Moving to the preparation phase requires tipping the balance of benefits and costs so that the costs of the addiction outweigh the benefits, and the benefits of change outweigh the costs. While the emotional significance of items in table 16.2 carries more weight than the sheer number of items,

TABLE 16.2 Ted's Costs/Benefits Analysis

	Benefits	*Costs*
Continue Drinking	Helps me not to worry Relaxes me Alone time	Less time with the kids Less productive at work Hangovers

Make a Change	More time with the kids
	Wife will be happier
	Less need to work
	  Saturday
	Feel less guilty
		How will I deal
		  with stress?

it looks like Ted is beginning to move closer to being prepared to do something about his drinking.

What the Addicted Person Can Do during the Contemplation Phase
Jonathan Diamond (2000), an innovative addictions therapist, has developed an simple but potent approach to generating a balanced exploration of the pros and cons of addiction and change. The deeper experiences of addiction are private and not easily shared in a conversation. To help give expression to the whole gamut of feelings, Diamond encourages his patients to write a good-bye letter to their addiction.

Remember that letter writing is an exercise of the imagination—not action. You don't need to change anything right now; just imagine what it would be like to say good-bye to your addiction.

What follows is an example of a letter that a young girl wrote for Diamond:

> ~~Dear~~ Narcotics, Pot (acid, alcohol) etc. thanks for all You've done for me. You've helped me forget my problems, You've made me feel good, You've made me see the world in a whole new perspective, You've made me fail out of my freshman year, You've made me Ruin the lining of my esophagus and stomach. You've made the Relationship with my Parents go down hill, You've given me a who gives a shit attitude — i've gotten fucked up Emotionally and Physically. (Relationship wise also) I've gotten used by abusing you: even after all those complaints I don't want to give you up Because i'll be alone. Miranda (Diamond, 2003, p. 180)

Miranda's ambivalence is apparent. Addiction helps her forget her problems, but at the same time ruins her health, relationships, and her freshman year at college. The only explicit outcome of change is negative—being alone. While she mentions no positive outcomes of change, these are implied by the loss of the negatives. In treatment, a counselor would want to help Miranda think about her goals and what would be gained should she decide to give up substance use.

Letter writing gives words to powerful and often unspoken experiences. Doing so creates a potentially new relationship to those experiences. They are less diffuse. There is distance between you and them. It is as if you and the addiction have developed a bit of a separation. Diamond (2003, p. 182) captures the effect of putting experiences into words: "I am the problem" becomes "I am up against a problem."

Like any good-bye letter, a common theme is loss; writing the letter does not erase the loss. Rather, giving expression is one way to understand the deeply felt ambivalence. This letter can be kept private or shared with others. Sharing this letter with a treatment provider or someone who is able to accept your feelings lessens the power of these lonely feelings and opens the way to experiencing some of the benefits of change.

Preparation and Action Phases

Tasks of the Preparation and Action Phases

Become familiar with the different treatment options.
Identify readily available resources and make this information available.
Develop a personalized plan of change.
Recognize that change begins with small, incremental changes.
Acknowledge and support desired changes.
Do not ignore or dismiss feelings of loss—they are part of the change process and not a return to the past.

During the preparation phase, addictive behavior is recognized to be a problem and the need for change is acknowledged. Ambivalence has not disappeared but the value of change has become more real, and there is some hope. Small, overt changes have been made. The alcohol abuser stops buying alcohol for the house. The addicted shopper destroys all credit cards. Often these initial self-directed changes are shortlived because the person has yet to fully commit to change or is unaware of where to go for help (To, 2006).

The preparation phase is the time to learn about the various change options such as psychotherapy, twelve-step programs, inpatient treatment, or speaking to an addiction counselor. Whatever plan is selected needs to be realistic. Seeing a counselor who is twenty miles a way is not a viable option for a person without transportation. Long-term inpatient treatment is probably not the best alternative for a single mother.

Typical Presentation Among a variety of other worries, Carol is concerned about her drinking. People have told her that she becomes a different person when she drinks. Despite overtly dismissing their expressions of concern, Carol has told friends never to let her have more than three drinks when they go out. This plan has not worked. It is not very realistic to expect friends to keep count of her drinks. Even if they do, Carol has been known to ignore their reminders and drink as much as she wants. Carol is still interested in making a change. When told by a friend about a local addiction treatment program with a good reputation, she made an appointment for an intake.

When an employee, friend, or relative is in the preparation phase, your task is simple: make sure that information about change options is available. You can find information about treatment options in the resource sections in each chapter in part II, as well as at the end of this chapter. Many professional treatments include those who are close to the addicted person, given that marital and family interventions have more successful outcomes than treating the addicted person individually (National Institute of Alcohol Abuse and Alcoholism, 2005; O'Farrell and Fals-Stewart, 1999). Although traditionally the focus is on formal treatment, reduction or cessation of addictive behaviors can happen without it. In *Sober for Good*, Anne Fletcher (2001) interviews recovered alcoholics to see what brought them to a better life. Some changed

During the action phase, consultation with a health care provider is recommended so that a formal diagnosis can be made. What appears to be an addiction could be symptomatic of another mental or physical disorder. Periodic problematic gambling can be one way of expressing the manic side of manic-depressive illness. Alcoholism may be self-medication for an anxiety disorder. Health care providers may not be adept at recognizing addictions, but once a potential problem is identified, they can help confirm a diagnosis, make a differential diagnosis (identifying which problem is the primary problem), and provide effective treatment.

on their own, others selected from one or more self-help programs, while still others sought help from a health care professional or lay counselor.

Two Philosophies of Addiction Treatment In the United States, the twelve-step philosophy has dominated the addictions treatment field. The origins of Alcoholics Anonymous, the first twelve-step program, took shape in the 1930s, when a small group of people, mostly men, sought help through fellowship with other alcoholics after medical-based interventions had failed. Their philosophy spread to the treatment of other substance and behavioral addictions, and by the 1970s, the twelve-step philosophy had been incorporated into most medical-based treatments. Known as twelve-step treatment, this approach begins with a period of detoxification, if needed, followed by a more extended rehabilitation program. Initially offered only in inpatient settings, treatment can now be completed as an outpatient. Daily attendance at twelve-step meetings and total abstinence from the addictive behavior are required as part of this treatment.

A less familiar approach to addiction treatment is known as harm reduction. Harm reduction is a relatively new philosophy of treatment (Denning, 2000; Marlatt, 1998; Tartarsky, 2002). Harm reduction initially arose in response to the growing spread of HIV infection among intravenous drug users; rather than insisting that they stop heroin, the focus was on reducing risk of infection by using clean needles.

Unlike twelve-step-based programs and treatments that require abstinence, the goal of reducing an addiction's harm rarely requires that the addictive behavior be eradicated. Other forms of harm reduction include drinking but never driving under the influence, adhering to strict financial limits when gambling, or destroying credit cards so that the addicted buyer

Alternatives to Twelve-Step Programs and Treatments

Twelve-step-based treatments and harm reduction represent two of the more general approaches to treatment. Other options include Rational Recovery, Moderation Management, spiritual-based approaches to change, Women for Sobriety, SOS (Secular Organization for Sobriety/Save Our Selves), and SMART (Self Management and Recovery Training). Melanie Solomon wrote *AA: Not the Only Way* (2005), which reviews alternatives to twelve-step approaches. It can be found at www.aanottheonlyway.com.

pays only with cash. When reduction in harm is maintained and new forms of harm do not emerge, family members, friends, and the addicted person may consider this an agreeable outcome. Maintaining reduced harm over long periods of time is less likely the further one has progressed along the addiction continuum. Once neuroadaptation has set in, it is more difficult to maintain control over the addictive behavior, and harmful levels of the behavior are likely to return.

Once a method of change and a goal (abstinence or harm reduction) are chosen, the stage is set for action. Concerted efforts are made to follow the plan, which includes changing not only oneself but also one's environment. Alternative ways of coping are explored. The addicted person makes an effort to avoid friends and locations that are associated with addictive activities. Setbacks in the action phase are simply temporary obstacles to be overcome; there is motivation to keep moving toward the goal despite difficulties. Others begin to notice there are changes.

Typical Presentation   Gary decided to forego formal inpatient treatment for his gambling addiction and instead attended Gamblers Anonymous (GA). He goes to one meeting a day, but if urges to gamble emerge, he attends a second meeting. He has a sponsor whom he calls every evening. He has made changes in his social network in order to avoid contact with other gamblers. He lives within ten miles of a casino; knowing this will be a temptation, he avoids this area of town. He has had a few slips; he played blackjack on the Internet and found himself placing mental bets on horse races. Although it was not easy for him, he told his sponsor and talked about these slips in GA meetings.

What Significant Others Can Do during the Preparation and Action Phases   As the person involved with someone who is addicted, you have relatively little to do after the preparation phase except to support change, by not impeding progress or encouraging a relapse. Inviting a newly sober person to a party where there will be liquor is a bad idea, just as it is a bad idea to insist that a person who is overcoming a running addiction go for a jog with you.

As someone close to the addicted person, you need to take a moment to examine how you have been affected by the addiction. How are you responding now that things are different? How has your way of communicating and relating to this person been affected by the addiction? Also, you will want to assess if you, like the addicted person, mourn the addiction's loss. As discussed in chapter 17, another person's addiction can have benefits for you. Often these benefits are unrecognized until the addiction is gone.

Complicated emotions underlie the "robust" changes and alterations in mood or self that drive an addiction. In his aptly titled book, *The Heart of Addiction* (2002), Lance Dodes homes in on these emotions. Whether you are struggling with an addiction or know someone who is addicted, this book will guide you to a deeper understanding of the psychology of addiction that comes with the action phase.

Being aware of what you have lost lessens the likelihood of inadvertently behaving in a way that supports a relapse.

As a significant other, your role extends beyond not getting in the way of recovery. You also support positive changes in the addicted person's life. The importance of supporting positive change emerged in an innovative set of interviews with people recently treated for alcoholism. They spontaneously described how important friends and family had been in supporting their ability to continue in treatment and maintain changes. Communication was more open; the addiction was talked about more freely (not kept a secret from each other) with less anger and hostility. Whereas in earlier phases, any encouragement to drink less was met with anger, in the action phase, the addicted person valued the family member's active support in keeping drinking under control.

Getting back into the "routine" of life is another way family and friends support positive change. The practical aspects of life have been neglected during the days of active addiction: cleaning, bill paying, grocery shopping, and eating regularly have been neglected. Family and friends can help the person return to a more healthy and normal way of living (Orford et al., 2006).

Maintenance and Relapse Phases

Tasks of the Maintenance and Relapse Phases

Adjust to living without the addiction.
Recognize that relapse is a normal part of change; it does not mean all gains are lost.

In the maintenance phase—whether the goal is abstinence or harm reduction—the focus is on consolidation of gains. Living without the addiction or avoiding harm gradually becomes more familiar and comfortable. Maintenance is as important a part of the change process as any other. This is because change is rarely permanent. Although relapse is a term associated with addictions, relapse occurs when changing any behavior. In the non-addictive realm, a person who gradually develops a routine schedule of healthy eating can, after several years, experience a disruption in this routine. It starts with a few potato chips and gradually more fatty and salty foods are consumed. Time passes before the person realizes this is a relapse. This recognition does not necessarily mean an immediate return to a healthier routine. The person examines on the effects of junk food: what has been lost (and gained) by eating it (contemplation phase). Initial steps to regain the old routine (preparation) may succeed or fail (relapse) before there is a full-fledged effort to return to healthy eating (action phase). The same back-and-forth movement through the phases of change occurs with addictive behaviors.

Autobiographies about Addiction

Reading about the experiences of living with and overcoming addiction provides valuable lessons that aid in recognition and preparation to change an addiction. This is true whether you are addicted or close to someone who is. Memoirs about addiction serve as mirrors that reflects one's own or another's addiction.

After reading Susan Cheever's *Note Found in a Bottle* (1999), one of my patients was dismayed to discover that her father had been an alcoholic. Cheever's description of how her alcoholic father, the author John Cheever, behaved turned out to be a portrayal of her own father's behavior. My patient had never linked her father's mood swings and withdrawal to alcohol consumption. Instead, she assumed they arose in response to his disappointment in her. Living with addiction, but not knowing it, is the focus of two books. David McCreery's *No Soft Landings* (2001) recounts his experiences growing up in an upper-middle-class family of alcoholics before he, too, succumbs to addiction. Chris and Toren Volkmann, in *From Binge to Blackout* (2006), are mother and son who, in alternating chapters, chronicle Toren's path from adolescent experimentation to severe alcoholism. The book describes the signs of early addiction that were overlooked because of Toren's good grades and his parents' acceptance of his assurances that everything was just fine.

The ways in which families and friends overlook or even sometimes support an addiction stand out in Christopher Kennedy Lawford's *Symptoms of Withdrawal* (2005) and Koren Zailckas's *Smashed* (2005). In *Broken* (2006), William Cope Moyers shows how his parents and wife keep looking right past his addiction to see some deeper emotional or spiritual problem, which is more acceptable than addiction.

Many memoirs demonstrate how easily the adverse consequences of addiction are undetected by health care professionals. Ann Marlowe's psychotherapist failed to see her growing heroin use in *How to Stop Time* (1999), while Elizabeth Wurtzel's cocaine and methamphetamine addiction is overlooked by her psychiatrist in *More, Now, Again* (2002). Depression effectively masks the recognition of sex addiction in *Love Sick* (Silverman, 2001). Similarly, Zailckas's adolescent alcoholism described in *Smashed* is misdiagnosed as depression at her annual physical.

Often, the ability to maintain professional competence keeps the addiction hidden. Caroline Knapp in *Drinking: A Love Story* (1996) continues her successful journalistic career while an alcoholic. It is not as if there were no negative consequences. The reader is allowed to see how drinking destroys her relationships and emotional well-being, although neither Knapp, her family, nor her therapist recognize that substance use is the problem. Moyers's (2006) in *Broken* and Augusten Burroughs in *Dry* (2003) continue in successful, high-powered careers while nightly becoming strung out on substances. Lawford never let drugs get in the way. "Hell, I managed to get three degrees and I was pretty much stoned through it all. When it is the addict's intention to remain functional, then the addict's use becomes geared to keeping in the addict game" (2005, p. 160).

Most memoirs center on substance use—usually polysubstance abuse and dependence. Several books chronicle the development and change of behavioral addictions. In *Lighting Up: How I Stopped Smoking, Drinking and Everything Else I Loved in Life Except Sex*, Susan Shapiro (2005) illustrates the fact that any behavior can become addictive. The book documents what Shapiro refers to as "addiction swapping." As psychotherapy helps her overcome one substance addiction and then another, she begins to recognize other addictive patterns emerging. Feeling ill, she takes the recommended dose of medication but then adds in an extra Sudafed or two. To control her weight, she turns to carrots, a low calorie food, but consumes two pounds of them to the point of becoming sick. She has a bout of constant shopping and also suspects she is addicted to therapy. Substituting one addictive behavior for another serves to help her escape long-standing feelings of emptiness and depression.

There are several books on gambling addiction. In *Double Down: Reflections on Gambling and Loss* (Barthelme and Barthelme, 1999), two brothers become addicted to gambling in order to avoid dealing with grief following the death of their parents. A more inwardly reflective work on gambling is provided by Bill Lee (2005) in *Born to Lose*. Katy Lederer's *Poker Face* (2003) provides the perspective of a family member surrounded by professional gamblers, although other addictions lurk in the family (her mother may be addicted to alcohol and her brother to overeating).

Two other behavioral addictions recounted in memoirs are shopping addiction in Karyn Bosnak's *Save Karyn: One Shopaholic's Journey to Debt and Back* (2003) and sex addiction in Sue William Silverman's *Love Sick: One Woman's Journey through Sexual Addiction* (2001). Although written by a woman, Silverman's book gives voice to men's experience of sexual addiction.

Reading about how an author's addiction destroyed relationships, careers, and health opens the door to seeing more sides of addiction's harm in one's own or another's life. As these authors describe their tactics for minimizing and distorting addiction, the reader becomes more aware of the addicted person's defensive maneuvers. Sometimes it is easier to deal with the pain of addiction when it is presented with humor. One of the best is *Dry* (2003), Burroughs's reflections on his years as a drunk in the world of New York City advertising.

Autobiographies about addiction are a valuable resource for learning about treatment options. You can visit a twelve-step meeting. The majority of treatment programs described in these autobiographies reflect this philosophy. You can find out who found this treatment approach essential for change and who did not and why. You can see what psychotherapy for addiction is like and learn about residential and outpatient treatments for addiction. Memoirs of addiction also convey another message that is important for all to remember: relapse is a typical part of the recovery process.

Resources

Intervention Resources

Substances and behavioral addictions:
  www.intervention.com/
  www.addictionintervention.com/
To learn more about addiction treatment informed by harm reduction philosophy, an alternative to twelve-step approaches, see
  www.harmreductiontherapy.org/

Web-Based Portals to Addiction Treatment Options

An extensive compilation of treatment options organized by type of addiction, type of person (e.g., age, gender), twelve-step and non-twelve-step based, and location within the United States. Resources address general substance-based addictions and addictions to specific substances, eating, and gambling.
  www.soberrecovery.com/
  www.soberrecovery.com/links/resources.html
Alternatives to twelve-step-based treatment approaches:
  www.aanottheonlyway.com

CHAPTER 17

Impediments to Effective Helping

Being in a close relationship with someone who is addicted is stressful to say the least. The strain is greatest if you live together; family members' physical and emotional health can be as adversely affected by addiction as the addict's (Dickson-Swift, James, and Kippen, 2005). A gambler's family suffers financial uncertainty along with the gambler. There is the strain of managing life with an alcoholic who is prone to unpredictable, angry outbursts and sullen withdrawals. An addicted sibling alters the whole fabric of family relationships. Awareness of addiction's insidious effects on all it touches comes with the desire to help rid the addicted person of the problem. Despite good intentions, family members, friends, colleagues, and relatives can inadvertently keep an addiction hidden and impede change.

Your Blinders to Seeing Addiction and Supporting Change

Living with an addicted person does not mean you see the problem for what it really is. You see a son or daughter, colleague or friend, who is struggling, but instead of seeing an addiction, you conclude that the person is depressed, anxious, lazy, obstinate, impulsive, secretive, arrogant, erratic, or lacking in motivation. Addiction's masks and disguises are as effective in hiding an addiction from the addict as they are in hiding an addiction from you. And some blinders do not fully mask the addiction, but instead lead you to minimize the addiction or get in the way of your ability to help. Lifting these blinders is essential in order to help the addicted person in your life make a change.

If you are reading this chapter, I assume you suspect that someone you know is addicted. In this chapter, I will help you examine personal factors that impede your ability to see the addiction fully and be effective in setting the stage for change. Some of these blinders require you to ask some difficult questions of yourself. At times you may not want to do this; you might even feel defensive. If this happens, I hope you can step back a moment and wonder what makes you want to dismiss what you read. Answering this question—and others that will be posed—ultimately will allow you to interact more effectively with the person you so very much want to help.

Blinder 1: Succumbing to Addiction's Masks and Disguises

The more you know about addiction's masks and disguises discussed in chapters 5 and 6, the better you will be at recognizing this problem. Several masks warrant special attention, particularly the mask of denial, where what appears to be denial is more often simply lying in order to avoid facing the shame that comes from having an addiction.

Family members are not immune to shame, and their shame can keep an addiction hidden. The journalist Bill Moyers was well aware that his son's drinking had led to an arrest. Drinking was also behind his son's auto accident during a drive in the country, but the Moyers family willingly accepted their son's explanation that a tractor was to blame. Years later, William Cope Moyers (2006) suspects that his parents avoided seeing his addiction because they were ashamed. "No parent wants to think of their child as a drug addict, no matter how obvious the signs, for most people (and my parents were no exception) believe that drug addiction is synonymous with weakness of character, personality disorder or a failure of willpower" (pp. 84–85). In the place of an addiction, they saw their son's problem as a "malady," an emotional and spiritual breakdown.

William Cope Moyers (2006) goes on to write that his family had other reasons for blindness to his addiction. "I wasn't an inherently lazy or weak person. I had a steady job, showed up for work on time, exercised regularly, went to church, owned a house (and paid the mortgage every month), and had a wife who loved me. I was never beaten, abused, or denied anything I needed or deserved—how would I possibly be a drug addict?" (p. 85). This quote should serve as a reminder to reconsider the masks of stereotypes

An Addiction's Perk

There is a truth about difficult relationships that is not easy to face. No one stays in a relationship that is totally without benefit. You stay because parts of the relationship remain valuable. When the benefit that keeps you in a relationship is linked to the addiction itself, I call it "an addiction's perk." An addiction's perk can prevent you from seeing the problem's severity or lead you to act in ways that maintain the addiction—despite voicing desire to have it change.

and demographics, so that your beliefs about who is addicted and how an addicted person behaves do not blind you to the problem.

Also take some time to reflect upon your family history of substance use and excess behavior—the mask of family excess. Those in recovery from addiction often describe growing up with a family member whose addiction was never identified, and this unidentified addiction created a distorted understanding of what was normal. Having observed a parent's nightly consumption of four whiskey sours or a six-pack of beer can, years later, blind you to the fact that difficulties in your current relationship are due to excessive alcohol. Or perhaps you were raised in a family that was plagued with chronic debt despite both parents making a good living. In this case, you may be prone to overlook signs gambling or shopping addictions in those you know.

Blinder 2: The Benefits of an Addictive Behavior

By the time their husbands get treatment, wives of pathological gamblers know if this addiction holds any perks. Despite remaining distraught and angry about all the money their husbands lost, some wives acknowledge missing the lifestyle and extravagant gifts that came with a winning streak (Rosenthal, 2005). Because of these benefits, it took them a long time to rec-

Blinders That Hide Addiction and Impede Change

Blinder 1: Succumbing to addiction's masks and disguises
Blinder 2: The benefits of an addictive behavior
Blinder 3: The attraction of addictive attributes
Blinder 4: Avoiding my problems through your addiction

ognize the severity of their husbands' gambling. Only after the savings and retirement accounts were drained and the debt was too much to cover did they recognize that what they had accepted as their husbands' pastime was a gambling addiction.

An addiction's perk blinded a man I was treating to his wife's exercise addiction. He was proud of his wife's attractiveness and devotion to her sport, which he described as "enthusiastic athleticism." A very independent woman, her frequent injuries resulting from excessive exercising left her bedridden and less able to be a partner to him. While overtly annoyed, over time, he discovered the secret enjoyment he took from her injuries. When injured, she became dependent on him. Although he felt guilty admitting it, he came to realize how much he enjoyed being able to take care of her and run the household the way he liked.

An addiction can hold out the promise of rewards that are not otherwise forthcoming in a relationship. For the gambler's wife, it was the hoped-for lavish life. For the exercise addict's husband, it was the reward of feeling needed by a beautiful woman. If someone close to you becomes a more appealing person when under the influence of an addiction—significantly friendlier, warmer, or sexier—you have less motivation to face the problem. The same process is in operation when elderly parents living with family members are allowed to drink too much or abuse their medication so that they are easier to care for. When significant others benefit from an addictive behavior, the problem will be allowed to continue.

Blinder 3: The Attraction to Addictive Attributes

Sometimes, the attributes you find most appealing in a partner are the exact same attributes that make an addiction more likely. A work addict's apparent strength of conviction and devotion to being a good provider can appeal to someone whose previous relationships were characterized by unpredictability. Yet the work addiction will ultimately make for a rocky relationship.

While science has yet to identify an addictive personality, there are several personality types that are prone to addiction—narcissistic personality is one. Remember the Greek myth of Narcissus staring at his beautiful reflection in a pond? We all expect to dislike this selfish and self-centered person; like the myth, this personality type is more common among men. Yet such personalities can be extraordinarily appealing upon first meeting. They appear calm and exceedingly self-assured. Their sense of self-importance (which is not always seen as grandiosity) conveys that they are successful achievers. Often they are successful; other times it is a lie.

Although self-absorbed and in need of adoration, a narcissist can be passionately aggressive when pursuing a desired relationship. The object of this desire feels adored while being showered with attention and gifts. Because narcissists believe that they are special people, being in such a relationship can make you feel special, too, and, at least for a while, you are just two people who adore each other and have found true love (Ekleberry, 1996; Kohut, 1987).

Over time, the true character begins to peek out. The narcissist requires that the other person feed his need for adoration, power, and attention. If a partner fails to meet these needs, the narcissist resorts to demeaning verbal attacks and, possibly, physical abuse. Relying on other people to feel good about oneself leaves this person vulnerable to intolerable disappointment. Herein lies the appeal of addiction. Mood-altering substances rarely disappoint; they are a way to create good feelings that are under personal control. People with narcissistic character traits are attracted to drugs like cocaine, which inflate self-image or provide a sense of power. Prone to perfectionism and high achievement, a narcissist can become addicted to work or seek esteem and power through his body and become addicted to exercise. Alcohol is appealing because it allows escape from the reality that no one is perfect (Ekleberry, 1996; Khantzian, 1997).

Being in a relationship with someone who is narcissistic is bound to be a roller-coaster ride of emotions as the partner shifts from being needy and demanding to adoring. For some, this roller coaster is experienced as passion and taken as evidence of true love. Once inside this dynamic, it can be hard to distinguish if this roller-coaster relationship is further fueled by addiction.

Blinder 4: Avoiding My Problems through Your Addiction

Just as an addictive behavior serves as a coping mechanism, a relationship with an addict can become your way to cope. Focusing on the addicted partner's problem provides an engaging distraction from your own concerns. Without the other's addiction to hold your attention, heretofore avoided feelings would come closer to the surface. Or, if you are the kind of person who often feels bored or understimulated, an attribute also common to gamblers and extreme sport enthusiasts, the ups and downs of living with an addict provide the desired stimulation, without requiring that you become directly involved in potentially dangerous activities. When another's addiction helps you to cope, the addiction is minimized or attempts to help are unproductive.

One man failed to see his wife's overspending as a buying addiction because it justified his long-standing sexual addiction. When the credit card bills came, he would become righteously indignant about her "wasteful" spending and leave the house to spend money on a prostitute. His wife's addiction became a justification for his behavior and allowed him to avoid the guilt he felt about his desires for sex outside the marriage. His wife, sensing his emotional distance, would soothe herself by buying and the cycle would continue.

Removing Blinders Created by Addiction's Perks

Usually the personal benefits found in a loved one's addiction are quite idiosyncratic. Even if previous examples do not resonate with your experience, they can help stimulate your thinking. If you suspect you might be under the influence of an addiction's perk, consider the following questions:

- What rewards or benefits does the addictive behavior provide you?
- Think back to what first attracted you to the addicted person. Is what you love about him or her in any way linked to the behaviors you now find problematic?
- In what ways do the negative consequences arising from addiction benefit you (serve as a distraction or a way to escape or cope)?

Often the full scope of an addiction's perk is unknown until the addiction lessens or ceases. Thus, how you benefit from another's addiction can be found by imagining what life would be like if the addiction went away. The first answers to come to mind will involve the loss of all the problems an addiction creates. You are happy to be rid of these. But what would you miss? What you miss is the addiction's perk.

My work with Joanne, whose husband was a severe alcoholic, illustrates how the full scope of an addiction's perk is unknown until the addiction stops.

Joanne had watched her husband's slide into severe alcoholism over a six-year period. His liver function was compromised, and he could not go a day without alcohol before withdrawal symptoms set in. For many years, Joanne had not recognized his alcoholism. She knew he drank nightly. This should have been a clue. His drinking was actually worse than it appeared; she was unaware that his nightly drinking was a continuation of drinking during the day. Although they fought often, the passion that came when they made up was well worth it to her (one of addiction's perks). Once his declining health made it impossible to ignore the severity of his alcoholism, she sought therapy for herself. This was the last resort after all attempts to get her husband into treatment had failed.

To meet Joanne's stated goal of getting her husband in treatment, we had to address some of the perks his addiction held for her. One benefit, noted above, was the passion of making up after a fight. Another benefit was that his problems kept her focused on the present and saved her from facing painful remnants of an abusive childhood. Our work together paid off, and he spent three months in an inpatient treatment center. They had long, loving conversations on the phone planning their "new" relationship, unencumbered by alcohol. She could hardly contain her excitement about his return home.

When he returned, their relationship was better than ever until he began looking for work. Almost immediately, Joanne began to experience anxiety and panic attacks. She could not understand what was happening. In therapy she had often spoken about how much she looked forward to her husband's return to work. This was the last piece of the puzzle in making their relationship truly normal. Why would this long-awaited event make her anxious? Joanne was willing to speculate that despite her positive expectations, there was something she feared about his getting a job. With careful questioning, Joanne realized that she was convinced that once he was able to leave the house, he would abandon her for another woman. As long as he was a drunk, he was all hers, and Joanne never had to look at her own low self-esteem when it came to men and fears of abandonment.

The Constraints of Guilt and Shame

Chapter 16 emphasized the importance of having your own support system before trying to help the addicted person in your life. If you have not taken this advice, but instead kept the addiction a secret and have been trying to help another while isolated, be sure to read this section. The feelings that lead you to act in isolation are the same feelings that lead an addicted person to hide an addiction. These feelings are guilt and shame. Guilt and shame also get in the way of implementing other recommendations made in chapter 16.

Feeling Responsible for the Addiction

One woman I treated was convinced that her husband's gambling was caused by her lifelong dream to take a cruise around the world. His job did not provide sufficient income for them to afford this luxury. Long after she saw that

Guilt and Shame Keep the Addiction a Secret

You feel responsible for the creation or maintenance of the addiction.
It's embarrassing to be involved with someone who has the stigma of an
  addiction.
You are unable to make the addicted person change.
You are caught in the web of lies that surround an addiction.
The problem feels as if it has gone on too long to ask for help.

his gambling was a problem, she kept it hidden, convinced that the addiction was all her fault. Her husband supported this belief by periodically blaming his inability to control his betting on his attempts to make her happy.

Although an addicted partner tries to blame you for the problem, in reality, no one causes another person's addiction. With this woman, it was fairly easy to point out the absurdity of her feeling responsible. If pleasing her was so important, her husband could have taken another job rather than attempting to raise cash through a risky activity like gambling. Why was she so ready to believe that his addiction was her fault?

As it turned out, she took some comfort in believing that she, rather than her husband, was the cause of problem. This gave her a sense of control over a situation where she felt terribly helpless. Seeing herself as responsible gave her hope that she had the power to do something about his problem. Of course, all her attempts to change him were ineffective.

The Shame of Being Unable to Fix the Problem

This woman's way of thinking is far from unique. It is common in intimate relationships to feel an inkling of responsibility when problems befall a partner. This feeling of responsibility is strengthened when the partner accuses you of being part of the cause, an accusation all too often made by an addict. The sex addict, upon being discovered, blames his partner's unattractiveness for his need to view pornography. This is not just mean-spiritedness on the addicted person's part. It is as if an addict, feeling helpless and out of control, is saying, "I can't do anything to help myself; maybe if you are responsible for my problem, you can get rid of it." As someone close to the person, you pick up on this implicit communication and begin to believe that there is something you can do to fix the problem. Even in the absence of such implicit communication, you are likely to believe you can do something to make him or her change. Despite being told otherwise, you cling to this belief because no one likes feeling powerless, helpless, or ineffective, especially when watching someone we love harm him- or herself.

This was true for Don, whose wife had placed the family in financial jeopardy because of her buying addiction. She used all of her income to make purchases, when her salary was needed to pay the bills and maintain the family's lifestyle. Don was consumed by self-blame and guilt. He was ashamed that his job was not more lucrative so that her spending did not have such detrimental effects. Adding to these bad feelings was his conviction that there was something he could say or do to alter her behavior.

As I emphasized in chapter 16, only the addicted person can change the behavior. As someone close to the addict who wants to be helpful, you should put your energies into helping that person prepare to change, and when change does occur, to help maintain it.

The Stigma of Being Involved with an Addicted Person

In a society that values individual autonomy and self-control, being addicted carries the connotation of being dependent and out of control. The addict is weak willed and immoral. Having married someone who later becomes addicted can induce shame. The addicted partner is seen as "damaged goods," a source of embarrassment to be kept hidden. While these negative impressions infuse every addiction, certain types of addiction bring added sources of shame. A woman whose husband is addicted to Internet pornography wonders what inadequacy of hers has led to his sexual infidelity. She avoids getting support for herself or for her husband in order to hide an embarrassing problem that feels is as much hers as his.

Imagining how others will respond once an addiction is shared within the larger family system is another reason for keeping it secret. One woman explained why she had not revealed her husband's gambling to her family: "If I went to my parents and told them how we are struggling financially because of Greg's gambling, I know they will just say 'told you so.' They think all my decisions are bad." This woman needs to stop hiding the problem from everyone because of how her parents will respond and look elsewhere for support.

Caught in the Addiction's Web of Lies

Any time your actions allow an addiction to continue or to be kept hidden, you are said to be an "enabler." Enabling occurs when you pay off the shopper's or gambler's debt or provide bail after a loved one is arrested when drunk. Any action that limits the adverse consequences of addictive behavior is enabling.

Enabling often involves lying. There are smallish lies, such as calling in to work to say a roommate or spouse is sick when in fact he or she is in bed with a hangover. There is covering up for exercise and substance-induced physical injuries by nodding in agreement when a friend or partner lies to the physician about having accidentally slipped off a curb. Other lies compromise relationships with close friends and relatives. A woman approaches her best girlfriend to borrow money for a "medical procedure" when the money actually is going to be used by her spouse for gambling.

Other times you become caught in the web of lies without ever lying. The addicted person in your life approaches friends and relatives without your knowledge and asks for money under the guise that you are "in need" but too uncomfortable to ask. If at some later date you find out that this has happened, chances are good you don't reveal the truth, because doing so brings with it the shame of admitting that you have an addict in your life. As addiction and its negative consequences continue to mount, you long to turn to family or friends, but because of the lies and complicity, you feel you cannot.

The Guilt of Waiting Too Long to Reveal the Problem

At some point, the burdens of being in a close relationship with an addicted person mount and you dearly long to tell someone. Feeling like you should have spoken out sooner becomes a source of guilt. Guilt is based on self-blame. You blame yourself for hiding the problem for so long. "If only I had gotten support, I would have been able to prevent the addiction from becoming so extreme."

There is an additional danger with feeling guilty: self-blame easily shifts into blaming others. Blaming them makes it even less likely that you will approach others for support. This happened to Don, whose wife's buying addiction was mentioned above.

The family's lifestyle had gone downhill as Don's wife purchased makeup and shoes for herself and extravagant presents for family members. They no longer went out to eat. The kids' clothing was purchased in secondhand stores. Don longed to get help but he was paralyzed by the shame of not having been able to solve the problem himself and the guilt about the amount of time that had already passed without saying anything. As a result, the family was in ter-

rible debt. His response to this shame and guilt isolated him further. His self-blame was transformed into being furious with friends and family for not doing anything. "What's with my parents and my best friend? Don't they see what has happened to us? Why don't they do something to help us?"

Becoming angry at his potential support system only led Don to further isolate himself and his family from the help they needed.

Facing Guilt and Shame

Guilt and shame are probably two of the most difficult feelings to overcome. Accepting these feelings is made easier by knowing that you are not alone; many people whose friends or partners are addicted have these feelings. But you can't know this until you go public with the problem. To do this, you need to recognize the powerful hold these feelings have and consider how their control is leading you to act in ways that serve to perpetuate an addiction. The following are some actions to take in order to move ahead despite feelings of guilt and shame:

- You can do a cost-benefit analysis like the one described for the contemplation phase in chapter 16. The benefit of keeping the addiction a secret is that you avoid guilt or shame. What are the detrimental effects (for you, for the addicted person, and for others involved with this person) of continuing to keep the problem a secret? What are the benefits of going public? Other than uncomfortable feelings, what problems arise from going public? Which creates worse consequences: going public or continuing to keep the problem hidden? Being criticized or getting the much-needed support you and the addicted person need?
- As the person close to an addict, you feel there are many reasons for being guilty or ashamed but rarely are they realistic. Recognizing that these feelings are grounded in unrealistic beliefs can help free you from them. Ask yourself, Is the source of shame realistic? Although it may feel like it is true, are you *really* the cause of the addiction? Although you may feel stigmatized because of your involvement with an addict, does everyone you know share this reaction or are you assuming that they feel this way?
- Reexamine who you can go to for support. Seeking help from those with similar problems lessens guilt and shame. Attending an Alcoholics Anonymous or Family Anonymous meeting does not require you to identify yourself, and you will be among people who know and understand what you are going through. Similarly, do you really

believe a health care provider will think less of you for being close to an addict?

Being "Too Helpful": When Helping Is Hurtful

If, despite your best efforts, you keep getting angry and insisting that the addict change, then chances are good that you are overly involved with another's addiction. Over-involvement can fall under the guise of "I'm just trying to be helpful." Distinguishing true helpfulness from over-involvement is not all that difficult.

Wanting to help a person who is struggling is normal; in the process, you may occasionally neglect your own needs. This normal approach to helping differs from over-involvement, where the desire to help is subverted into something else: a desire to control another's behavior. The focus is on single-handedly containing the addiction and making the person cease the harmful behavior. Beer cans are carefully counted in the garbage, receipts are retrieved from the trash to see what has been purchased, or you follow the person to see where he or she is going. When the helper becomes so absorbed in "being helpful" that he or she is acting in a self-harming manner, the helper has crossed the line into over-involvement. This kind of helping can be part of a larger way of relating known as codependency.

Codependency is considered a type of addiction. Instead of being pre-occupied with a substance or activity, the codependent is dependent on or preoccupied with the addict. Both addict and codependent are involved in self-injurious behaviors. Just as the addict feels powerless and unable to manage the addictive behavior, the codependent ultimately feels powerless and unable to manage the addict.

In the popular press, codependency is a woman's disorder. While women are socialized to be caretakers and place greater value on relationships, there is nothing to preclude a man from behaving in a codependent manner. Codependency has more to do with family history and personal feelings than one's gender. Codependents often grow up in highly stressed families where at least one family member was addicted or ill. Early learning teaches that intimate relationships are premised upon one person being in need with the other being the caretaker. The helper is self-effacing and places her or his needs second to the other person's needs.

Codependency may be a component of all of one's close relationships, or it may be confined to the addicted person. In the latter case, codependent ways of relating develop as a consequence of accommodating to changes in a relationship that occur as a moderate addiction becomes more severe and efforts to stop the decline grow in intensity.

Rising above this overly involved way of helping can be as simple as recognizing the tendency to place yourself second or to attend to another's needs while neglecting your own. Learning less engaged and more independent forms of helping—like those presented in chapter 16—provide an alternative to codependent relating. However, if you can't turn this knowledge into action, then you will want to return to the discussion of addiction's perks to see if any of these are getting in the way of implementing more effective helping strategies. Another alternative is to join a self-help group or try psychotherapy.

Your Own Phases of Change

As someone who wants to help an addicted person, you need to prepare yourself to become a change agent. The phases of change that help ready an addict to address an addiction also prepare you to be a more effective facilitator of change.

Precontemplation Phase

You have experienced some negative consequence created by another's addiction, but these have not yet coalesced and you do not identify the problem as an addiction. Occasional adverse effects are seen as flukes or isolated incidents. As these seemingly isolated incidents begin to accumulate, you start to wonder if there is an addiction. Or, perhaps, you suspect the problem is an addiction but feel helpless to do anything about it. The precontemplation phase ends when you strongly suspect that there is an addiction and plan to pursue the matter.

Contemplation Phase

With greater clarity about the scope of negative consequences has come the recognition that something needs to change. There is no clear understanding or plan for how to go about it. You begin to learn more about addiction and methods of change. At the same time, you may be trying to eliminate the problem yourself by pressuring the person to cut back or stop. You have yet to accept that you are powerless to make the person change.

Although you are only aware of wanting the addiction to go away, chances are good you have some ambivalence. You may not become aware of this ambivalence until later when you find yourself unable to follow through on the phases of change in chapter 16 or when you routinely act in ways that undermine the progress the addicted person has made. Some sources of ambivalence discussed above include addiction's various perks (benefits of addiction) and sources of shame and guilt (costs of change). To help you move beyond ambivalence, create your own cost-benefit analysis outlining the pros and cons of keeping the addiction and supporting its change (see table 16.1).

Preparation Phase

You will have stopped trying to change the addiction on your own. This is the time for actively gathering information about treatment options. Before going into action and assisting the addicted person prepare for change, assess your level of stress and how well you are coping. Too often family members neglect themselves as the addict becomes the focus of their existence: they stop seeing friends, begin hiding what is happening at home, and become preoccupied with worrying about the addict or the addiction's effects.

Be sure you have enough support. There are many readily available sources: health care professionals, Alcoholics Anonymous, or friends and relatives. To find the right support for you, simply type "support for friends and family of addicts" into an Internet search engine. Self-help groups—such as Alcoholics Anonymous for adults and Alateen for teenagers—are available across the country and online. Although described as groups designed for people involved with alcoholics, these meetings remain a valuable, free, and readily accessible resource for anyone affected by another's addiction.

Action Phase

In light of what you have learned about addictions and getting ready to change, you begin to act on the information provided in chapter 16. Your attempts to help are not overdone (i.e., they do not represent codependence). More and more attention is turned to yourself and other family members who have been neglected while attention was focused on the addicted person.

Becoming less engaged with the addicted person is necessary for your own health and for their recovery. One of the first lessons of Alcoholics Anonymous is "keep the focus on yourself." Family members of addicted relatives who have utilized such support often remark that "it made me realize I've got a life of my own" (Templeton, Zohhadi, and Velleman, 2004, p. 17).

Resources

Where family members affected by a loved one's addiction can meet:
www.familiesanonymous.org/
www.al-anon.alateen.org/english.html
Information and help for codependency:
www.codependents.org/
www.helpself.com/directory/codependency.htm
A portal to resources for families and the addicted person:
http://ncadistore.samhsa.gov/catalog/referrals.aspx?topic=83&h=resources

An Overview of Addiction-Induced Psychological and Physical Changes

Substances and behaviors with psychoactive effects have the potential to create symptoms that mimic physical and psychological disorders. This mimicry occurs at all phases of the addictive process: in the acute or active phase (when the person is under the influence of the substance), with prolonged or chronic use, and as a result of withdrawal.

The best-known addictive substances are grouped into classes (see appendix II). Each class of drug creates a specific set of physical and psychological effects. Revealing an addiction is easier when you know about how active addiction or withdrawal creates symptoms that disguise the problem.

Alcohol and Sedatives

Alcohol is the best known of the sedatives, which also include such frequently prescribed medications as Valium and Xanex.

Sedatives depress nervous system functioning. When taken frequently and in high doses, sedatives actually alter how the nervous system functions (i.e., neuroadaptation; see chapter 2); in their absence, the nervous system operates in a way that creates anxiety and low moods. Who would think that unpleasant anxious feelings are the result of a drug initially taken to reduce such feelings? In response, more sedatives are required to relieve the renewed bad feelings.

Sedating substances increase the risk of accidents, especially car accidents and accidental overdoses. Ongoing or extensive use of alcohol can lead to memory lapses, which in extreme cases result in blackouts. Blackouts do not refer to loss of consciousness but rather loss of memory of what happened. When in a blackout, a person appears to be drunk yet functional (e.g., walking, talking, dancing), but will have no memory for what happened.

Chronic sedative use is associated with disturbed sleep patterns, stomach irritation, sadness, anxiety, irritability, and difficulty concentrating. These aftereffects are easily mistaken for physical disorders, such as ulcers or irritable bowel syndrome, and psychological problems, such as depression, anxiety, and generalized stress.

Alcoholism also may be mistaken for what is referred to as a borderline personality disorder. The symptoms they share are erratic behavior, especially in interpersonal relationships, poor control over anger, suicidal or dramatic behavior, and disturbances in one's sense of identity (e.g., a confident person one day becomes filled with self-loathing the next) (Lilenfeld and Kaye, 1996).

Once dependent on sedatives, reduction in use brings withdrawal symptoms. Withdrawal from sedatives is associated with a wide array of symptoms ranging from mild physical discomfort and a sense of not being quite right to convulsions. The longer one has been taking sedating substances and the more quickly the substance is stopped, the more severe the symptoms. Never suddenly stop using alcohol or other sedating substances unless under medical care. Once addicted, these are the most dangerous drugs to withdraw from. Sudden cessation can result in convulsions and even death.

Stimulants

Caffeine is the most readily available and best-known stimulant. As the most widely used psychoactive substance, caffeine use is not considered a diagnosable addiction. As a result, its psychological effects are easily overlooked. Caffeine's acute effects include anxiety, sleep disturbances, mood change, and cardiovascular complaints (heart palpitations) that can be experienced as symptomatic of panic attacks. Withdrawal from caffeine is associated with headaches and irritation.

Cocaine and amphetamines are two other popular stimulants. In the acute phase, stimulants induce increased alertness and improved attention. Other immediate effects include an improved sense of well-being, restlessness, and mood swings. Under their influence, a person can be highly effective followed by a crash when little is accomplished. A stimulant high is easily mistaken for a manic episode followed by a low period. This pattern can be misdiagnosed as evidence of a manic-depressive disorder.

In the presence of an undiagnosed heart condition, stimulants can set off life-threatening heart arrhythmias and heart attacks. Stimulants, when routinely snorted, create nasal and sinus problems that a doctor or parent may misinterpret as frequent colds or allergies. In the more chronic phases, paranoid thoughts can develop that in turn lead to aggressive behavior.

Among some men, cocaine acts as an aphrodisiac. Initially, cocaine facilitates sexual arousal, but with chronic use, an inability to maintain an erection and an inability to orgasm may occur. Sixty percent of men with cocaine addiction also report sexual addictions, often involving excessive use of pornography (Washton, 1989). Cocaine-induced sexual problems may be misdiagnosed as organic in nature or mistakenly tied to relationship problems. Women who use cocaine addictively may do so because of its desired effects on concentration (see Wurtzel's *More, Now, Again* [2002]). Among younger women, especially those with concerns about body size, cocaine may be used to control weight.

Amphetamines with brand names like Ritalin, Concerta, and Adderall are psychostimulants that are prescribed to treat attention related disorders such as attention deficit disorder (ADD) or attention deficit hyperactivity disorder (ADHD). Students without attention problems, especially college students, are drawn to these drugs, which can improve concentration and alertness when studying late into the night. Amphetamines are also a popular appetite suppressant among those with eating disorders or those whose appearance is a major component of self-esteem. Stimulants used for these purposes are usually procured illegally or from acquaintances willing to share some medication from their valid prescriptions. The latter practice is so commonplace that psychostimulants account for a major portion of the epidemic in prescription medication abuse.

Withdrawal symptoms following cessation of regular use include lowered energy, poor concentration, and a general withdrawal from life, where there is less pleasure and interest in daily activities. These withdrawal symptoms mimic depression and can last eighteen weeks or longer. This prolonged time frame often contributes to the mistaken conclusion that low energy and mood are purely psychological in origin rather than the result of an ongoing withdrawal process.

Cannabis

Marijuana is the most frequently used illicit drug. The relaxed and calm feeling it creates has resulted in marijuana becoming the equivalent of the evening cocktail in some circles. White-collar professionals who smoke marijuana regularly agree that this substance is not conducive to keeping one's professional edge and thus adhere to the rule of no smoking before or during work (Kurutz, 2003). Chronic use of marijuana is associated with an amotivational syndrome. The symptoms of low energy, blunted affect, apathy, and sexual dysfunction are easily mistaken for depression.

Opioids

Opioids are no longer a class of drug associated with urban and/or poor communities. Abuse of the pain reliever oxycodone and the street drug, heroin, have become popular among young, affluent city dwellers and suburbanites. Instead of injecting heroin, with its risk of transmitting HIV, this group prefers to snort the drug. Ann Marlowe's autobiography, *How to Stop Time: Heroin A to Z* (1999), tells their story.

In the acute phase, opioids create compelling euphoric feelings. Marlow captures heroin's appeal as follows: "The deep satisfaction of your first cup of coffee in the morning" that cannot be recaptured in the second cup (p. 9). Snorting heroin does not get in the way of Marlow's busy daily schedule of work, exercise, and meeting friends. For those who inject heroin, the experience is more lethargic.

The psychoactive effects of opioids are rarely mistaken for other physical or psychological disorders. Withdrawal brings flulike symptoms (achy joints, runny nose) and extreme psychological discomfort. Although withdrawal from opioids can be physically and emotionally painful, it is not life threatening in the way unregulated withdrawal from sedatives, such as alcohol, can be.

The only opioid users who may misattribute the emotional discomfort of withdrawal to psychological causes are intermittent heroin users (e.g., weekend warriors) and abusers of opioid-based prescription painkillers. Upon stopping use altogether, anxiety has been noted to increase over the course of several weeks. These symptoms can be mistaken for a generalized anxiety disorder (Myrick and Brady, 2003).

Hallucinogens

While LSD, popular in the 1960s and early 1970s, is still produced, newer forms of hallucinogens, such as Ecstasy and MDMA, have replaced it in popularity. Hallucinogens create breaks from reality with the most salient effect being hallucinations.

If disturbing enough, these hallucinations may lead a user to seek help, usually through a hospital emergency room. Appropriately trained medical professionals will not mistake drug-induced hallucinations for a psychotic episode. This is because drug-induced hallucinations are usually visual and tactile whereas hallucinations accompanying schizophrenia are auditory (M. Johnson, Heriza, and St. Dennis, 1999).

Behavioral Addictions

Behavioral addictions can be disguised as routine physical and psychological problems. Addictive exercising that leads to physical injuries is seen as a consequence of normal exercise rather than the outcome of excessive physical activity. Gambling is associated with sleep disturbances, stomachaches, and back and leg problems, as well as depression. Sexual and cybersex addictions lead to a declining sexual interest in a partner, which is interpreted as a relationship problem. Computer addiction, especially in adolescents, can lead to decreased interest in family and social life, where real-time interpersonal relations are replaced by gaming or other online activities. A parent may assume this isolation represents normal adolescent preoccupations.

Withdrawal from a behavioral addiction can produce symptoms typical of depression or anxiety. An often-overlooked fact about withdrawal is that it can last much longer than expected. One rule of thumb is that withdrawal symptoms usually subside in two weeks; others argue that they can continue up to several months (Schuckit, 1998). Extended withdrawal effects include nervousness, sleeping problems, and a general sense of unease as the body adjusts to life without routine exposure to a substance or behavior. If not correctly linked to withdrawal, such feelings could be mistaken for anxiety or depression. For those with a history of managing feelings through addictive behaviors, the unease created by a protracted withdrawal can trigger a relapse.

Common Addictive Substances

Alcohol

Drug name: ethanol (ETOH)
Some popular names: brew, booze, juice, hooch
Method of use: swallowed
Potential for physical dependence: high
Potential for psychological dependence: high
Effects: reduced inhibitions, impaired judgment, slurred speech, impaired memory and learning, impaired coordination
Direct negative consequences: organ damage, especially liver and heart; fetal alcohol syndrome; blackouts; increased accidents; reduced effectiveness of medications; increased risk of overdose when mixed with depressants; anxiety; depression; severe withdrawal syndrome

Cannabis

Drug names: marijuana, hashish, THC
Some popular names: grass, pot, weed, dope, reefer, joint, ganja, sinsemilla
Method of use: smoked, less commonly swallowed
Potential for physical dependence: low
Potential for psychological dependence: moderate
Effects: relaxed; good feelings; hilarity; reduced inhibitions; hunger; altered perception
Direct negative consequences: lung damage, agitation, paranoia, amotivational syndrome, impaired judgment

Cocaine

Drug name: cocaine
Some popular names: coke, snow, blow, crack, candy cane, dust
Method of use: snorted as a powder; crack is smoked, less often swallowed
Potential for physical dependence: possible
Potential for psychological dependence: moderate for cocaine, high for crack
Effects: alertness, increased concentration and sense of well-being, diminished appetite
Direct negative consequences: insomnia; anxiety; depression; lung, sinus, and nasal passage damage

Sedatives/Hypnotics/Depressants

Drug names:
1. barbiturates
2. benzodiazapines
3. methaqualone
Some popular names:
1. Seconol, Amytal, Phenobarbytol, yellow jackets, reds, goofballs
2. Valium, valleys, Atavin, Xanex, Tranxene
3. Quaaludes, ludes, spoor
Method of use: usually swallowed, sometimes injected
Potential for physical dependence: high
Potential for psychological dependence: high
Effects: relaxation, drowsiness
Direct negative consequences: impaired performance and judgment, confusion, slurred speech, memory impairment, respiratory distress, increased overdose potential when mixed with alcohol

Stimulants

Drug names:
1. amphetamines/methylphenadate
2. methamphetamine
3. MDMA
4. PCP
5. caffeine and ephedrine
Some popular names:
1. Dexedrine, Ritalin, Adderall, speed, uppers, pep pills, bennies, black beauties

2. crystal (meth)
3. Ecstasy, X, Adam
4. angeldust, dust

Method of use: swallowed or may be injected
Potential for physical dependence: possible for 1, 2
Potential for psychological dependence: high for 1, 2
Effects: altered consciousness, energized, appetite loss, grandiosity
Direct negative consequences: nervousness, irritability, sleeplessness, panic, hallucinations, heart attack, stroke, heart arrhythmia

Opioids/Narcotics

Drug names: opium, morphine, heroin, synthetic drugs resembling opium (e.g., Percodan, oxycodone, codeine, Fentanyl, Vicodin, Demeral)
Some popular names: junk, smack, syrup
Method of use: swallowed or injected
Potential for physical dependence: high
Potential for psychological dependence: high
Effects: euphoria, "rush," pain relief, laissez-faire attitude, sleepiness, decreased appetite
Direct negative consequences: increased risk of infection when injected, high risk of overdose, constipation, uncomfortable withdrawal syndrome, respiratory depression, coma

Hallucinogens

Drug names:
1. Psilocibin
2. Mescaline
3. Phenacyclidine (PCP)
4. Dextromethorphan (DXM) found in cough syrups/cold medication
5. Ketamine

Some popular names:
1. LSD, acid, purple haze
2. magic mushrooms
3. PCP mixed with marijuana, supergrass, killer hog
4. Candy, C-C-C Dex, Red Devils, Robo, Rojo, Skittles, vitamin D

Method of use: swallowed; PCP is smoked, snorted, or injected
Potential for physical dependence: possible
Potential for psychological dependence: unknown
Effects: altered perceptions/altered sense of reality, visual hallucinations, illusion of heightened insight, detachment, confusion

Direct negative consequences: fear, anxiety, paranoia, flashbacks, psychosis, irregular heartbeat

Inhalants

Drug names:
1. cleaning agents, solvents, adhesives
2. amyl/butyl nitrite
3. nitrous oxide

Some popular names:
1. gasoline, airplane glue, paint thinner, dry cleaning fluid
2. poppers, snappers, locker room
3. laughing gas, whippets

Method of use: inhaled; sniffed sometimes from cotton, ampoules, plastic/paper bags

Potential for physical dependence: unknown

Potential for psychological dependence: unknown

Effects: euphoria, reduced inhibitions, lightheadedness

Direct negative consequences: impaired reflexes, slowed thought, lack of coordination, violent behavior, nerve damage, suffocation, kidney failure, heart arrhythmia, anoxia

References

Adams, J., and R. J. Kirby. (2002). Excessive exercise as an addiction: A review. *Addiction Research and Theory* 10: 415–38.

American Psychiatric Association. (2000). *Diagnostic and statistical manual of mental disorders.* 4th text revision ed. Washington, DC: American Psychiatric Association.

Associated Press. (2006). Ashley Judd Treated for Addictive Behaviors. July 5. Retrieved on 3/12/07 from www.addictioninfo.org/articles/907/1/Ashley-Judd-treated-for-addictive-behaviors/Page1.html.

Bamber, D., I. M. Cockerill, S. Rodgers, and D. Carroll. (2000). "It's exercise or nothing": A qualitative analysis of exercise dependence. *British Journal of Sports Medicine* 34: 423–30.

Bancroft, J., and Z. Vukadinovic. (2004). Sexual addiction, sexual compulsivity, sexual impulsivity or what? Toward a theoretical model. *The Journal of Sex Research* 41: 225–34.

Barthelme, F., and S. Barthelme. (1999). *Double Down: Reflections on Gambling and Loss.* Boston: Houghton Mifflin.

Becker, E. (1973). *Denial of Death.* New York: Free Press.

Becker, L. K., and B. Walton-Moss. (2001). Detecting and addressing alcohol abuse in women. *Nurse Practitioner* 26: 13–25.

Benson, A. (Ed.). (2000). *I Shop, Therefore I Am.* New York: Jason Aronson.

Blow, F. C., K. J. Brower, J. E. Schulenberg, L. M. Demo-Dananberg, J. P. Young, and T. P. Beresford. (1992). The Michigan Alcoholism Screening Test-Geriatric Version (MAST-G): A new elderly specific screening instrument. *Alcoholism: Clinical and Experimental Research* 16: 372.

Blumberg, E. S. (2003). The lives and voices of highly sexual women. *Journal of Sex Research* 40: 146–57.

Bosnak, K. (2003). *Save Karyn: One Shopaholic's Journey to Debt and Back.* New York: HarperCollins.

Bradley, K. A., J. Boyd-Wickizer, S. H. Powell, and M. L. Burman. (1998). Alcohol screening questionnaires in women: A critical review. *Journal of the American Medical Association* 280: 166–71.

Brems, C., and M. E. Johnson. (1997). Clinical implications of the co-occurrence of substance use and other psychiatric disorders. *Professional Psychology: Research and Practice* 28: 437–47.

Brown, R. I. F. (1997). A theoretical model of the behavioural addictions—applied to offending. In J. E. Hodge, M. McMurran, and C. R. Hollin (Eds.), *Addicted to Crime?* Chichester, West Sussex, England: John Wiley.

Burroughs, A. (2003). *Dry: A Memoir.* New York: St. Martin's Press.

Cadoret, R. J., E. Troughton, T. W. O'Gorman, and E. Heywood. (1995). Adoption study demonstrating two genetic pathways to drug abuse. *Archives of General Psychiatry* 42: 1131–36.

Carnes, P. (2001). *Out of the Shadows: Understanding Sexual Addiction.* Center City, MN: Hazelden.

———. (2005). *Facing the Shadow: Starting Sexual and Relationship Recovery.* Carefree, AZ: Gentle Path Press.

Center for Substance Abuse Treatment. (2004). *Issues in the Treatment of Women.* (Treatment Improvement Protocol Series). Bethesda, MD: Substance Abuse and Mental Health Services Administration.

Chan, C., and H. Grossman. (1988). Psychological effects of running loss on constant runners. *Perceptual and Motor Skills* 66: 875–83.

Charlton, J. P. (2002). A factor-analytic investigation of computer "addiction" and engagement. *British Journal of Psychology* 93: 329–44.

Cheever, S. (1999). *Note Found in a Bottle: My Life as a Drinker.* New York: Simon and Schuster.

Cherpital, C. J. (1997). Brief screening instruments for alcoholism. *Alcohol Health and Research World* 21: 348–51.

Christenson, G. A., R. J. Faber, M. de Zwaan, N. C. Raymond, S. M. Specker, M. D. Ekern, T. B. Mackenzie, R. D. Crosby, S. J. Crow, E. D. Eckert, M. P. Mussell, and J. E. Mitchell. (1994). Compulsive buying: Descriptive characteristics and psychiatric comorbidity. *Journal of Clinical Psychiatry* 55: 5–11.

Christo, G., S. L. Jones, S. Haylett, G. M. Stephenson, R. M. H. Lefever, and R. Lefever. (2003). The Shorter PROMIS Questionnaire: Further validation of a tool for simultaneous assessment of multiple addictive behaviours. *Addictive Behaviors* 28: 225–48.

Coleman, E., N. Raymond, and A. McBean. (2003). Assessment and treatment of compulsive sexual behavior. *Minnesota Medicine* 86. Retrieved on 1/5/07 from http://www.mmaonline.net/publications/MNMed2003/July/Coleman2 .html.

Collins, J., W. Skinner, and T. Toneatto. (2006). Beyond assessment: The impact of comorbidity of pathological gambling, psychiatric disorders and substance use disorders on treatment course and outcomes. Ontario Problem Gambling Research Centre.

Committee on Substance Abuse and Council on School Health. (2007). Testing for drugs of abuse in children and adolescents: Addendum—testing in schools and at home. *Pediatrics* 119: 627–30.

Cooper, A. (Ed.). (2000). *Cybersex: The Dark Side of the Force*. Philadelphia, PA: Brunner-Routledge.

Cooper, A., D. L. Delmonico, and R. Burg. (2000). Cybersex users, abusers, and compulsives: New findings and implications. In A. Cooper (Ed.), *Cybersex: The Dark Side of the Force*. Philadelphia, PA: Brunner-Routledge.

Cooper, A., N. Galbreath, and M. A. Becker. (2004). Sex on the Internet: Furthering our understanding of men with online sexual problems. *Psychology of Addictive Behaviors* 18: 223–30.

Cooper, A., C. Scherer, S. S. Boies, and B. Gordon. (1999). Sexuality on the Internet: From sexual exploration to pathological expression. *Professional Psychology: Research and Practice* 30: 154–64.

Cooper, M. L., M. R. Frone, M. Russell, and P. Mudar. (1995). Drinking to regulate positive and negative emotions: A motivational model of alcohol use. *Journal of Personality and Social Psychology* 69: 990–1005

Csikszentmihalyi, M. (1999). If we are so rich, why aren't we happy? *American Psychologist* 54: 821–72.

Currie, S. R., D. C. Hodgins, J. Wang, N. el-Guebaly, H. Wynne, and S. Chen. (2006). Risk of harm among gamblers in the general population as a function of level of participation in gambling activities. *Addiction* 101: 570–80.

Dai, X., J. Thavundayil, and C. Gianoulakis. (2005). Differences in the peripheral levels of beta-endorphin in response to alcohol and stress as a function of alcohol dependence and family history of alcoholism. *Alcoholism: Clinical and Experimental Research* 29: 1965–75.

Dean, J. C., and F. Rud. (1984). The drug addict and the stigma of addiction. *International Journal of Addictions* 19: 859–69.

DeJong, W. (2001). Finding common ground for effective campus prevention. *Psychology of Addictive Behaviors* 15: 292–96.

Denning, P. (2000). *Practicing Harm Reduction Psychotherapy: An Alternative Approach to Addictions*. New York: Guilford Press.

Derevensky, J. L., R. Gupta, and K. Winters. (2003). Prevalence rates of youth gambling: Are the current rates inflated? *Journal of Gambling Studies* 19: 405–25.

DeSarbo, W. S., and E. A. Edwards. (1996). Typologies of compulsive buying behavior: A constrained clusterwise regression approach. *Journal of Consumer Psychology* 5: 231–62.

Diamond, J. (2000). *Narrative Means to Sober Ends: Treating Addiction and Its Aftermath.* New York: Guilford Press.

———. (2003). Editorial: Situating myself. *Janus Head*, 6: 179–89. Retrieved on 6/1/06 from http://www.janushead.org/6-2/index.cfm.

Dickson-Swift, V. A., E. L. James, and S. Kippen. (2005). The experience of living with a problem gambler: Spouses and partners speak out. *Journal of Gambling Issues* 13. Retrieved on 7/27/06 from http://www.camh.net/egambling/issue13/jgi_13_dicksonSwift.html.

DiClemente, C. C. (2003). *Addiction and Change: How Addictions Develop and Addicted People Recover.* New York: Guilford Press.

Dodes, L. (1996). Compulsion and addiction. *Journal of the American Psychoanalytic Association* 44: 815–35.

———. (2002). *The Heart of Addiction.* New York: HarperCollins.

Donovan, D. M., and G. A. Marlatt. (1988). *Assessment of Addictive Behaviors.* New York: Guilford Press.

Duke, A. (2005). *Annie Duke: How I Raised, Folded, Bluffed, Flirted, Cursed, and Won Millions at the World Series of Poker.* New York: Hudson Street Press.

Edwards, E. A. (1993). Development of a new scale for measuring compulsive buying behavior. *Financial Counseling and Planning* 4: 67–84.

Ekleberry, S. (1996). Dual diagnosis: Addiction and axis II personality disorders. *The Counselor* March/April: 7–13. Retrieved on 11/17/06 from http://www.toad.net/~arcturus/dd/shart1.htm.

Faber, R. J., and G. A. Christenson. (1996). In the mood to buy: Differences in the mood states experienced by compulsive buyers and other consumers. *Psychology and Marketing* (Special issue: Aberrant Consumer Behavior) 13: 803–20.

Faber, R. J., G. A. Christenson, M. de Zwaan, and J. Mitchell. (1995). Two forms of compulsive consumption: Comorbidity of compulsive buying and binge eating. *Journal of Consumer Research* 22: 296–304.

Faber, R. J., and T. C. O'Guinn. (1992). A clinical screener for compulsive buying. *Journal of Consumer Research* 19: 459–69.

Feldman, S. R., A. Liguori, M. Kucenic, S. Rapp, A. W. Fleischer, W. Lang, and M. Kaur. (2004). Ultraviolet exposure is a reinforcing stimulus in frequent indoor tanners. *Journal of the American Academy of Dermatology* 51: 45–51.

Ferris, J., and H. Wynne. (2001). The Canadian Problem Gambling Index: Final Report. Ottawa: Canadian Centre on Substance Abuse. Retrieved on 1/14/07 from www.ccsa.ca/NR/rdonlyres/58BD1AA0-047A-41EC-906E-87F8FF46C91B/0/ccsa0088052001.pdf.

Fink A., M. Tsai, R. D. Hays, A. A. Moore, S. C. Morton, K. Spritzer, and J. C. Beck. (2002). Comparing the Alcohol-Related Problems Survey (ARPS) to traditional alcohol screening instruments in elderly outpatients. *Archives of Gerontology and Geriatrics* 34: 55–78.

Fischer, C. (1987). *Postcards from the Edge.* New York: Pocket Books.

Fletcher, A. M. (2001). *Sober for Good.* Boston: Houghton Mifflin.

Flores, P. (2004). *Addiction as an Attachment Disorder.* New York: Jason Aronson.

Forchuk, C. (1984). Cognitive dissonance: Denial, self-concepts and the alcoholic stereotype. *Nursing Papers* 16: 57–69.

Freimuth, M. (2005). *Hidden Addictions.* New York: Jason Aronson.

———. (In press). Another missed opportunity: Recognition of alcohol use problems by mental health providers. *Psychotherapy.*

Frey, J. (2003). *A Million Little Pieces.* New York: Anchor.

Gavin, D. R., H. E. Ross, and H. A. Skinner. (1989). Diagnostic validity of the Drug Abuse Screening Test in the assessment of DSM-III drug disorders. *British Journal of Addiction* 84: 301–7.

Goldman, D., and A. Bergen. (1998). General and specific inheritance of substance abuse and alcoholism. *Archives of General Psychiatry* 55: 964–65.

Goldsmith, T., and S. L. McElroy. (2000). Diagnosis, associated disorders, and drug treatment. In. A. Benson (Ed.), *I Shop, Therefore I Am.* New York: Jason Aronson.

Goodman, A. (1993). Diagnosis and treatment of sexual addiction. *Journal of Sex and Marital Therapy* 19: 225–51.

———. (1998). *Sexual Addiction: An Integrated Approach.* Madison, CT: International Universities Press.

Greenberg, J. L., S. E. Lewis, and D. K. Dodd. (1999). Overlapping addictions and self-esteem among college men and women. *Addictive Behaviors* 24: 565–71.

Griffiths, M. D. (1995). Technological addictions. *Clinical Psychology Forum* 76: 14–19.

———. (2001). Sex on the Internet: Observations and implications for Internet sex addiction. *The Journal of Sex Research Research* 38: 333–43.

———. (2003). Internet abuse in the workplace: Issues and concerns for employers and employment counselors. *Journal of Employment Counseling* 40: 87–96.

Griffiths, M. D., and R. T. A. Wood. (2000). Risk factors in adolescence: The case of gambling, videogame playing, and the Internet. *Journal of Gambling Studies* 16: 199–225.

Grohol, J. M. (2003). Internet Addiction Guide. Retrieved on 12/18/06 from http://psychcentral.com/netaddiction/.

Grucza, R. A., C. R. Cloninger, K. K. Bucholz, J. N. Constantino, M. I. Schuckit, D. M. Dick, and L. J. Bierut. (2006). Novelty seeking as a moderator of familial risk for alcohol dependence. *Alcoholism: Clinical and Experimental Research* 30: 1176–83.

Hall, A. S., and J. Parsons. (2001). Internet addiction: College student case study using best practices in cognitive behavior therapy. *Journal of Mental Health Counseling* 23: 312–28.

Hamill, P. (1994). *A Drinking Life: A Memoir.* Boston: Little, Brown.

Hansen, G. R. (2002). In drug abuse, gender matters. *NIDA Notes* 17: 3–4.

Hasin, D. S., M. A. Schuckit, C. S. Martin, B. F. Grand, K. K. Bucholz, and J. E. Helzer. (2003). The validity of DSM-IV alcohol dependence: What do we know and what do we need to know? *Alcoholism: Clinical and Experimental Research* 27: 244–52.

Hausenblas, H. A., and D. Symons Downs. (2002). Relationship among sex, imagery, and exercise dependence symptoms. *Psychology of Addictive Behaviors* 16: 169–72.

Hodgins, D. C., and K. Makarchuk. (2003). Trusting problem gamblers: Reliability and validity of self-reported gambling behavior. *Psychology of Addictive Behaviors* 17: 244–48.

Howard, M., C. McMillen, L. Nower, D. Elze, T. Edmond, and J. Bricout. (2002). Denial in addiction: Toward an integrated stage and process model—qualitative findings. *Journal of Psychoactive Drugs* 34: 371–83.

Insel, T. R. (2003). Is social attachment an addictive disorder? *Physiology and Behavior* 79: 351–57.

Institute of Medicine. (1997). Dispelling the Myths about Addictions. Washington, DC: National Academy Press. Retrieved on 11/18/06 from http://www.nap.edu/openbook/0309064015/html/20.html.

Jersild, D. (2002). *Happy Hours: Alcohol in a Woman's Life.* New York: Perennial.

Johansson, K., I. Akerlind, and P. Bendtsen. (2005). Under what circumstances are nurses willing to engage in brief alcohol interventions? A qualitative study from primary care in Sweden. *Addictive Behavior* 30: 1049–53.

Johnson, J. G, R. L. Spitzer, J. B. Williams, K. W. Kroenke, M. Linzer, D. Brody, F. deGruy, and S. Hahn. (1995). Psychiatric comorbidity, health status, and functional impairment associated with alcohol abuse and dependence in primary care patients: Findings of the PRIME MD-1000 study. *Journal of Consulting and Clinical Psychology* 63: 133–40.

Johnson, M. D., T. J. Heriza, and C. St. Dennis. (1999). How to spot illicit drug abuse in your patients. *Postgraduate Medicine* 106: 199–200, 203–6, 211, and 214.

Johnston, L. D., P. M. O'Malley, and J. G. Bachman. (2003). Monitoring the future national survey results on adolescent drug use: Overview of key findings, 2002. (NIH Publication No. 03–5374). Bethesda, MD: National Institute on Drug Abuse.

Kafka, M. P., and R. Prentky. (1992). Fluoxetine treatment of nonparaphilic sexual addiction and paraphilias in men. *Journal of Clinical Psychiatry* 53: 351–58.

Kalichman, S. C., and D. Rompa. (2001). The Sexual Compulsivity Scale: Further development and use with HIV-positive persons. *Journal of Personality Assessment* 76: 376–95.

Kalichman, S. C., R. R. Johnson, V. Adair, D. Rompa, K. Multhauf, and J. A. Kelly. (1994). Scale development and predicting AIDS-risk behavior among homosexually active men. *Journal of Personality Assessment* 62: 385–97.

Kandel, D. B. (1982). Epidemiological and psychosocial perspectives on adolescent drug use. *Journal of the American Academy of Child and Adolescent Psychiatry* 20: 328–47.

Kasser, T., and Kanner, A. D. (Eds.) (2003). *Psychology and Consumer Culture: The Struggle for a Good Life in a Materialistic World.* Washington, DC: American Psychological Association.

Kessler, R. C., R. M. Crum, L. A. Warner, C. B. Nelson, J. Schulenberg, and J. C. Anthony. (1997). Lifetime co-occurrence of DSM-III-R alcohol abuse and dependence with other psychiatric disorders in the National Comorbidity Study. *Archives of General Psychiatry* 54: 313–21.

Keyes, M. (1998). *Rachel's Holiday.* New York: Harper Collins.

Khantzian, E. J. (1997). The self-medication hypothesis of substance use disorders: A reconsideration and recent applications. *Harvard Review of Psychiatry* 4: 231–44.

Knapp, C. (1996). *Drinking: A Love Story.* New York: Dial Press.

Knight, J. R., L. A. Shrier, T. D. Bravender, M. Farrell, J. Vander Bilt, and H. J. Shaffer. (1999). A new brief screen for adolescent substance abuse. *Archives of Pediatric Adolescent Medicine* 153: 25–30.

Kohut, H. (1987). *The Kohut Seminars on Self Psychology and Psychotherapy with Adolescents and Young Adults.* Ed. M. Elson. New York: Norton.

Koran, L. M., R. J. Farber, E. Aboujaoude, M. D. Large, and R. T. Serpe. (2006). Estimated prevalence of compulsive buying in the United States. *American Journal of Psychiatry* 163: 1806–12.

Kraut, R., M. Patterson, V. Lundmark, S. Kiesler, T. Mukopadhyay, and W. Scherlis. (1998). Internet paradox: A social-technology that reduces social involvement and psychological well-being? *American Psychologist* 53: 107–31.

Kuczynski, A. (2006). *Beauty Junkies: Inside Our $15 Billion Obsession with Cosmetic Surgery.* New York: Doubleday.

Kurutz, S. (2003). White-collar stoner. *Details,* August: 72, 74.

Ladd, G. T., and N. M. Petry. (2002a). Gender differences among pathological gamblers seeking treatment. *Experimental and Clinical Psychopharmacology* 10: 302–9.

———. (2002b). Disordered gambling among university-based medical and dental patients: A focus on Internet gambling. *Psychology of Addictive Behaviors* 16: 76–79.

Larimer, M. E., and C. Neighbors. (2003). Normative misperception of the impact of descriptive and injunctive norms on college student gambling. *Psychology of Addictive Behaviors* 17: 235–43.

LaRose, R., C. A. Lin, and M. S. Eastin. (2003). Unregulated Internet usage: Addiction, habit, or deficient self-regulation. *Media Psychology* 5: 225–53.

Lasch, C. (1978). *The Culture of Narcissism: American Life in an Age of Diminishing Expectations.* London: W. W. Norton.

Lawford, C. K. (2005). *Symptoms of Withdrawal: A Memoir of Snapshots and Redemption.* New York: HarperCollins.

Lederer, K. (2003). *Poker Face: A Girlhood among Gamblers.* New York: Crown.

Lee, B. (2005). *Born to Lose: Memoirs of a Compulsive Gambler.* Center City, MN: Hazeldon.

Lejoyeux, M., J. Ades, V. Tassain, and J. Solomon. (1996). The phenomenology and psychopathology of uncontrolled buying. *American Journal of Psychiatry* 153: 1524–29.

Lejoyeux, M., V. Tassain, J. Solomon, and J. Ades. (1997). Study of compulsive buying in depressed patients. *Journal of Clinical Psychiatry* 58: 169–73.

Leonard, K. E., and P. Mudar. (2003). Peer and partner drinking and the transition to marriage: A longitudinal examination of selection and influence processes. *Psychology of Addictive Behaviors* 17: 115–25.

Lesieur, H. R., and S. B. Blume. (1987). The South Oaks Gambling Screen (SOGS): A new instrument for the identification of pathological gamblers. *American Journal of Psychiatry* 144: 1184–88.

Lilenfeld, L. R., and W. H. Kaye. (1996). The link between alcoholism and eating disorders. *Alcohol Health and Research World* 20: 94–99.

Marlatt, G. A. (Ed.). (1998). *Harm Reduction: Pragmatics Strategies for Managing High Risk Behaviors.* New York: Guilford Press.

Marlow, A. (1999). *How to Stop Time: Heroin from A to Z.* New York: Basic.

Matano, R. A., C. Koopman, S. F. Wanat, S. D. Whitsell, A. Borggrefe, and D. Westrup. (2003). Assessment of binge drinking of alcohol in highly educated employees. *Addictive Behaviors* 28: 1299–310.

Matthews, C. R., L. A. Schmid, A. A. Conclaves, and K. H. Bursley. (1998). Assessing problem drinking in college students: Are counseling centers doing enough? *Journal of College Counseling* 12: 3–9.

Mayfield, D., G. MacLeod, and P. Hall. (1974). The CAGE Questionnaire: Validation of a new alcoholism screening instrument. *American Journal of Psychiatry* 131: 1121–23.

McCormick, R. A. (1987). Pathological gambling: A parsimonious need state model. *Journal of Gambling Behavior* 3: 257–63.

McCreery, D. (2001). *No Soft Landings: A Memoir.* Vancouver, BC: Trafford.

Menninger, J. A. (2002). Assessment and treatment of alcoholism and substance-related disorders in the elderly. *Bulletin of the Menninger Foundation* 66: 166–83.

Miles, H., A. Winstock, and J. Strang. (2001). Identifying young people who drink too much: The clinical utility of the five-item Alcohol Use Disorders Identification Test (AUDIT). *Drug and Alcohol Review* 20: 9–18.

Miller, W. R., and S. Rollnick. (2002). *Motivational Interviewing: Preparing People for Change.* 2nd ed. New York: Guilford Press.

Mitchell, J. E., J. Redlin, S. Wonderlich, R. Crosby, R. Faber, R. Miltenberberg, J. Smyth, M. Stickney, B. Gosnell, M. Burgard, and K. Lancaster. (2002). The relationship between compulsive buying and eating disorders. *International Journal of Eating Disorders* 32: 107–11.

Moehringer, J. R. (2006). *The Tender Bar: A Memoir.* New York: Hyperion.

Moore, A. A., J. C. Beck, and T. F. Babor. (2002). Beyond alcoholism: Identifying older, at risk drinkers in primary care. *Journal of Studies on Alcohol* 63: 316–24.

Morahan-Martin, J., and P. Schumacher. (2000). Incidence and correlates of pathological Internet use among college students. *Computers in Human Behavior* 16: 13–29.

Moriarty, J. (2001). *Liquid Lover: A Memoir.* New York: Alyson.

Moyers, W. C. (2006). *Broken: My Story of Addiction and Redemption.* New York: Viking.

Myrick, H., and K. Brady. (2003). Editorial review: Current review of the comorbidity of affective, anxiety, and substance use disorders. *Current Opinion in Psychiatry* 16: 261–70.

National Center on Addiction and Substance Abuse at Columbia University. (1998). *Under the Rug: Substance Abuse and the Mature Woman.* New York: The National Center on Addiction and Substance Abuse at Columbia University.

———. (2000). *Missed Opportunity: National Survey of Primary Care Physicians and Patients on Substance Abuse.* New York: The National Center on Addiction and Substance Abuse at Columbia University.

National Gambling Impact Study Commission. (1999). Final Report. Washington, DC: US Government Printing Office. Retrieved on 02/05/07 from http://govinfo.library.unt.edu/ngisc/.

National Institute of Alcohol Abuse and Alcoholism. (2005). Module 10J: Alcohol and the Family. Retrieved on 11/19/06 from http://pubs.niaaa.nih.gov/publications/Social/Module10JFamilies/Module10J.html.

Nichols, L. A., and R. Nicki. (2004). Development of a psychometrically sound Internet Addiction Scale: A preliminary step. *Psychology of Addictive Behaviors* 18: 381–84.

Nova Scotia Office of Health Promotion. (2004). Nova Scotia Gambling Prevalence Study: Final Report. Retrieved on 12/28/06 from http://www.gov.ns.ca/hpp/repPub/2003Gambling_Prevalence_Study_Report.pdf.

O'Dea, J. A., and S. Abraham. (2002). Eating and exercise disorders in young college men. *Journal of American College Health* 50: 273–78.

O'Farrell, T. J., and W. Fals-Stewart. (1999). Treatment models and methods: Family models. In B. S. McCrady and E. E. Epstein (Eds.), *Addictions: A Comprehensive Guidebook*. New York: Oxford University Press.

Orford, J., R. Hodgson, A. Copello, B. John, M. Smith, R. Black, K. Fryer, L. Handforth, T. Alwyn, C. Kerr, G. Thistlethwaite, and G. Slegg. (2006). The client's perspective on change during treatment for an alcohol problem: Qualitative analysis of follow-up interviews in the UK Alcohol Treatment Trial. *Addiction* 101: 60–68.

Orzack, M. H., and C. J. Ross. (2000). Should virtual sex be treated like other addictions? In A. Cooper (Ed.), *Cybersex: The Dark Side of the Force*. Philadelphia, PA: Brunner-Routledge.

Palahniuk, C. (2001). *Choke*. New York: Anchor.

Peele, S. (Ed.). (1985). *The Meaning of Addiction: A Compulsive Experience and Its Interpretation*. Lexington, MA: Lexington.

———. (1999). Is sex *really* addictive? *Contemporary Psychology* 44: 154–56.

Petry, N. (2002). How treatments for pathological gambling can be informed by treatments for substance use disorders. *Experimental and Clinical Psychopharmacology* 10: 184–92.

———. (2003). A comparison of treatment-seeking pathological gamblers based on preferred gambling activity. *Addiction* 98: 645–55.

Petry, N. M., and B. D. Kiluk. (2002). Suicidal ideation and suicide attempts in treatment-seeking pathological gamblers. *Journal of Nervous and Mental Disorders* 190: 462–69.

Pomery, E. A., F. X. Gibbons, M. Gerrard, M. J. Cleveland, G. H. Brody, and T. A. Wills. (2005). Families and risk: Prospective analysis of familial and social influences on adolescent substance use. *Journal of Family Psychology* (Special issue: Sibling Relationship Contributions to Individual and Family Well-Being) 19: 560–70.

Prochaska, J. O., J. C. Norcross, and C. C. DiClemente. (1994). *Changing for Good*. New York: William Morrow.

Randall, C. L., J. S. Roberts, F. K. Del Coca, K. M. Carroll, G .J. Connors, and M. E. Mattson. (2002). Temporal sequencing of alcohol-related problems, problem recognition, and help-seeking episodes. *Addictive Behaviors* 27: 659–74.

Recovery Institute. (1998). *The Road to Recovery: A Landmark National Study on Public Perceptions of Alcoholism and Barriers to Treatment*. San Francisco: The Recovery Institute.

Reiger, D. A., M. E. Farmer, D. S. Rae, B. Z. Locke, S. J. Keith, L. L. Judd, and F. K. Goodwin. (1990). Comorbidity of mental disorders with alcohol and other drug abuse. *Journal of the American Medical Association* 264: 2511–81.

Reis, J., and W. L. Riley. (2000). Predictors of college students' alcohol consumption: Implications for student education. *Journal of Genetic Psychology* 161: 282–91.

Rhee, S. H., K. John, J. K. Hewitt, S. E. Young, R. P. Corley, T. J. Crowley, and M. C. Stallings. (2003). Genetic and environmental influences on substance initiation, use, and problem use in adolescents. *Archives of General Psychiatry* 60: 1256–64.

Robins, L. N., D. H. Davis, and D. W. Goodwin. (1974). Drug use by U.S. enlisted Army men in Vietnam: A follow-up on their return home. *American Journal of Epidemiology* 99: 235–49.

Rosenker, D. C. (2002). Heroin reaches the well-to-do adolescent population. *Brown University Child and Adolescent Behavior Letter* 18: 3–4.

Rosenthal, R. J. (2005). Staying in the action: The pathological gambler's equivalent of the dry drunk. *Journal of Gambling Issues* 13. Retrieved on 10/15/06 from http://www.camh.net/egambling/issue13/jgi_13_rosenthal.html.

Rotunda, R. J., S. J. Kass, M. A. Sutton, and D. T. Leon. (2003). Internet use and misuse: Preliminary findings from a new instrument. *Behavior Modification* 27: 484–504.

Sachs, M. L., and D. Pargman. (1984). Running addiction. In M. L. Sachs and G. W. Buffone (Eds.), *Running as Therapy: An Integrated Approach.* Lincoln: University of Nebraska Press.

Saunders, J. B., O. G. Aasland, T. F. Babor, J. R. De La Fuente, and M. Grant. (1993). Development of the Alcohol Use Disorders Identification Test (AUDIT): WHO Collaborative Project on early detection of persons with harmful alcohol consumption. *Addiction* 88: 381–89.

Schneider, J. P., and B. Schneider. (2004). *Sex, Lies, and Forgiveness.* 3rd ed. Tucson, AZ: Recovery Resource Press.

Schottenfeld, R. S. (1994). Assessment of the patient. In M. Galanter and H. D. Kleber (Eds.), *Textbook of Substance Abuse Treatment.* Washington, DC: American Psychiatric Press.

Schuckit, M. A. (1998). *Educating Yourself about Alcohol and Drugs: A People's Primer.* Cambridge, MA: Perseus.

Schuckit, M. A., G. P. Danko, E. B. Raimo, T. L. Smith, M .Y. Eng, K. K. T. Carpenter, and V. M. Hesselbrock. (2001). A preliminary evaluation of the potential usefulness of the diagnosis of polysubstance dependence. *Journal of Studies on Alcohol* 62: 54–61.

Shaffer, H. (1999). Strange bedfellows: A critical view of pathological gambling and addiction. *Addiction* 94: 1445–48.

Shaffer, H. J., D. A. LaPlante, R. A. LaBrie, R. C. Kidman, A. N. Donato, and M. V. Stanton. (2004). Toward a syndrome model of addiction: Multiple expressions, common etiology. *Harvard Review of Psychiatry* 12: 367–74.

Shaffer, H. J., M. N. M. Hall, and J. VanderBilt. (1999). Estimating the prevalence of disordered gambling behavior in the United States and Canada: A research synthesis. *American Journal of Public Health* 98: 1369–76.

Shapiro, S. (2005). *Lighting Up: How I Stopped Smoking, Drinking and Everything Else I Loved in Life Except Sex.* New York: Bantam Dell.

Shewan, D., P. Dalgarno, A. Marshall, and E. Lowe. (1998). Patterns of heroin use among a non-treatment sample in Glasgow, Scotland. *Addiction Research* 6: 215–34.

Silverman, S. W. (2001). *Love Sick: One Woman's Journey through Sexual Addiction.* New York: W. W. Norton.

Solomon, M. (2005). *AA: Not the Only Way.* Venice, CA: Capolo Press.

Stanton, M. D. (1997). The role of the family and significant others in the engagement and retention of drug-dependent individuals. In L. S. Onken, J. D. Blaine, and J. J. Boren (Eds.), *Beyond the Therapeutic Alliance: Keeping the Drug Dependent Individual in Treatment.* NIDA Research Monograph 165. Rockville, MD: National Institute on Drug Abuse.

Starace, G. (2002). New "normalities," new "madness." *British Journal of Psychotherapy* 19: 21–32.

Steinberg, H., B. R. Nicholls, E. A. Sykes, and N. LeBoutillier. (1998). Weekly exercise consistently reinstates positive mood. *European Psychologist* 3: 271–80.

Stromberg, G., and J. Merrill. (2005). *The Harder They Fall: Celebrities Tell Their Real-Life Stories of Addiction and Recovery.* Center City, MN: Hazeldon

Substance Abuse and Mental Health Services Administration. (1999). Substance Use and Mental Health Characteristics by Employment Status. Retrieved on 3/16/08 from http://www.oas.samhsa.gov/NHSDA/A10.pdf.

———. (2002). *Results from the 2001 National Household Survey on Drug Abuse.* Volume 1: *Summary of National Findings.* Office of Applied Studies, NHSDA Series H-17, DHHS Publication No. SMA02-3758. Rockville, MD: U.S. Department of Health and Human Services.

———. (2003). The NSDUH Report: Quantity and Frequency of Alcohol Use. Retrieved on 1/15/07 from http://www.oas.samhsa.gov/2k3/AlcQF/AlcQF.cfm.

Tartarsky, A. (2002). *Harm Reduction Psychotherapy: A New Treatment for Drug and Alcohol Problems.* New York: Jason Aronson.

Templeton, L. S. Zohhadi, and R. Velleman. (2004). Working with Family Members in SDAS: Findings from a Feasibility Study. Retrieved on 5/26/06 from http://www.bath.ac.uk/mhrdu/drug-alcohol/sdas%20feasibility%20study%20final%20report.pdf.

Terry, A., A. Szabo, and M. Griffiths. (2004). The Exercise Addiction Inventory: A new brief screening tool. *Addiction Research and Theory* 12: 489–99.

Thom, B., and C. Tellez. (1986). A difficult business: Detecting and managing alcohol problems in general practice. *British Journal of Addictions* 81: 405–18.

Thornton, E. W., and S. E. Scott. (1995). Motivation in the committed runner: Correlation between self-report scales and behaviour. *Health Promotion International* 10: 177–84.

To, S. E. (2006). Alcoholism and pathways to recovery: New survey of results on views and treatment options. *Medscape General Medicine* 8. Retrieved on 1/9/07 from http://www.medscape.com/viewarticle/518483.

Tonigan, J. S., W. R. Miller, and J. M. Brown. (1997). The reliability of FORM 90: An instrument for assessing alcohol treatment outcome. *Journal of Studies on Alcohol* 58: 358–64.

U.S. Department of Health and Human Services. National Institute on Alcohol Abuse and Alcoholism. (2000). NIH publication 00–1583.

———. National Institute on Alcohol Abuse and Alcoholism. (2005). *Helping Patients Who Drink Too Much: A Clinician's Guide.*

Vaillant, G. E. (1995). *The Natural History of Alcoholism Revisited.* Cambridge, MA: Harvard University Press.

Volkmann, C., and T. Volkmann. (2004) *Our Drink: Detoxing the Perfect Family.* Seattle, WA: Elton-Wolf.

———. (2006) *From Binge to Blackout: A Mother and Son Struggle with Teen Drinking.* New York: New American Library.

von Ranson, K. M., M. McGue, and W. G. Iacono. (2003). Disordered eating and substance use in an epidemiological sample: II. Associations within families. *Psychology of Addictive Behaviors* 17: 193–202.

Washington State Department of Health. (2002). Substance Abuse during Pregnancy: Guidelines for Screening. Olympia: Washington State Department of Health. Retrieved on 1/19/07 from http://www.doh.wa.gov/Publicat/ Screening_Guidelines.pdf.

Washton, A. M. (1989). Cocaine abuse and compulsive sexuality. *Medical Aspects of Human Sexuality* 23: 32–39.

Wasilow-Mueller, S., and C. K. Erickson. (2001). Drug abuse and dependency: Understanding gender differences in etiology and management. *Journal of the American Pharmaceutical Association* 41: 78–90.

Wechsler, H., and T. F. Nelson. (2001). Binge drinking and the American college student: What's five drinks? *Psychology of Addictive Behaviors* 15: 287–91.

Weinberg, N. M., E. Rahdert, J. D. Colliver, and M. D. Glantz. (1998). Adolescent substance abuse: A review of the past 10 years. *Journal of the American Academy of Child and Adolescent Psychiatry* 37: 252–61.

Weisner, C., and H. Matzger. (2003). Missed opportunities in addressing drinking behavior in medical and mental health settings. *Alcoholism: Clinical and Experimental Research* 27: 1132–41.

Wholey, D. (1984). *The Courage to Change: Hope and Help for Alcoholics and Their Families.* Boston: Houghton Mifflin.

Whybrow, P. C. (2005). *American Mania: When More Is Not Enough.* New York: W.W. Norton

Williams, A. (2006). Hooked on online psychics. *New York Times,* March 5, sec. 9, pp. 1–2.

Wills, T. A., G. McNamara, D. Vaccaro, and A. E. Hirky. (1996). Escalated substance use: A longitudinal grouping analysis from early to middle adolescence. *Journal of Abnormal Psychology* 105: 166–80.

Wilsnack, R. W., N. D. Vogeltanz, S. C. Wilsnack, and T. R. Harris. (2000). Gender differences in alcohol consumption and adverse drinking consequences: Cross-cultural patterns. *Addiction* 95: 251–65.

Winn, M. (2002). *The Plug-In Drug: Television, Computers and Family Life.* New York: Penguin.

Wurtzel, E. (2002). *More, Now, Again: A Memoir of Addiction.* New York: Simon and Schuster.

Young, K. (1998). Internet addiction: The emergence of a new clinical disorder. *CyberPsychology and Behavior* 1: 237–44.

Yurchisin, J., and K. K. P. Johnson. (2004). Compulsive buying behavior and its relationship to perceived social status associated with buying, materialism, self-esteem, and apparel-product involvement. *Family and Consumer Sciences Research Journal* 32: 291–314.

Zailckas, K. (2005). *Smashed: A Story of a Drunken Girlhood.* New York: Viking.

Zinberg, N. (1994) *Drug, Set, and Setting: The Basis for Controlled Intoxicant Use.* New York: Yale University Press.

Zuckerman, M., and D. M. Kuhlman. (2000). Personality and risk-taking: Common bisocial Factors. *Journal of Personality* (Special issue: Personality Perspectives on Problem Behavior) 68: 999–1029.

Index

AA (Alcoholics Anonymous), 224, 234, 253. *See also* twelve-step programs
abstinence, 139, 234
abuse. *See* polysubstance use, abuse, dependence; substance abuse/dependence; trauma and addiction
action phase, 232–36, 253; addiction treatment philosophies, 234–35; for significant others, 235–36; tasks of, 232; typical presentation, 233–34, 235. *See also* treatment
ADD/ADHD (attention deficit hyperactivity disorder), 128, 257
addiction: addictive disorder, 27–28, 91, 208; any behavior as, 26, 34, 56, 68; as behavior gone wild, 24–25; compulsion as distinct from, 21, 30–33, 80, 143; as coping mechanism, 41–42; cultural factors, 43–45, 63, 184, 192; defined, 21–28; disease concept, 2, 11, 207–8; disguised by mental health or physical disorders, 70–72; and DSM-IV, 19–20; early detection, 4, 17, 35, 113–14, 138–39; engagement as distinct from, 55, 161–62; excessive

behavior as distinct from, 21–22; failure to recognize, 13, 14–15; habit as distinct from, 28–30, 32–33; help for, 207–39; impediments to help for, 240–54; labeling, 222–24; learned behavior as, 37–41; loss and, 32, 226, 229, 236; mood- and/or self-altering effects, 31–32, 37, 39, 42–43, 70–72, 80–81; myths about, 67–69; negative consequences, 25–26, 51–52; out-of-control behavior, 24–25, 67; paradox of, 39–41, 144, 226; perks of, 242, 245–46; as physical dependence, 22–24, 68; positive, 26, 195; psychological dependence, 23–24; recognizing, 26–28; recognizing without screening tools, 88, 90–91, 208; relationships as replacement for, 83–84; resources for, 111–12, 129, 140, 155, 168, 182, 193, 239, 254; risk factors, 49–50; role of genetics, 34–37, 128, 139, 196; role of quantity/frequency, 49, 52, 82, 89, 106–7, 122, 169, 175; role of reinforcement, 37–39, 158; self-identification of, 11, 62–63; as self-medication, 90, 128, 137, 159,

178, 198, 233; as source of stimulation, 37, 128, 244; statistics on, 2;
stereotypic views of, 4, 7–9, 15;
stigma of, 19, 60–63, 71, 128, 247–48;
subtle signs of, 16, 78–85, 138, 154,
177; three C's of, 26–27; and trauma,
139, 171, 179; under-diagnosed, 11,
131, 136–38. *See also* adolescent
behavioral addictions; adolescent
substance addictions; autobiographies about addiction; behavioral
addiction; buying addiction; computer addiction; continuum of
addiction; cybersex addiction;
denial; depression; development of
addiction; exercise addiction; gambling addiction; masks of addiction;
older adults' addiction; risk factors;
sexual addiction; unidentified
addictions
addictive personality, 76, 243
addictive potential, 37–38, 195, 261–64;
form of intake as function of, 68; not
a property of drug or behavior, 35
addictive substances. *See* substances
adolescent behavioral addictions: buying
addiction, 185; computer addiction,
161–62, 166, 259; exercise addiction,
205; gambling addiction, 142,
153–55; sexual addiction, 171,
176–77
adolescent substance addictions, 113–29;
assessment of, 117–23; binge drinking, 120–23, 129; case example, 111;
CRAFFT Screen, 118–19; dangers,
115, 121, 128; and denial, 116; developmental consequences, 113, 115,
118; differences from adult addictions, 113, 117; early detection,
113–15, 128; experimentation, 38, 83,
113–14, 116–17, 118, 184; gateway
theory, 127; gender differences, 121,
135; guidelines for parents, 45,
114–16, 123–27; negative consequences, 117, 119; parents' dilemma,
114–16, 123–27; prescription med-

ication misuse, 111; prevention programs, 116; rapid course of, 114, 116;
resources for, 129; risk factors, 83,
119, 127–29; and role of parental
addiction, 42, 128, 139; screening for,
117–19; self-reports, 89; signs of,
116–17; toxicology screens, 119–20
alcohol consumption: binge drinking,
54, 82, 103, 107, 120–23; blackouts,
62, 256; blood alcohol level (BAL),
101, 102, 103, 120, 136; differences
in response to, 22, 99, 121, 131–32,
135–36; DUI/DWI, 95, 126, 137; and
genetics, 36–37, 40, 42, 139; interaction with medication, 73–74, 111,
132; mood-altering effects, 40, 80, 84,
98, 103, 137, 233; negative consequences, 40, 60, 64, 70, 71, 74, 89, 97,
102, 108, 131, 137, 255–56; and pregnancy, 140; psychological and physical effects, 52, 70–71, 255–56; safe use
standards, 21, 99–101, 126–27, 136;
withdrawal, 73–74, 256
Alcoholics Anonymous (AA), 224, 234,
253. *See also* twelve-step programs
ambivalence about loss of addiction,
225–32; resolving, 215, 222, 229
amphetamines. *See* stimulants
antisocial personality, 68, 128
anxiety: caused by addiction, 16, 70, 102,
132, 150, 170, 255; compulsions and,
30–31; denial, 58; self-medicated by
addiction, 32, 80, 90, 98, 118, 156,
178, 185, 233, 255
attachment, 45, 83–84, 227
attention deficit hyperactivity disorder
(ADD/ADHD), 128, 257
autobiographies about addiction,
124–25, 237–39; *Annie Duke: How
I Raised, Folded, Bluffed, Flirted,
Cursed, and Won Millions at the
World Series of Poker,* 147, 152;
*Beauty Junkies: Inside Our $15 Billion
Obsession with Cosmetic Surgery,* 19;
*From Binge to Blackout: A Mother and
Son Struggle with Teen Drinking,* 12,

117, 129, 237; *Born to Lose: Memoirs of a Compulsive Gambler*, 65, 81, 85, 144, 147, 238; *Broken: My Story of Addiction and Redemption*, 42, 117, 125, 128, 227, 229, 237, 241; *Double Down: Reflections on Gambling and Loss*, 148, 238; *Drinking: A Love Story*, 24, 37, 84, 238; *Dry: A Memoir*, 214–15, 238–39; *How to Stop Time: Heroin from A to Z*, 55, 199–200, 237; *Lighting Up: How I Stopped Smoking, Drinking and Everything Else I Loved in Life Except Sex*, 238; *Liquid Lover: A Memoir*, 24, 37, 62; *Love Sick: One Woman's Journey through Sexual Addiction*, 170–71, 178–79, 181, 238–39; *A Million Little Pieces*, 8; *More, Now, Again: A Memoir of Addiction*, 98, 237, 257; *No Soft Landings: A Memoir*, 237; *Note Found in a Bottle: My Life as a Drinker*, 59, 66, 67, 237; *Our Drink: Detoxing the Perfect Family*, 129; *Poker Face: A Girlhood among Gamblers*, 147, 238; *Postcards from the Edge*, 72; *Save Karyn: One Shopaholic's Journey to Debt and Back*, 184–86, 238; *Smashed: A Story of a Drunken Girlhood*, 14, 61, 121, 125, 237–38; *Symptoms of Withdrawal: A Memoir of Snapshots and Redemption*, 41, 125, 237, 238

BAL (blood alcohol level), 101, 102, 103, 120, 136
behavioral addiction, 13, 19–21, 68, 259; cross-addictions, 74–76; cross-tolerance, 74; as excessive behavior, 13, 82, 161–62; masks unique to, 150–55, 166–68, 179–82, 192–93, 203–5; negative consequences, 259; withdrawal, 23, 259. *See also* adolescent behavioral addictions
binge drinking, 120–23; assessment, 122–23; as at-risk drinking, 82, 103; case example, 54, 122; defined, 121;

negative consequences, 121, 123; screening tool, 107, 122; as social norm, 82
blackouts, 62, 256
blinders to recognizing addiction, 61, 240–45; approaching addicted person, 114–16; as impediments to recovery, 131, 212, 213, 240–54; phases of change, 252–53. *See also* communication skills; unidentified addictions
blood alcohol level (BAL), 101, 102, 103, 120, 136
borderline personality disorder, 256
boredom: alleviation by addiction, 37, 41, 118, 144, 158, 159; risk factor for addiction, 128; by significant others, 244
bottoming out, 207
breathalyzer, 76, 102, 120
buying addiction, 183–93; autobiography about, 184–85; case examples, 75, 248–49; continuum, 189–90, 191; co-occurring disorders, 193; diagnostic criteria for, 187–88; disguised as hobby, 184; gateway theory, 184; gender differences, 185, 186, 192; impulsive buying, 186, 190; masks and disguises, 190, 192; mood- and/or self-altering effects, 33, 185, 186; negative consequences, 148, 186, 187–88, 190; prevalence, 186; purchase types, 184, 185–86; resources for, 193; risk factors, 189–90; role of cultural values, 183, 184, 186, 192; screening tool, 188–89; and shame, 189–90; subtle signs, 84, 187; tolerance, 23, 190–91

caffeine, 73, 97, 256, 262
cannabis, 23, 48–49, 68, 93, 101, 114–15, 124, 257–58, 261–62; case examples, 11–13, 110–11, 218–21; gateway drug, 127
change, phases of, 216–37; for addicted person, 216–37; for significant others, 252–53; vs. "stages," 216. *See also*

action phase; contemplation phase; maintenance phase; precontemplation phase; preparation phase; relapse phase

cigarettes. *See* nicotine

cocaine, 8, 16, 68, 93, 256–57, 262; case examples, 223, 227, 237; mood-altering effects, 39, 44, 97, 244; and sexual addiction, 74, 257

codependency, 223, 251, 254

communication skills, 213–16, 219

compulsion, as distinct from addiction, 21, 30–33, 80, 143

computer addiction, 156–68; and alternative reality, 158; and benefits of anonymity, 158; case examples, 84, 156–57, 167; computer-mediated relationships, 84; continuum of, 163–66; co-occurring disorders, 166–67; as coping mechanism, 84, 158, 164; diagnostic criteria for, 160; engagement as distinct from, 22, 55, 161–62; gateway theory, 159; gender differences, 159–60, 166; immediate gratification with, 158–59; and instant gratification, 158–59; masks and disguises, 166–68; mood- and/or self-altering effects, 37, 50, 84, 157–58; motivation for computer use, 159; negative consequences, 52, 55, 160–61, 163–66, 167; online gaming, 154; origins of, 157; reasons for, 157–59; resources for, 168; risk factors, 159, 162–63; role of anonymity, accessibility, and affordability, 158, 163, 172; screening tool, 162–63; as secondary addiction, 166–67, 179, 181, 184; self-medicating effects, 157–59, 164; technology addiction, 157; and time online, 160–61; tolerance, 165–66; virtual vs. face-to-face interactions, 157–58; withdrawal, 163, 165; in work settings, 167–68. *See also* cybersex addiction

contemplation phase, 224–32; for addicted person, 231–32; and

ambivalence, 227–31; case example, 224, 228, 230–31; cost/benefit analysis, 226, 231; good-bye letter to addiction, 231–32; for significant other, 226–31, 252–53; tasks of, 224; typical presentation, 224–26

continuum of addiction, 12, 48–53; at-risk level, 49, 83; chart, 52–53; vs. dichotomous view, 47; fully addicted level, 50, 84–85; negative consequences, 51–52; problematic level, 49–50, 82, 83; recreational level, 48–49. *See also specific addictions*

cost/benefit analysis. *See* contemplation phase

cough medicine/DXM, 73, 93, 97, 126, 127, 263

crack. *See* cocaine

cravings, 26–27, 30–33, 53, 54–55, 69, 84, 167, 169, 211

cross-addictions, 74–76

cross-tolerance, 73–74, 111, 152

cybersex addiction, 171–73; access, anonymity, affordability (three A's) of, 172; case examples, 75, 181; continuum, 175–79, 180; diagnostic criteria for, 173–74; and gender, 173; masks and disguises, 179–82, 259; resources for, 182; risk factors, 177; screening tools, 174–75, 182; Sexual Compulsivity Scale (SCS), 174–75; subtle signs, 16; time online, 175; two types of, 175. *See also* computer addiction; sexual addiction

denial, 58–61; alternative interpretations, 11, 59, 62, 76–77, 218; case examples, 8; defined, 58–59, 63; in late stage addiction, 53, 63, 218; vs. lying, 59, 144; and misconceptions, 63–64; as response to criticism, 61; as response to shame, 60–61, 241; role in masking addiction, 241; by significant other, 59–60, 61, 65; treatment implications, 76 dependence: physical, 22–24, 68, 255–59; psychological, 23–24, 255–59. *See also* addiction; substance addictions

depressants. *See* sedatives

depression: case examples, 108, 131–32, 137–38, 220–23; created by alcohol, 14, 16, 68, 131, 132; created by behavioral addiction, 150, 153, 170; as mask, 9, 16, 30, 63, 66, 88, 166, 171, 193, 238; risk factor for addiction, 128; self-medicated by addiction, 85, 90, 118, 143–44, 155, 178, 185, 198; women, 137

development of addiction, 47–48; biology, 34–36; and brain's reward system, 35, 43, 227; environment, 43–46; genetics, 36, 37, 40, 42, 128; limited coping mechanisms, 41–42; mode of intake, 68; neuroadaptation, 34–35, 211, 235, 255; punishment, 40–41; reinforcement, 37–43, 49; role of access, 44, 72, 75, 98, 115, 135, 141, 159, 172; role of mood- and/or self-altering effects, 43–44; role of relationships, 83; self-regulation, 45; sociocultural factors, 45–46

diagnosis of addiction. *See specific addictions*

discrepancies, developing, 215, 222, 229

disease concept of addiction, 127, 207–8

disguises of addiction. *See* masks of addiction

drugs. *See specific drugs*; substances

DUI (driving under the influence), 95, 126, 137

early detection: importance of, 4, 17, 75, 132, 138–39; role of subtle signs, 78–79

eating disorders, 20, 90, 193, 204–5, 257

elderly. *See* older adults' addiction

empathy, 214, 228

enabling, 248–49

engagement, high: addiction vs., 19, 113, 116–17, 118, 161–62; risk factor for addiction, 162–63

excessive behavior: addiction as distinct from, 21–22, 186; and cross-addictions, 74; family norms, 66–67, 242; social norms, 82–83, 183

exercise addiction, 194–205; adolescents, 205; case examples, 48, 75, 197–200, 198–99, 201–2, 204, 205, 243; vs. committed athlete, 200–202; continuum, 197–200, 201–2; co-occurring disorders, 74, 204; diagnostic criteria, 196; and eating disorders, 204–5; effect on appearance, 194, 195, 198, 205; endorphins, 39, 83, 196, 198, 200, 201, 203; injuries due to, 196, 201; masks and disguises, 87, 203–5; mood- and/or self-altering effects, 37, 48, 195, 198; negative consequences, 161, 195, 196, 199; Olympic/elite athletes, 161, 194, 198, 200–201; as positive addiction, 26, 195, 263; risk factors, 39, 194, 198, 201–2, 244; screening tool, 197; subtle signs, 199; tolerance, 199, 202; withdrawal, 199, 200, 201–2

family and significant others: being "too helpful," 251–52; resources for, 254; role in addiction development, 83; role in supporting recovery, 208, 250; shame and guilt, 61, 128–29, 241, 246–50; standards of addiction learned from, 242. *See also* blinders to recognizing addiction

gambling addiction, 141–55; adolescent, 142, 153–55; autobiographies, 65, 81, 85, 144, 147, 148, 238; blinders to seeing, 242–44, 246–49; Canadian Problem Gambling Index, 145–46; case example, 56, 167, 235; continuum of, 85, 146–50; co-occurring problems, 74, 150, 233; covert gambling, 151–52; defined, 142; denial vs. lying, 144; diagnostic criteria for, 142–43; DSM-IV criteria for, 20, 142–43; early recognition, 150;

financial consequences, 51, 147, 148, 153; gateway to, 141; masks and disguises, 65, 70, 150–55; mood-altering effects, 43, 144, 147; negative consequences, 147, 149, 161; online gambling, 142, 154–55, 160, 166; prevalence, 142, 152; vs. professional gambling, 146–47; reinforcement, 39, 41; resources for, 155; risk factors, 44, 50, 155, 184; screening tools, 145–46; shame, 151, 246; South Oaks Gambling Screen (SOGS), 145; subtle signs, 82–85, 154–55; suicide risk, 150, 155; withdrawal, 23, 71; women, 152–53

gateway theory, 127, 141, 159

genetics, role of, 34–37, 128, 139, 196

government standards for safe alcohol use, 99–101

grief and grieving, 132, 238

guilt. See shame

habits. See addiction

hallucinogens, 23, 97, 126, 184, 258–59, 263–64

harm reduction treatment, 112, 219, 234–35, 239

health care providers. See unidentified addictions

heroin: addictive potential, 35–36, 43, 68; adolescent use, 113, 115; autobiography about heroin use, 55, 199–200, 237; case example, 55; controlled use, 35, 42, 101; endorphins, 206; harm reduction, 234; intrinsic reinforcement, 38–39; physical dependence, 23–24; psychoactive effects of, 43; tolerance, 199; toxicology screens, 120; use by soldiers in Vietnam, 24

hypnotics. See sedatives

inhalants, 23, 73, 97, 264

Internet addiction. See computer addiction

intervention, 221

levels of addiction. See continuum of addiction

LSD. See hallucinogens

lying, 58, 151, 211; vs. denial, 60–62, 144, 241; by significant others, 248–49

maintenance phase, 236–37; tasks of, 236

marijuana. See cannabis

masks of addiction, 58–69; absence of physical markers, 76; demographic information, 64, 77, 152–55, 166; denial, 58–61, 76; emotional distress, 90, 166, 170, 192; ignorance about addictions, 61–63; misconceptions, 63–66; moderation, 72–75, 203; myths about addictions, 67–69; norms of family excess, 66–67; one addiction masking another, 166, 204; role of gender, 136–37, 152–53, 192; shame, 151; stereotypes and cultural norms, 4, 7–9, 15, 64–65, 192, 203; unique behavioral addictions, 150–55, 166–68, 179–82, 192–93, 203–5

misdiagnosis. See unidentified addictions

misinformation about addictions, 67–69. See also masks of addiction

motivational interviewing, 213

myths about addiction, 67–69

narcissism, 45, 243–44

narcotics. See opiates/opioids

neuroadaptation, 34–37. See also development of addiction; withdrawal

nicotine, 73, 97, 114, 124, 127, 198

older adults' addiction, 130–35; adverse effects of alcohol use, 131; alcohol, 130–33; ARPS medication checklist (Alcohol Related Problem Survey), 134–35; case example, 29–30, 89, 131; family blinders, 131; misdiagnosis, 26, 131, 132; prescribed medications, 2, 74, 130, 133–35; safe drinking limit, 130; screening tools, 132–35;

Short Michigan Alcoholism Screening
Test—Geriatric Version (S-MAST-G)
132–33; substances, 130–35
opiates/opioids, 258, 263; medication
abuse, 98; original model of addiction, 36; oxycodone, 98, 258
overdose, 11, 40, 61, 72, 74, 256
oxycodone. *See* opiates/opioids

paradox of addiction, 39–41, 144, 226
parents. *See* family and significant others
phases of change. *See* change, phases of
polysubstance use, abuse, dependence,
72–73; autobiographies about, 238;
case example, 111; toxicology screen
for, 127
positive addiction, 26, 195
precontemplation phase, 218–24; for
addicted person, 222; admitting to
addiction, 222–24; case example, 218,
220; intervention, 221; for significant
others, 219–22, 252; tasks of, 218;
typical presentation, 218
preparation phase, 232–36; addiction
treatment philosophies, 234–35; for
addicted person, 232; case example,
233; for significant others, 227,
235–36, 253; tasks of, 232; typical
presentation, 233–34, 235
preparing to change, 209, 212–16. *See
also* change, phases of
prescription medication: adolescent substance abuse, 111; case examples, 54,
69, 98, 111; most commonly abused
forms, 72, 93, 257; negative interaction with sedating substances, 11, 74,
132; older adults addicted to, 2, 130,
133; and polysubstance abuse, 72–73
psychoactive effects: and behavioral
addictions, 68, 81, 259; and substance
use, 34–35, 37, 39, 43, 57, 84, 255–59

reinforcement. *See* development of
addiction
relapse, 216, 235, 236, 239, 259
relapse phase, 217, 236–37; tasks of, 236

risk factors, 41, 43–44, 49–50; computer
addiction, 159, 162–63; cybersex
addiction, 177; exercise addiction, 39,
194, 198, 201–2, 244; gambling
addiction, 44, 50, 155, 184; subtle
signs, 79–85; trauma history, 139
roll with resistances, 214–15. *See also*
communication skills

safe drinking limits, 82, 106–7, 130
screening tools, 89–92; 5P's scale for
women's alcohol use, 139–40; addictive buying screen, 188; addictive
disorder screen, 91; Alcohol Use Disorder Identification Test (AUDIT),
105–6; ARPS medication checklist
(Alcohol Related Problem Survey),
134–35; CAGE, 9, 103, 105; Canadian
Problem Gambling Index, 145; computer addiction screen, 162; CRAFFT,
117–19; Drug Abuse Screening Test
(DAST), 109–10; exercise addiction
inventory, 197; and interpreting
screening outcome, 89–90; quantity/
frequency questionnaire, 106–7, 122,
134; reliability of, 90; self-report
accuracy, 88–89; sexual compulsivity
scale, 174–75; S-MAST-G (Short
Michigan Alcoholism Screening
Test—Geriatric Version), 132–33;
South Oaks Gambling Screen
(SOGS), 145; toxicology, 119–20;
validity, 90
sedatives, 73–74, 255–56, 262. *See also*
alcohol consumption
self-assessments: alcoholism, 64; discovering psychoactive effects, 81; drinking, 82; drug addiction, 65;
identifying addictions from
vignettes, 18–19, 54–57; stereotypes
of addiction, 63; subtle signs, 79; vulnerability to addiction, 50
self-help groups, 239; adolescent substance abuse, 129; buying addiction,
193; computer addiction, 168; family
members affected by loved one's

addiction, 253–54; gambling addiction, 155; older adults and women, 140; sex and cybersex addictions, 182; substance addictions, 111–12. *See also* twelve-step programs
sexual addiction, 169–82; adolescent, 176; autobiography about, 170–71, 178, 181; blaming partner for, 182; case examples, 169, 179, 181, 244; cocaine and, 257; continuum, 175–80; diagnostic criteria for, 173–74; vs. frequent sex, 169; gender differences, 173; history of abuse, 171, 176, 179; vs. illegal/immoral acts, 170; masks and disguises of, 90, 171, 179, 181–82; mood- and/or self-altering effects, 43, 49, 178; negative consequences, 169–70, 177, 180–81; and power, 178–79; prevalence, 171; relationship problems created by, 181; resources for, 182; risk factors, 176–77; screening tool, 174–75; Sexual Compulsivity Scale (SCS), 174–75; shame, 170; tolerance, 177, 180. *See also* cybersex addiction
shame: addicted person's, 60–61, 170, 189, 211, 217, 223; as mask, 151; overcoming, 250, 252–53; of significant other, 128, 241, 246–50
shopping addiction. *See* buying addiction
significant others. *See* family and significant others
sociopath. *See* antisocial personality
spouses. *See* family and significant others
steroids, 74, 97
stigma of addiction, 19, 60–63, 71, 128, 247–48
stimulants, 98, 256–57, 262–63; autobiography about, 237, 257; toxicology screening, 120
substance abuse/dependence, 93–97. *See also* substance addictions

substance addictions, 93–140; abuse, 94–95; adolescent, 113–29; Alcohol Use Disorder Identification Test (AUDIT), 105–6; CAGE Screen, 103; case examples, 10–15, 55, 65, 114–15, 122, 137–38, 218–21, 223, 227, 237; common forms of, 93, 97, 261–64; continuum of, 97–103, 104; dependence, 95–97; distinguishing abuse and dependence, 108, 110–11; Drug Abuse Screening Test (DAST), 109–10; DSM-IV criteria for, 19, 94–95, 96–97; functional addict, 64, 65, 66; gender differences in, 135–38; older adults', 130–35; quantity/frequency questionnaire, 106–7; resources for, 111–12; screening tools, 103–7, 109–10, 117–19, 132–33. *See also* adolescent substance addictions; older adults' addiction; *specific substances*; tolerance; withdrawal
substances: common names, 261–64; effects, 255–59; major categories, 97, 255–59
subtle signs of addiction, 78–85, 138, 154, 177
suicide risk, 150, 155

technology addiction, 157. *See also* computer addiction
tolerance: buying addiction, 23, 190–91; cross-tolerance, 72, 73–74; defined, 23; exercise addiction, 199, 202; heroin, 199; role in defining addiction, 24, 53, 68, 104; sexual addiction, 177, 180
toxicology screens, 119–20
trauma and addiction, 139, 171, 179
treatment: alternative approaches, 112, 233–35; gender differences, 137; interventions, 222; obstacles to, 216–17, 233; philosophies of, 234–35; role of toxicology screens, 120; traditional approaches, 76, 207–8, 234

twelve-step programs: alternatives to, 234, 239; philosophy of, 224, 234; resources, 111, 129; for significant others, 213, 253

under-diagnosed addictions, 11, 131, 136–38
unidentified addictions, 3, 14, 218–19; alcoholism, 136; in autobiographies, 12, 14, 17, 65–66; cases, 3, 10, 11, 61; demographic characteristics, 63–64, 77; development of, 62–63; in general population, 11, 62; missed diagnoses by health care professionals, 1–2, 7, 13–15, 71–72, 78, 114, 153, 171, 193, 204, 237

withdrawal, 255–59; behavioral addictions, 23, 163, 165, 201–2, 259; dangers of with alcohol/sedatives, 73–74; defined, 23; neuroadaptation and, 35; prolonged, 259; signs and symptoms of, 23; substances, 256–58
women: 5P's Screening Tool, 140; alcohol screen, 139–40; buying addiction, 185, 186, 192; computer addiction, 160; exercise addiction, 195–96, 204–5; gambling, 150, 152–53; prescription medication use, 2, 133; resources for, 129, 140; sexual addiction, 179; substance addictions, 135–40